COLLABORATION IN PUBLIC POLICY AND PRACTICE

Perspectives on boundary spanners

Paul Williams

First published in Great Britain in 2012 by

The Policy Press
University of Bristol
Fourth Floor
Beacon House
Queen's Road
Bristol BS8 1QU
UK

t: +44 (0)117 331 4054
f: +44 (0)117 331 4093
tpp-info@bristol.ac.uk
www.policypress.co.uk

North American office:
The Policy Press
c/o The University of Chicago Press
1427 East 60th Street
Chicago, IL 60637, USA
t: +1 773 702 7700
f: +1 773-702-9756
sales@press.uchicago.edu
www.press.uchicago.edu

British Library Cataloguing in Publication Data
A catalogue record for this book is available from the British Library.

Library of Congress Cataloging-in-Publication Data
A catalog record for this book has been requested.

ISBN 978 1 84742 847 9 paperback
ISBN 978 1 44730 030 4 hardcover

Cover design by The Policy Press.
Front cover: image kindly supplied by istock.com
Printed and bound in Great Britain by TJ International, Padstow.
The Policy Press uses environmentally responsible print partners.

Contents

List of tables, figures and boxes   iv

About the author   v

Acknowledgements   vi

one   Introduction   1

two   Policy context: intra and intersectoral collaboration   9

three   Structure and agency   23

four   The role and competencies of boundary spanners   37

five   Challenges in the boundary spanning role   63

six   Learning from the private sector   83

seven   We are all boundary spanners now?   95

eight   Implications for policy and practice   119

nine   Reflections and conclusion   139

References   155

Index   173

List of tables, figures and boxes

Tables

2.1	A history of collaborative working in the UK	9
3.1	The components of structure	27
4.1	A model of trust in romantic relationships	48
4.2	Roles and competencies	58
5.1	Collaborative knowledge and experience	65
5.2	Desirable personal characteristics of boundary spanners	67
6.1	Profile of alliance managers	88
7.1	Network management roles and behaviours	97
7.2	Competencies for collaborative managers	99
7.3	Leadership theories	101
8.1	Job description for a boundary spanner	128
8.2	Collaborative leadership competencies	134
9.1	Summary of boundary spanners' profiles	142

Figures

2.1	Partnership structure in Cardiff	11
3.1	The interlocking forces of structure, agency and ideas	26
4.1	Boundary spanning roles	38
8.1	Methods of knowledge conversion in collaboration	122

Boxes

| 5.1 | Sources of accountability | 74 |
| 5.2 | Multiple interpretations of the locality model | 78 |

About the author

Dr Paul Williams is Reader in Public Management and Collaboration at the School of Management, Cardiff Metropolitan University. He combines an extensive career of working as a public sector manager in Welsh local government for over 20 years, with academic experience as a researcher, lecturer and consultant in public policy and management. He has undertaken research for a wide range of agencies at local and national government levels in Wales on topics such as equality, sustainable development, community strategies, the role of elected members and collaborative working. He has a record of publications in these policy areas and his research interests are predominantly focused on integration between health and social care, leadership for collaboration and the role of individual agents in the collaborative process.

Acknowledgements

This book is the product of my sustained research interest in collaborative working over the last decade. During this time I have been involved in a number of research studies in different policy fields, predominantly in Wales, the fieldwork for which has brought me into contact with numerous people from different sectors – practitioners, managers, directors, professionals, politicians, community representatives and others. These have found time in busy schedules to engage with me in detailed conversations about collaboration in general and boundary spanning in particular. I am extremely grateful to all of them for their time and insights.

I have been influenced by the work of many academics during the preparation of this book, none more so than Professor Helen Sullivan with whom I have collaborated on many research studies, and who has always been a critical and valued friend.

Finally, this book is dedicated to my wife and daughter – Jan and Sophie. Jan has been incredibly supportive and inspirational during my academic career, encouraging me to strive to high standards, and along the way providing valuable contributions drawn from her long experience of senior management in the NHS. I am equally proud of Sophie who has already demonstrated her proficiency as a high academic achiever. My love and thanks to them both.

ONE

Introduction

This book concerns a particular set of individual actors who work within theatres of collaboration – settings that involve agencies uniting to design and deliver public services both within and between sectors. These individual actors are referred to as 'boundary spanners' because they engage in 'boundary spanning' activities that cross, weave and permeate many traditional boundary types, including organisational, sectoral, professional and policy.

Collaboration in the UK has proliferated across all areas of public policy, particularly in response to the interconnected and complex nature of policy issues. As Luke (1998, p 5) observes: 'in the last twenty years, a quiet crystallization of interdependencies has set in that has changed the way we engage in public action. We are now tied into multiple webs of interconnections never before witnessed in human history'. As a consequence, the breadth and depth of collaboration has expanded over the last decade, and has emerged as an integral component of the design and delivery of public services. New forms of governance and management arrangements have developed which challenge existing practices and demand different skills and capacities. The success of this model of public policy is critical to the quality of life for many service users and citizens who are often disadvantaged by a lack of coordination and duplication between service providers in dealing with their complex and interrelated needs. Forms of collaboration are central to the efficiency and effectiveness of scarce public resources, particularly during periods of unprecedented financial restraint. This book, therefore, has been written at an opportune time where the imperatives of collaboration are being experienced across the range of public policy and practice, and insights and lessons contained within the book will hopefully inform the practical design of collaborative solutions.

Policy makers and practitioners are eager to search for 'what works' in a dynamic policy field replete with complexity, ambiguity and tension. While the broad thrust and benefits of collaboration are accepted, delivery in practice is highly problematic. Negotiating and enacting common purpose among multiple and diverse agencies with different cultures, management systems, accountabilities and purposes is complex, and understanding the structural and agential determinants of success is difficult to unravel. What limited robust evidence exists suggests that collaboration has not yielded its potential in many areas leading to frustration, conflict and an inefficient use of public resources.

Although this book is grounded primarily in a public sector context, perspectives from other sectors, particularly the private sector, are explored as a means of learning both to establish whether any useful practical lessons can be transferred between sectors, and also as an opportunity to interrogate the relevance of any theorising based on evidence from the private sector. The importance of intersectoral learning is particularly appropriate in contemporary public policy collaboration because of the involvement of agencies from different sectors and the increasingly blurred and shifting boundaries between them. While public and private contexts can be viewed as fundamentally different in terms of purposes, value base and accountabilities, the motivations to collaborate are often similar, and the consequent governance and management challenges faced stemming from differences in culture, style and strategic purpose are common to both sectors. But care is needed when drawing direct comparisons between sectors because of the strength of contrasting contextual and structural factors.

The book's focus on public policy and practice is underpinned by a robust academic enquiry into an important and hitherto relatively under-researched area. A central theme is that, although the theoretical and empirical literature on collaboration is extensive and multidisciplinary, its focus is unbalanced, being pitched primarily at a macro level and neglectful of the role of individual agents. This assertion applies equally across different sectors. Referring to the private sector, Hutt et al (2000, p 51) comment that: 'surprisingly, human or people factors appear to have remained unconsidered or, at worst, dismissed, in the alliance research tradition'; in relation to public–private partnerships (PPPs), Noble and Jones (2006, p 891) argue that: 'the PPP literature is dominated by institutional and organizational level discourses to the detriment of analyses of the dynamic role of individual actors in the management of this form of inter-organizational relationship'; and in relation to the public sector, Williams (2002, p 106) affirms that: 'the fixation at the inter-organizational domain level understates and neglects the pivotal contribution of individual actors in the collaboration process'. This book aims to counter this perceived imbalance with a focus on the role and behaviour of the boundary spanners in the process of collaboration. It aims to achieve this, not only via a micro-level examination, but also through a balanced approach that situates individual agency within its dynamic interplay within institutional, organisational and other macro-level contextual forces. An analytical framework is introduced to ground and explore relationships between structure, agency and ideas, and to pose questions, some of which can be examined with the help of existing evidence, and others which must remain the research topics for future enquiry.

This book adopts a predominantly UK focus and draws greatly on the author's own research in Wales. However, it presents relevant literature from other countries, particularly the US and Northern Europe, because collaborative forms of governance and management have emerged as a result of similar forces to the UK, including the complexity of policy issues, restrictions on public finances, the changing boundaries between public and private spheres and an increasing focus on the needs of the citizen. While the context may be different in terms of institutional and organisational structures, financial and accountability frameworks and the nature of government intervention, and while the drivers for collaboration and type of stakeholders involved may result in different local approaches, the challenges for managers and practitioners have much in common. Hence, the potential for transferable learning between different countries is significant.

In terms of structure, the book opens with an overview of the policy context with a short history of the nature and extent of collaboration in UK public policy. It explores some of the main influences driving this form of governance and its problematic nature. A synopsis of the situation internationally is included to highlight the emergence of recent trends and practices in a number of countries. Questions of terminology and definitions which often bedevil any discussion of collaboration are addressed, before the chapter proceeds with a review of the complex and diverse motivations underpinning collaboration, and an examination of its costs and benefits. It is suggested that there is a questionable hegemony about this form of working which needs to be exposed, partly stemming from competing roots of collaboration which, on the one hand, emphasise a process that is driven by self-interested motivations and bargaining, and on the other, by a vision that transcends the individual in an integrative search for the common good (Emerson, 2009). Lastly, a short literature review is included which identifies the main theories, models and concepts that are advanced to explain collaboration at a macro level of analysis. This material is multidisciplinary in nature but lacks integration. Nevertheless, it provides an opportunity of anchoring emerging micro-level perspectives on the boundary spanner considered in later chapters.

In the absence of balance and coherence in the literature on collaboration, Chapter Three turns to the structure–agency debate underpinning the study of social sciences to provide both a theoretical and practical framework in which to position the present study. Although contributions on this discussion are highly contested, the theories that suggest a high degree of interaction and interplay between the two basic components are illuminating, and attribute a greater role for individual agency than is acknowledged in other quarters. The equation is complicated by the introduction of 'ideas' as an additional major component to structure and agency, and this presents a highly rewarding set of new relationships particularly between the agency–ideas axis. It stimulates a discussion on the role of framing and sensemaking by individuals that assumes paramount importance in the congested and contested 'ideas' terrain of collaboration, and links to theories of the policy process such as the Advocacy Coalition Framework (ACF) that fully incorporates the role of individual actors and their systems of beliefs, values and preferences. Although much of the focus is on the interrelationships between structure, agency and ideas, Emirbayer and Mische's (1998) contribution allows a more in-depth exploration of agency – a route that is embraced in this book. A much wider examination of the entire framework is outside the realms and resources of the current project.

Before the in-depth exploration of the role and nature of boundary spanners is undertaken, the thorny question of definition is tackled. Who can be classed as a boundary spanner? Can they be clearly differentiated from other actors? And is this a useful or confusing construct? It is suggested that there are broadly two types of boundary spanner. First, there are the individual actors who have a dedicated position and job role to operate within multiorganisational settings, and whose formal duties are wholly devoted to boundary spanning activities. And second, there is a significantly larger cohort of people who increasingly undertake boundary spanning activities as part of mainstream public management. The underlying proposition here is that as a consequence of the interrelated nature of policy problems, multilevel governance and the imperatives of user-focused models of service design and delivery, public managers are required to engage in collaborative management to achieve their objectives. This type of boundary spanner can be found at different levels in the organisational hierarchy – at the top with leaders, people occupying managerial positions, and at the frontline with practitioners delivering services to users and citizens. The subsequent discussion and analysis is informed by literature and research evidence relevant to leaders and managers. Although certain groups of practitioners can lay a legitimate claim to being a boundary spanner, against a background of a limited body of research, this book does not directly consider their contribution. However, the seminal work of Lipsky (1980), which centres on the life and work of 'street-level' bureaucrats, offers important insights into the practical challenges and dilemmas faced in delivering services at the interface between agencies and users. Here, the ambiguities and tensions flowing from the juxtaposition of bureaucratic imperatives and the needs of citizens result in a high degree of discretionary behaviour. Petchey et al (2007) have recently adopted this perspective by referring to 'street-level policy entrepreneurs' and their role in developing local cancer care innovations, and Rugkasa et al (2007) emphasise the 'downward' spanning focus of some boundary spanners and their engagement with citizens and communities. They suggest that much of the work of the 'downward spanner' has much in common with community development practice.

Chapters Four and Five focus on the dedicated class of boundary spanner operating in public sector collaboration. The material that forms the substance for an exploration of their role and competencies is partly gathered from the author's own research and partly from a range of diverse perspectives from an interdisciplinary literature. The discussion is structured around four main roles that boundary spanners discharge – reticulist, entrepreneur, interpreter/communicator and coordinator. It is argued that each of these has a number of competencies associated with them, although both the individual roles and competencies are highly interrelated. Following this in-depth investigation, a number of questions are posed and addressed relating to knowledge, experience and personality. First, whether there is a discrete body of knowledge, expertise and experience that is necessary for boundary spanners to acquire, and second, whether personality is an important factor. Are boundary spanners born or bred? Is there a set of traits that predispose certain types of actors to be effective boundary spanners? Or is the debate wrongly posed and personality is not a material issue? Finally, the discussion moves on to consider the challenges boundary spanners face which are manifested in a number of tensions, paradoxes and ambiguities – managing in and across multiple modes of governance, the blurring of personal and professional relationships, the dilemmas of multiple accountabilities and appreciating multiple framing processes.

Although the focus of this book is set within a public sector context, potentially valuable perspectives and insights can be extracted from the private sector. Although early perspectives on boundary spanners were confined to activities related to managing the interface between businesses and their external environments, a significant body of material has been accumulated on the functions and activities of alliance managers working in the context of joint ventures, strategic partnerships and other forms of cooperative behaviour, particularly Public Private Partnerships (PPPs). Alliance managers here look to manage across different firms and cultures, building trust through personal relationships, developing effective links and networks and communicating both internally and externally. The tensions and ambiguities involved in different forms of accountability are emphasised, but an important point is made that effective alliance management can lead to improved company performance. A short discussion looks at the comparisons and contrasts between boundary spanners in the public and private realms.

Chapter Seven takes up a broader interpretation of a boundary spanner to encompass managers and leaders operating within arenas requiring 'collaborative public management'. While many of the role elements and competencies are similar to those discussed previously, the key challenge for this group is how to balance their function and responsibilities within formally prescribed positions inside an organisation, with those as agent or representative in forms of collaboration. Coping with sources of tension, paradox and ambiguity are an ever-present part of this job. This chapter is influenced by the emerging literature on 'collaborative public management' as well as the more traditional material on network management, and explores a range of perspectives on individual actors. Finally, the focus is shifted to leaders operating in this context, and the boundary spanning skills and behaviours that are needed to be effective. The discussion is framed within a broader overview of leadership for collaboration and critically reviews the relevance of different theories and approaches to leaders and leadership processes. While the literature on leadership in general is voluminous, expanding and contested, comparatively little attention has been accorded to leadership for collaboration. What little exists is unconsolidated but illuminating in parts and relevant to the main thrust and central arguments contained in this book.

An important aim of this book is to ground the research and theoretical exploration of boundary spanners in the realities of public policy and practice, and this is the focus of Chapter Eight. 'What works' and 'evidence-based practice' were key New Labour mantras that reflected a need to encourage a more effective resonance between the respective academic and research communities, and the practical needs of policy makers and practitioners. The thrust of this trend has more recently been translated into the development of the new Research Excellence Framework (REF) which controls the amount and direction of public funding into UK universities including the requirement to evidence research impact. This book concerns a highly influential set of actors performing within governance arrangements that have, and continue to spread across the public policy landscape. What then are the implications of the previous chapters for the design and practice of collaboration? What impact do different structural arrangements have on the ability of boundary actors to operate effectively? Do we need to install a greater number of dedicated boundary spanners into the system, or is the longer-term strategy one of developing the boundary spanning capabilities of all public managers and operators? How should we train and develop boundary spanners and with which competencies? This chapter also considers the mechanisms and frameworks for learning and knowledge management in collaborative settings because, without these, the lessons identified through empirically generated and other research are unlikely to be accepted and embedded. Boundary spanners have a key role in learning and knowledge management processes but this needs to be contextualised within institutional and other factors that have an impact on these phenomena.

The concluding chapter takes stock of the main themes and arguments presented in the book and looks forward to the trajectory of future collaborative action in the public domain and the likely role of boundary spanners. It advances a research agenda with questions that need to be addressed to enable a much fuller, richer and nuanced account of the work of boundary spanners to be assembled than currently exists.

This book has been written for two main audiences. First, it is designed to appeal to a multidisciplinary academic audience of researchers, lecturers and students interested in this field of study from public policy and administration, business and management, social policy, organisational studies, economics and political science. Case study material is included where appropriate throughout the text to exemplify aspects of the discussion. At the end of each chapter, the main learning points are summarised for the reader, together with suggested further reading on the specific topics covered. Lastly, as an aid to classroom discussion, a number of questions are posed on key points of debate and deliberation. Although the book favours an academic audience, it is not overly theoretical in tone and content, and is designed to be accessible, and of practical assistance to a broad policy and practitioner community, particularly those who are engaged in management development and other forms of career development and learning. Lessons for practice and 'what works' are legitimate concerns of this treatise, and generic lessons about effective collaborative practice are highlighted.

In summary, this book has been written with a number of objectives in mind:

- First, within the overall context of collaboration, to address an imbalance in the theoretical and empirical literature by focusing on the role of agency through the theory and practice of boundary spanners.
- Second, to provide a practical contribution to policy makers and practitioners tasked with designing and delivering public services in collaboration.

- Third, to highlight and value the potential of learning through an approach that is multidisciplinary, drawing on different theoretical approaches and traditions, and interrogating material from different policy areas, sectors and countries.
- Fourth, to set out a future research agenda consisting of key questions that need to be addressed to accumulate a body of evidence in this area that is theoretically robust, consolidated, conceptually integrated within a macro-level framework of structure and agency, and providing practical insights and lessons for public policy and practice.

It can be argued that this book is highly original, provides a comprehensive and integrated work on the nature and role of boundary spanners, and fills a gap in the general literature on collaboration that hitherto has been focused at a macro level. Its analysis and messages are likely to stand the test of time because collaboration, albeit in constantly evolving and changing manifestations, will be a permanent feature of the public policy landscape. The ultimate value of this text might be judged against the extent to which it prompts further research and enquiry into this comparatively neglected aspect of collaboration in the future.

TWO

Policy context: intra- and intersectoral collaboration

Introduction

Intra- and intersectoral collaboration is now an established feature of the UK public policy landscape evidenced in a mosaic of different permutations between the public, private and third sectors. This form of working can be traced back over 50 years and during that time it has altered in its shape, breadth and depth. As illustrated in Table 2.1, the early focus was primarily directed towards the alleviation of poverty, social malaise and the inner cities, through a combination of area-based and community development approaches.

Table 2.1: A history of collaborative working in the UK

Era	Partnerships
1960s and 1970s Emphasis on Poverty and the problems of the Inner Cities	Educational Priority Areas; Housing Action Areas; General Improvement Areas; Area Management; Inner Area Studies; Urban Programme; Community Development; Comprehensive Community Development
1980s Conservative years focusing on economic regeneration involving the private sector, and some limited activity around the health and social care interface	Urban Development Corporations; Urban Task Forces; Inner city Partnerships; Joint Planning and Joint Consultative Committees for health and social care.
1990s and first decade of 21st Century Development of partnerships across a wide policy front promoted by the government mantra of 'joined-up' governance, continuation of public private partnerships and explosion of initiatives.	Single Regeneration Budgets; Estate Action; City Challenge; Local Strategic Partnerships; People in Communities; Communities that Care; Communities First; Drug and Alcohol Partnerships; Community Safety Partnerships; Community Strategy Partnerships; SureStart; OnTrack; Youth Offending Teams; Local Agenda 21; Health, Social Care and Wellbeing Partnerships; Health Action Zones; Employment Action Zones; Education Action Zones; Early Years Partnerships; Children and YoungPeople's Partnerships; Local Area Agreements; Multi-Area Agreements; Total Place Programme; Sustainable Communities Partnerships.

This was succeeded in the Thatcher years by partnerships concerning economic regeneration and urban development, coupled with some joint working around the health and social care interface. The involvement of business in economic regeneration initiatives was the forerunner of a much greater role for the private sector in the design and delivery of public services in subsequent years. The election of a New Labour administration in 1997 heralded a proliferation of collaborative initiatives across a wide policy front amounting to a distinctive public policy paradigm. This approach, typically referred to as 'joined-up government' (Pollitt, 2003), has been rolled out and practised in most areas of social, economic and environmental policy – crime and community safety, health, housing, education, transport and urban regeneration (Sullivan and Skelcher, 2002) – and has continued unabated albeit with frequent changes in emphasis and approach. Since devolution in Wales and Scotland, a similar range of partnerships have been developed across most policy areas. The goals of joined-up government are essentially to increase the effectiveness and efficiency of policies, to create synergy and foster innovation through joint production of effort and expertise and to secure seamless and integrated services at the point of delivery. The true extent and complexity of this phenomenon can be gauged by an audit of partnership arrangements in Cardiff undertaken in 2010 that revealed the existence of over 118 partnership groups with 560 individuals involved (see Figure 2.1).

Dowling et al (2004, p 309) reflect that: 'it is difficult to find a contemporary policy document or set of good practice guidelines that does not have collaboration as the central strategy for the delivery of welfare'. Although devolution offers the potential for policy divergence to the constituent countries of the UK, here too, collaboration remains central to their approaches in different ways.

Collaborative models of public policy can be seen as part of a long tradition in the UK of attempting to secure better coordination in government (Peters, 1998). In part, this stems from the fragmentation of public services and the creation of multiple agencies with differing forms of accountability; from the constant need by government to make the best use of resources and secure economic efficiency; as a result of trends towards decentralisation and devolution which make problems of coordination and policy coherence across different tiers of governance highly problematic; and finally, as a consequence of the increasing globalisation of many policy issues which cannot be contained within national boundaries. A particular driver of collaboration is the analysis of many policy problems such as health inequalities, obesity, low educational attainment, crime and disorder, poverty, sustainable development and an ageing population as 'wicked' (Rittel and Weber, 1973; Grint, 2005) – problems that are complex, interdependent and weave across organisational, professional and sectoral boundaries. Their causes and solutions are the subject of differential framing by multiple stakeholders, and critically are not capable of being managed by single agencies acting autonomously. In the words of Kooiman (2000, p 142):

Figure 2.1: Partnership structure in Cardiff

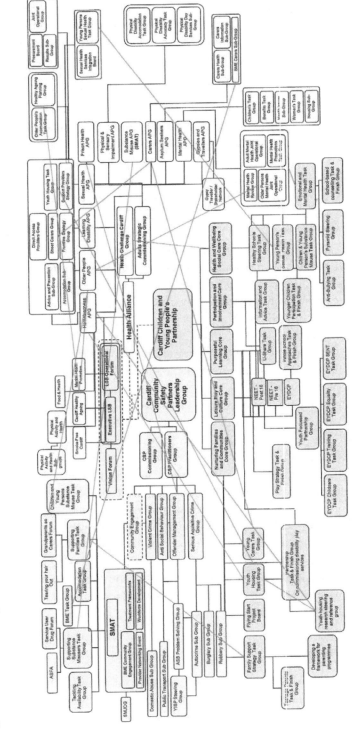

Source: City and County of Cardiff (2010)

> ... no single actor, public or private, has the knowledge and information required to solve complex, dynamic, and diversified problems; no actor has an overview sufficient to make the needed instruments effective; no single actor has sufficient action potential to dominate unilaterally.

The argument therefore is that effective public policy interventions should be predicated on intra- and intersectoral collaboration, expressed in the notion of 'governance' which refers to a set of institutions and actors drawn from, but also beyond, government, and reflecting the blurring of boundaries and responsibilities between public, private and third sector interests (Stoker, 1998). Although major parties across the political spectrum concede a role for the private sector in the public realm – to provide choice in previously monolithic bureaucracies and to lever additional resources into the public sector – the means of achieving these ends are highly contested. Under the stewardship of successive Conservative administrations of the 1980s and 1990s, new public management, with its focus on private sector management methods, in combination with new institutional economics, with its aim of introducing competition into the public sector, were used to justify the dismantling of public sector monopolies, and creating new service sector markets for private companies. Although political control at national level changed in 1997, and the language and rhetoric centred on the term 'partnership', the involvement of the private sector remained an important plank of New Labour government policy. The private finance initiative (PFI), public–private partnerships (PPPs) and the government's modernisation programme gave clear expression to this approach.

UK government approaches to collaboration have been multifaceted and have altered frequently. They include a mixture of coercion, exhortation and prescription involving a plethora of initiatives and experiments, legislation and statutory duties aimed at forcing organisations to work together, and discretionary funding streams and competitive bidding predicated on partnership working. Although the imposition of duties to 'consult and cooperate' on named bodies, such as those introduced by the Local Government and Public Involvement in Health Act 2007 in relation to the preparation of Local Area Agreements in England, are intended to coerce agencies to work together, the interpretation of the duties in practice is open to much discretion. Perri 6 (2004) suggests that although there are examples of bottom-up, opportunistic and organic forms of joined-up government, the main thrust is undoubtedly hierarchical and centralist in nature.

International trends

Subsequent chapters of this book refer to material from countries other than the UK, particularly the US and Northern Europe. It is therefore appropriate to offer some brief observations on the prevailing policy context in those areas, especially in relation to public governance and management. In general, Friedman (2005, p 201) suggests that the effects of globalisation have encouraged a move from 'a primarily vertical (command and control) value-creation model to an increasingly horizontal (connect and collaborate model)' with significant implications for intersectoral roles and relationships, and 6 (2004, p 119) argues that there is 'a widespread political commitment throughout the western world and beyond to co-ordination and integration'. New public management reforms represent a branch of this trend that have been manifested in different ways in different countries and with varying degrees of success (Pollitt, 2002), but generally reflecting a greater influence of private sector practices including more emphasis on performance measurement, markets, choice, competition and private sector management styles. In addition, there has been a greater focus on the involvement of customers and citizens with implications for accountability and openness.

While new public management focused on management, more recent trends suggest a shift towards new public governance models in a number of countries, reflecting a web of relationships between government, business and civil society (Lynn, 2010). Governance has become more multilayered in nature (Peters and Pierre, 2001), and horizontal institutional capacity has increased, both challenging the way in which the state and its capacities have an impact on society. Processes have become less hierarchical and more negotiated and decentralised, with decision making enmeshed in complex patterns of relationships and networks between state and non-state actors. In the Netherlands, for instance, there is a discernible emphasis on the development of policy networks and integrated services (Kickert, 1997), both for service administration and implementation. This involves less direct government intervention, an external orientation and the adoption of a steering role.

6 (2004) argues that the approach to coordination and integration in the US has been individualistic, voluntary, emergent and innovative in nature, primarily rooted at state rather than national level. However, there is equally a long tradition of programmes, for example, in health and welfare, that are premised on partnership working and which have been mandated in a top-down fashion by central government. Interestingly as well, examples of high profile leaders (tsars) being appointed to encourage better coordination in particular policy fields can be detected, for example, drugs and civil defence. Koliba et al (2011) also maintain that interorganisational, intergovernmental and intersectoral collaboration has been an important part of US administration, but now a number of contemporary trends – namely moves to devolve, privatise, partner and regulate – are contributing to the increasing importance of mixed-form network governance, aligned to one or more policy areas but typically drawing on actors from different sectors and geographic planes. These trends, coupled with societal changes in terms of increased diversity, fragmentation, dispersed power, the growth of networks, the permeability of structures and processes, interdependency and the nature of complex issues, has stimulated changes in public governance paralleling those in the UK. These are reflected in references to the emergence of 'collaborative public management' which Agranoff and McGuire (2003, p 4) define as a 'process of

facilitating and operating in multi-organizational arrangements to solve problems that cannot be solved or easily solved by single organizations'; and 'collaborative governance' defined by Donahue (2004, p 2) as an 'amalgam of public, private, and civil-society organizations engaged in some joint effort'. Cooper et al (2006, p 76) extend the former notion to one of 'citizen-centred collaborative public management' to emphasise the role of the public in these processes, again mirroring the focus on citizen-centred and user-focused approaches promoted in the UK. Innovation is a feature of this new public policy landscape, with a wide range of models used for the design and delivery of public services, frequent shifts in power relationships between different actors, a greater use of indirect policy tools by government, and now, 'far from being episodic or occurring in just a few programs, collaboration in public management is as common as managing bureaucracies' (McGuire, 2006, p 403)

Terminology and definitions do matter

The study of collaboration is bedevilled by problems of definition, language and terminology. These cannot be dismissed as mere academic indulgence because, not only is there no common or accepted definition of collaboration, it is also confused with other terms that are used to describe forms of interorganisational relationships such as partnership, alliance, integration and coordination. Such terms are often used interchangeably but mean different things to different people. Although as McLaughlin (2004) argues, a lack of definitional clarity can be helpful in some circumstances because its very ambiguity invites multiple interpretations, and therefore does not immediately exclude potential stakeholders, it does have the potential to be highly problematic in practice when consensus is sought on collective action. There is evidence that many forms of collaboration encounter difficulties that stem from different interpretations of the nature and purpose of collaboration (Sullivan and Williams, 2009). As will be discussed in later chapters, this is a product of the framing processes (Schon and Rein, 1994; Benford and Snow, 2000) of different actors who make sense of policy issues and organisational realities in different ways.

A few definitions of collaboration are helpful in understanding the essence of the notion. Bardach (1998, p 8) suggests that it is 'any joint activity by two or more agencies that is intended to increase public value by their working together rather than separately', and Sullivan (2010, p 3) defines collaboration as a 'more or less stable configuration of rules, resources and relationships generated, negotiated, and reproduced by diverse yet interdependent actors that enable them to act together in the pursuit of public purposes'. Both definitions place an emphasis on the creation of 'public value' (Moore, 1995) and of releasing the potential for synergy. Gray's (1989, p 228) spin on collaboration as 'a mechanism by which a new negotiated order emerges among a set of stakeholders' highlights the process of collaboration which may result in a different form of governance or institutional arrangements, and can be emergent, exploratory or developmental, and a vehicle for learning in action.

Lawrence et al (1999, p 481) offer a comprehensive definition of collaboration as follows:

> A co-operative, interorganizational relationship that relies on neither market nor hierarchical mechanisms of control but is instead negotiated in an ongoing communicative process. Whereas hierarchies are associated with a willingness on behalf of members to submit to both direction and monitoring of their superiors, collaboration involves the negotiation of roles and responsibilities in a context where no legitimate authority sufficient to manage the situation is recognised.

As with Gray, the emphasis is again placed on collaboration as a negotiated process but importantly, where the mediation mechanism is not price or authority. This presents an important contextual challenge for people managing in these kinds of environments as will hopefully become clearer in later chapters. Lastly, Thomson et al (2009, p 25), strongly influenced by the definition of Wood and Gray (1991), compile a definition that attempts to reflect the multidimensional nature of collaboration by stressing five key dimensions: 'two of which are structural in nature (*governance and administration*), two of which are social capital dimensions (*mutuality and norms*), and one of which involves agency (*organizational autonomy*)' emphasis in original.

Collaboration is therefore a complex notion that attracts different interpretations and emphasis, and can be conceived as a means to an end or an end in itself – a set of principles to guide the conduct of public governance and management, or a project that is ultimately manifested in new forms and structures. Definitional clarity is particularly important when measuring performance and outcomes (Thomson et al, 2009). If you are not able to understand what it means, how can you measure its effectiveness? Lasker et al (2001, p 199), in the context of community health partnerships, argue that it is critically important to conceptualise collaboration, to know what it is, how it functions and what determinants and processes are likely to achieve the outcome of synergy, which they refer to as the 'unique advantage of collaboration'.

Motivation and drivers

The motivations underpinning collaborative behaviour are numerous and varied, including the desire to create synergy, transformation or budget enlargement (Mackintosh, 1992), and particularly in the private sector, risk reduction, economies of scale or technological exchange (Contractor and Lorage, 1988). Aiken and Hage (1968) consider that, basically, it involves organisations chasing resources, notably money, skills and manpower, although as Kogut (1988) points out in relation to strategic alliances, the opportunity for acquiring organisational learning and the transfer of tacit knowledge are also important considerations.

Oliver (1990) offers a useful framework for understanding the critical contingencies of relationship formation. The first is equivalent to the mandated agenda pursued by UK government, whereas the others are voluntary interactions determined by asymmetry, reciprocity, efficiency, stability or legitimacy. Oliver emphasises the point that decisions to interact with other agencies can be determined by more than one contingency, although one may predominate at any one time, and also that motivations can be dynamic and change as a result of the experiences of collaboration or other external environmental influences.

Cooperative behaviours are also evident at an individual level and motivated by personal, professional or work-related reasons. Citizen-centred and client-focused models of public service design and delivery, and other altruistic values evoking a public service ethos, often drive individual actors and managers. Frontline professionals and practitioners faced with the realities of interorganisational incoherence can work creatively across boundaries to deliver care to vulnerable groups and service users.

Costs and benefits

The case for collaborative working is compelling but sometimes overstated in relation to its potential downside. It offers the prospect of interventions that are not only superior in quality and innovation through the combined knowledge, expertise and resources of different agencies working together, but also facilitates the delivery of solutions through mechanisms and frameworks based on participation, ownership and stakeholder involvement (McQuaid, 2010). It addresses the challenge of 'wicked issues', the problem of the fragmentation and duplication of public agencies, and aims at maximising the efficiency of scarce resources through the pursuit of quality and cost-effectiveness. Payne (2000) argues that partnership working helps by bringing together skills, sharing information, achieving continuity of care, apportioning responsibility and accountability, coordinating resource planning and focusing on the needs of service users, and McLaughlin (2004) refers to the whole process being greater than the sum of the individual parts. In the private sector, cooperative strategies such as joint ventures and strategic alliances are pursued as a means of securing competitive advantage.

However, despite the attraction of collaborative working, it has been found to be both complex and problematic, resulting in a reported high rate of failure in the private sector (Child et al, 2005; Parise and Prusak, 2006; Hansen, 2009). The situation is similar in the public sector and 'partnership is seen, generally as "a good thing" although very little empirical work has been done to justify either the claim that policies in the past failed because of a lack of partnership or that new partnership arrangements have demonstrably improved outcomes' (Ling, 2002, p 82). There is often an unquestioning belief in the virtues of collaboration rather than a hard-headed assessment of its relevance to particular circumstances.

As Alter and Hage's (1993) calculus of interorganisational collaboration highlight, there are very real costs to this activity, and any decision on joint working should not be taken lightly or in ignorance of the balance between the costs and benefits. Interorganisational working has a number of potential disadvantages. Working with other organisations risks a loss of status and legitimacy. It can be perceived as a sign of weakness in an organisation's ability to manage in a particular area, with potential future repercussions in terms of government funding or a reorganisation of functions. This form of working can also result in a loss of stability, control and autonomy, and produce a measure of confusion in customers and clients about who is responsible for particular aspects of service design and delivery. Power relationships between partnering organisations are invariably reconfigured, with accountability arrangements often unclear and opaque. Interorganisational arenas increase the potential for conflict over domain, goals and methods leading to lengthy and tortuous decision-making processes and delays over finding solutions and taking action. Lastly, there are very real risks for organisations taking a collaborative route in being linked with possible failure, not necessarily of their own making, but because of the performance of one of their partners. This can lead to a loss of reputation, status and financial position. At an individual level, Glasby and Lester (2004) highlight the negative effect of partnership working on staff morale and job satisfaction as a result of confused organisational identities, threats to professional roles and lack of clarity surrounding managerial responsibilities.

The collaborative imperative has continued unabated particularly over the last decade, despite these and other potential drawbacks. However, at a strategic level, concerns have been voiced about questions of multiple and different forms of accountability, coupled with a general lack of transparency and questionable democratic legitimacy (Skelcher, 1998; Morgan and Mungham, 2000). A major problem lies in evaluating and assessing the impact and effectiveness of collaboration, and the steady proliferation of different types of collaboration at both national and local levels has led to accusations of duplication and lack of coordination. 6 (1997) refers to a condition of 'fragmented holism' – both congestion and fragmentation at the same time. Indeed, it often appears that there is a strong presumption to create new forms of collaboration rather than to consider the appropriateness of existing structures, and that collaboration is seen as an outcome rather than a means to an end. The hegemonic nature of collaboration results in collaboration being used as an inappropriate response to particular issues and policy problems.

Theorising collaboration

Although the focus of this book is on individual agency within the process of collaboration, it is instructive to interrogate the theoretical frameworks that exist at a macro level in order to search for explanations that may have some resonance for individual-level behaviours. It also provides a range of perspectives, factors and context that may influence the role, nature and behaviour of individual agents.

However, although a considerable investment has been made by academics and policy makers to understand how and why collaboration works, this has generated a largely diverse literature that is characterised by 'a cacophony of heterogeneous concepts, theories, and research results' (Oliver and Ebers, 1998, p 549). This problem stems in part from the multidisciplinary attention that this field of study has attracted at a macro level, particularly by economists, sociologists and political scientists (Grandori, 1997).

The interorganisational literature in sociology offers a range of perspectives including the exchange perspective (Levine and White, 1961), power/resource dependency perspectives (Aldrich, 1979) and the political economy approach (Benson, 1975). The exchange perspective refers to organisations voluntarily cooperating in the exchange of resources considered to be essential to their goal attainment, including finance, status, legitimacy and assets. Exchange depends on the degree of consensus among organisations about goals, functions, ideologies, cultures and customers; the motivation to exchange is internal to each organisation based on choosing to interact, and organisations perceive mutual benefits or gains from interacting. In contrast, power/resource dependency perspectives assume more realistically that there is competition among organisations for scarce resources such as functions, finance and status. Hence, power is important here and the motivation to interact is likely to be asymmetrical, with one or more organisations inducing or forcing others to interact. The process is characterised by bargaining and conflict. Lastly, the political economy approach (Benson, 1975) is critical of the two previous models, maintaining that they falsely assume rationality and are without contextualisation in the wider socioeconomic structure of society. This approach considers that interorganisational activity is a function of the power relations between various structured interests in a particular policy sector, such as the users of services, service providers, managers, professional groups and politicians.

A number of theories appear in the economics literature to explain interorganisational relationships between firms typically resulting in joint ventures, alliances, trade associations and consortia. Transaction cost economics is prominently represented (Barringer and Harrison, 2000), and this centres on how an organisation manages its boundary spanning activities so as to minimise the sum of its production and transaction costs. The interorganisational option is seen as the alternative to the market or organisational hierarchy when it minimises the transaction costs for participating firms. It helps reduce the costs of opportunism and monitoring inherent in market transactions, and avoids the need to create additional bureaucracy where core competencies may be absent or difficult to arrange. Other theoretical perspectives appearing in the economics literature include resource dependence, strategic choice, stakeholder theory of the firm and organisational learning.

The third main macro-level approach to collaboration focuses on the 'network' that straddles a number of disciplinary areas. However, theoretical stances tend to be polarised between advocates of a social network perspective that concentrates on the structural properties of networks, and the political science preoccupation with governance (Oliver and Ebers, 1998). The social network approach, with its concentration on patterns of relationships and core concepts such as embeddedness, social capital, structural holes and centrality (Burt, 1982), has the potential to link macro and micro levels. The notion of 'governance' attracts a number of different interpretations (Jones et al, 1997) and it can be confusing because of its use in different contexts ranging from policy networks, new public management and corporate governance. A key characteristic of governance as networks expounded by Rhodes (2000) and Stoker (2000) is the differentiation made between this and other forms of governing structures – notably, markets and hierarchies. Network structures exhibit interdependence between actors that can be drawn from different sectors; interactions between members driven by resource exchange and the negotiation of shared purpose; and trust as the primary mechanism of interrelationships. Critically, there is no single source of sovereign power; rather it is negotiated, shared, dispersed and contested. The growth of networks in the UK is considered to be a major contributing factor to a 'hollowing out of the state' (Rhodes, 1996); 'governance without government' (Peters and Pierre, 1998); and the need for the state to concentrate on 'steering' rather than 'rowing' (Osbourne and Gaebler, 1992).

In addition to these macro-level theories, there are numerous other models and conceptual frameworks that are advanced to explain collaboration, including those based on type, structural form, phase and factor. Examples of partnership types include Gray's (1989) exploratory, advisory, confederative and contractual partnerships, and 6 et al's (1999) different forms of relationships between agencies such as mergers, strategic alliances, joint ventures and unions. Some models envisage a spectrum from weak to strong forms of relationships (Mattessich and Monsey, 1992). At the 'weak' end of the spectrum, reference is made to 'cooperation' where interactions are characterised by shared information and mutual support. 'Coordination' is the next along the line evidenced in efforts to reduce duplication, pool resources and pursue shared goals. More intense relationships and stronger ties feature in 'collaboration' with integrated strategies and collective purpose, and finally, integration or co-adunation (Gajda, 2004) is evidenced by unified structures and combined cultures.

In contrast to models based on structure, the process of collaboration is the basis of Gray's (1989) three-phase model that refers to problem definition, direction setting and implementation, and Wilson and Charleton's (1997) extension to five stages. Both models imply a false degree of linearity that does not fully represent the 'messiness' of the policy process. The stagist model is given an inventive twist by Lowndes and Skelcher (1998), with links being made between stages in the partnership lifecycle and predominant mode of governance.

Another set of models consists of factors, dimensions or themes considered to be influential in determining the shape, nature and success of collaboration. For instance, Mattessich and Monsey (1992) refer to factors relating to the environment, membership characteristics, process/structure, communication, purpose and resources, and Huxham and Vangen (2005) list key themes in collaborative practice such as trust, power, managing aims, negotiating purpose and leadership. In similar territory is Lasker et al's (2001) view of collaboration as fundamentally a matter of the creation of partnership synergy that is a product of resources, partner characteristics, relationships among partners, partnership characteristics and the external environment. Also, Mitchell and Shortell (2000) propose a typology/taxonomy of community health partnerships based on seven dimensions: nature of the problem addressed, partnership composition, differentiation, coordination and integration, accountability, centrality and alignment. The problem with these models is that they are inherently weak theoretically because the factors and themes are largely presented as simple lists, and they are underdeveloped in terms of the order, strength, compatibility and interrelationships of the individual components. Finally, there are many other and diverse theories offering explanations of collaboration including those based on discourse (Lawrence et al, 1999), negotiated order (Gray, 1989) and constitutive value (Cropper, 1996).

Conclusion

Theorising about collaboration is characterised by interdisciplinary variety and ambiguity. As Wood and Gray (1991, p 143) conclude, following an attempt to devise a comprehensive theory of collaboration, 'we have only succeeded in suggesting some overarching issues that transcend individual theories' and 'a welter of definitions'. However, despite the absence of any agreed synthesis, a variety of theories and models do exist which are helpful in offering possible explanations linking to, or integrating with, theorising at the level of the individual actors. The issues of motivation and purpose are clearly fundamental, as is the nature of exchange relationships. The prominence of the notion of power reflects the dynamic and contested relationships between different interests within collaborative arenas, and the inevitable consequence of the need for bargaining and negotiation in the search for collective action. Theories of collaboration that visualise it as a form of network governance have a number of interesting implications. For instance, both Agranoff and McGuire (2001) and Kickert et al (1997) suggest that managing in networks is different from managing within other forms of organising; Ebers (1997) argues that the benefit of network as a metaphor is that it can act in an integrative fashion between levels of analysis, particularly in relation to resource and information flows and trust; and finally, Jessop (1997) indicates that networks exist at individual, interorganisational and systemic levels.

Different models of collaboration emphasise particular key characteristics. Motivation is the focus for some, while form and type are referred to by others, although the measures used to generate various classifications are not always clear. Certainly, there is a common view that collaboration is manifested in various ways along a continuum from weak to strong relationships. A number of models highlight the dynamic nature of interorganisational activity and conceptualise it as a process that proceeds through a number of distinct stages or life cycles. Others highlight key factors that influence the nature and course of collaborative activity, both those that encourage and those that hinder success. Factors such as leadership, communication, trust, power and accountability are typical inclusions of this type of model.

This critique invites a number of interesting questions about the relationship between these macro-level theories and the behaviour and role of individual actors operating within collaborative settings. For instance, do different types or forms of collaboration demand specific boundary spanning roles? What influence do particular stages in the collaborative process have on the requirement for distinctive boundary spanning competencies? And are the key drivers for collaboration similar at both an organisational and individual level? Lastly, some of the theories examined in the literature alight on certain key factors that influence and help shape the outcomes of collaborative endeavours, notably leadership, trust, power and accountability. Are these equally important in explaining effective individual agency?

Review of main points

- Forms of collaboration have a long history in the UK, although over the last decade they have increased in depth, extent and intersectorality.
- Collaboration has been pursued in various guises – as policy coordination, joined-up government and partnership – and UK government approaches have been multifaceted and dynamic, and prosecuted through a mixture of prescription and exhortation.
- Terminology is problematic with consequent conceptual confusion. In the absence of universally agreed definitions, it is important to clarify meaning and the use of terms.
- Different motivations induce people and organisations to collaborate. These can be dynamic and multiple, complementary and conflictual.
- There are clearly costs and benefits to collaborative working. It is not the answer to all public policy challenges and public services, and should be carefully scrutinised.
- Macro-level theorising about collaboration is multidisciplinary in nature and lacks integration. It has spawned a range of theories particularly from sociology, economics and political science.
- The network governance approach resonates especially well with recent UK government's prescription for the design and delivery of public services involving a mixture of public, private and third sector interests.
- A range of models exist that highlight different determinants of collaborative working – structural type and form, processes through stages and phases and critical factors and themes. The key themes include deliberation about purpose and aims, developing trust and sharing power, leadership, and managing accountability and performance.

Questions for discussion

1. Given the variety of approaches to, and explanations of 'collaboration', should attempts be made to integrate the field of study or should we accept the richness of multidisciplinarity and theoretical diversity?
2. Which theory(ies) best explain collaboration?
3. Trace the drivers of and key motivations to collaboration over the last 25 years in UK public policy. In what form has it been managed and manifested?
4. What aspects and perspectives of the macro-level literature on collaboration might be instructive for individual actors operating in this environment?

Suggested further reading

6, P. (2004) 'Joined-up government in the Western world in comparative perspective: A preliminary perspective literature review and exploration', *Journal of Public Administration Research and Theory*, vol 14, no 1, pp 103-38.

Cropper, S., Ebers, M., Huxham, C. and Smith Ring, P. (2009) *The Oxford handbook of inter-organizational relations*, Oxford: Oxford University Press.

Gray, B. (1989) *Collaborating*, San Francisco, CA: Jossey-Bass.

Huxham, C. and Vangen, S. (2005) *Managing to collaborate: The theory and practice of collaborative advantage*, London: Sage Publications.

Ling, T. (2002) 'Delivering joined-up government in the UK: dimensions, issues and problems', *Public Administration*, vol 80, no 4, pp 615-42.

Sullivan, H. and Skelcher, C. (2002) *Working across boundaries: Collaboration in public services*, Basingstoke: Palgrave Macmillan.

THREE

Structure and agency

Introduction

A defining characteristic of the literature on collaboration is that it favours an organisational and institutional focus at the expense of micro-level examination. Although some of the models and theories make some reference to individual actors in the process, there is a need to search for a better balance between macro and micro-level explanations and perspectives. This line of argument is endorsed by practitioner perspectives that assert that the role of individual actors is often understated in the course of collaborative working. Poxton (1999, p 3), for instance, commenting on the reorganisation of health services, argues that: 'a new policy environment and new organizational arrangements should make co-operation and collaboration easier than it has been in the past. But real success will depend as much on the determination and creativity of practitioners and managers as it will on Government edict and structural change', and a Department for Transport, Local Government and the Regions (DTLR, 2002, p 125) report on area-based activities in local government concludes that: 'the evidence is that joined up delivery has occurred extensively but in an ad hoc, almost accidental manner dependent on the energy and imagination of individuals'.

In the course of a range of research that the author has been involved with in Wales, particularly in health and social care and community strategies, feedback from diverse individuals engaged in collaborative working consistently championed the pivotal role of key individuals in shaping outcomes. A typical response was: 'the thing that makes it work in any type of structure is the commitment of the person – structures can be enabling or difficult' (NLIAH, 2009, p 10). Perversely, when politicians and policy makers perceive failures in the system, they invariably reach for the 'structural toolkit' to induce change and modify behaviour, rather than taking steps to influence agency more directly. Frequent reorganisations and 'initiativitis' (Fitzpatrick, 1999, p xiii) bear witness to this behaviour. Although it is difficult to find comparable public sector evidence, research from the private sector makes a clear link between effective agency and performance, as illustrated in the following observation by Bamford et al (2003, p 202): 'alliance managers play key roles in nurturing relationships with partners. Because of this, establishing the position of alliance manager has become the single most common step that companies take to improve the performance of their alliances'.

The structure–agency dichotomy

One framework that can help to rebalance and frame the dilemma suggested above exists in the form of the traditional structure–agency debate (Hay, 1995) which is not merely an academic issue but is 'an "everyday" issue, which deals with the fundamental question of to what extent we, as individuals, have the ability to direct our lives in the face of sometimes enormous constraints' (McAnulla, 2002, p 291). The essence of the debate concerns the position that structuralists adopt, believing that social, political and economic outcomes can be explained by 'structure' relating to form, function, context and setting, as opposed to intentionalists or behaviouralists who argue that agency is the determining factor defined as the 'ability or capacity of actors to act consciously ... and to realise his/her intentions' (Hay, 1995, p 94).

Although protagonists from either side of the divide adopt firm positions, some argue that this debate is unnecessarily polarised and arguably falsely set up as 'oppositional'. Alternative approaches are posited by Giddens (1984) in his theory of structuration, which conceptualises a duality of structure, and considers that the interplay between structure and agency is more dynamic, emphasising the mutually important processes involved where 'individual actors carry out practices that are simultaneously constrained and empowered by existing social structure (Scott, 2001, p 75). Crosby and Bryson (2010, p 227 agree that 'structuration theory provides an ideal theoretical framework for understanding how actions and practices create, recreate, and stabilize the structures that then provide rules and resources to draw on and guide' collaborative action. Jessop (1996), also taking a strategic-relational approach, avoids the dualism of structure and agency by focusing on the interaction between strategic actors and the strategic context. Sewell (1992, p 27) suggests that agency is implied in the existence of structure, and that 'agents are empowered by structure, both by the knowledge of cultural schemas that enables them to mobilize resources and by access to the resources that enables them to enact schemas'. Agents are empowered differentially by structures such as position in an organisational hierarchy, social class and professional status. In collaborative settings where structures intersect and are often blurred, the potential exists for key actors to exert influence outside prevailing schemas. Marchington and Vincent (2004, original emphasis) take a pragmatic view by arguing that interorganisational relationships involve 'an *interplay of forces*' at different levels (institutional, organisational and interpersonal); Williams and Sullivan (2009) adopt the position that while actors manufacture outcomes, the parameters of their capacity to act – the constraints and opportunities – is set by the structured context within which they operate; and Martin et al (2009) reach a similar conclusion in their exploration of leadership within public service networks, arguing that structure provides the 'space' for individual actors to perform, and that the relationship between structure and agency is synergistic.

These views resonate with Bogason's (2000) rejection of actors as 'structural dopes' in favour of a compromise referred to as the 'actor-cum-institution (or structure)', where institutional or structural arrangements act as both constraints and assets or resources for future action. This emphasises the role of cognitive processes in actors making sense of the world, and of their ability to set priorities, act as mediators in the creation of strategic capabilities and as bearers of socialisation within organisations. An example of where actors, operating within institutional parameters, attempt to alter constraints into capabilities is where collaboration occurs across organisational boundaries. Here, actors frame strategic action through a new collective understanding.

Archer (1989) counsels against the trend to conflate structure and agency because, in his view, the constituent elements cannot be examined separately. Emirbayer and Mische (1998) take up this challenge with a forensic examination of the notion of 'agency' and a new way of conceiving the relationship between structure and agency. They advance a definition of agency which emphasises its dynamic nature, suggesting that it has three components – iteration, projective and practical-evaluative – each having orientations to the past, future and present. Human agency is defined as: 'temporally constructed engagement of actors of different structural environments – the temporal-relational contexts of action – which, through the interplay of habit, imagination, and judgement, both reproduces and transforms those structures in interactive responses to the problems posed by changing historical situations' (p 970). In relation to iteration, the primary locus of agency revolves around schematisation of social experiences including mental categories, embodied practices, habitual practices, routines and traditions; the projective element includes processes of framing which are considered in more detail below; and finally, the practical-evaluative element is situated in the present, and refers to the contextualisation of social experiences through communication and deliberation with others, providing the ability to exercise agency in a mediation fashion.

Emirbayer and Mische (1998) tackle the structure–agency relationship by forwarding the notion of the double constitution of agency and structure where temporal/relational contexts support particular agentic orientations, which in turn provide different structuring relationships of actors to their environments. In this conception, there is no time when actors are freed from structure, but it does open up a range of interesting empirical propositions about how particular contexts support particular agentic orientations. For instance, what encourages the maintenance of past practices as opposed to provoking more innovation and creativity? Emirbayer and Mische suggest that actors positioned at the 'intersection of multiple-relational contexts' – and this could be collaborative settings – can develop a greater capacity for creativity and critical intervention, particularly through the agentic activities of brokers who operate in this domain. Here, the context itself invites more critical discourse and a search for alternatives than is typically the case in more routinised, intraorganisational hierarchies.

Although structural and agential factors can be used to explain social, economic and political outcomes, Hay (2002) argues that ideational factors also have a significant role to play because, in the absence of perfect information, actors have to interpret the dense and complex world in which they act. This offers an additional set of factors, which, combined with those of agency and structure, offer a comprehensive framework to explore the interplay, direction and force of individual factors that constitute collaborative working (see Figure 3.1).

Figure 3.1: The interlocking forces of structure, agency and ideas

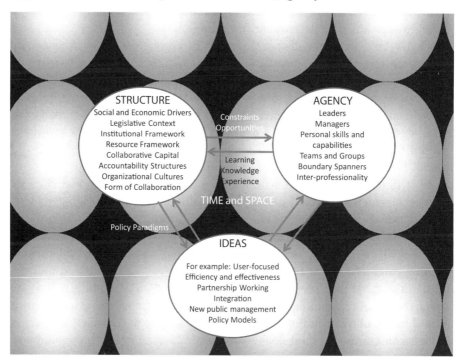

Source: Author's diagram

An examination of each of these sets of factors in turn enables a detailed analysis to be undertaken of a host of individual elements. In terms of context, the important elements are illustrated in Table 3.1. The individual elements that comprise agency include leadership, professionality and interprofessionality, teamwork, and personal skills, capabilities and experience. Ideational influences vary widely particularly at a micro level and in the context of particular policy areas, but certain narratives, stories, policy paradigms and ideas often play a large part in influencing the approach to policy design and implementation. The discourse of 'joined-up' government is a prime example in recent years. Others relate to the role of professionalism, the primacy of citizens and service users, the role of the private and third sectors, devolution and localism, and the future size and role of the state, which is likely to be a preoccupation of the new Conservative/Liberal Democrat administration. Schon (1973) discusses the way in which new ideas float to the surface and become accepted – ideas that are 'often fluid, mutable, changing itself and its environment as it moves' (Freeman, 2006, p 371). Ideas are sometimes seen to travel in the form of metaphors, being communicated through both formal and informal diffusion processes.

Table 3.1: The components of structure

Components	Key features
Social, economic and environmental drivers	Population trends, evidence of social malaise and need, economic recession, social justice and inequality, sustainable development
Statutory context	Legislation and duties, for example, general powers of wellbeing, health flexibilities, duties of partnership
Institutional framework	Configuration of public agencies and organisations, duties and responsibilities, coterminosity of boundaries, devolution and decentralisation, role of private and third sectors
Collaborative capital	History and culture of collaboration between people and agencies, social capital and networks
Financial and resource framework	National initiatives and programmes, availability of pump-priming finance, pooled budgeting, funding for dedicated personnel and administration
Accountability and governance structures	Methods of accountability – democratic, representative, participatory; relationship to users and citizens; single or multiple frameworks
Organisational cultures and management systems	Public or private, local government or NHS, civil service and local government, national and local, policy field
Performance management frameworks	Single or combined

The influence of ideas is strongly felt in particular policy areas where the views of different interests collide:

- in the health sector, with models of health being construed as essentially a matter of dealing with sick people (the medical model) as opposed to being determined by social and environmental factors (the social model);
- in sustainable development, the notion of which is the subject of wide interpretations ranging from simply the natural environmental to a broad-based policy imperative concerning balancing economic growth with social justice over intergenerational time frames;
- in the field of equality which is variously conceived as equal treatment, equality of outcome or integration.

This conflagration of ideas invariably occurs at sites of collaboration where different parties assemble in pursuit of joint purpose. The literature on environmental policy and sustainability, where a wide variety of interests come together, has numerous examples where ideas clash and framing processes are central to the understanding of policy action (Triandafyllidou and Fotiou, 1998; Gray, 2003; Lubell, 2005).

There is, of course, a high degree of interaction both within the sets of structure, agency and ideas, and between them. The building blocks of structure – institutions, organisations and resources – provide a structure that is enabling or constraining for individual actors. It can provide opportunities for action – new duties, policy tools and programmes – or it can represent barriers that inhibit effective collaborative working. In the opposite direction, agency supplies learning and knowledge based on the experiences of individual working practices. Unfortunately, as will be discussed in Chapter 8, the mechanisms for generating, embedding and transferring learning and knowledge management are far from effective, often serendipitous rather than the product of planned strategies. Posner (2009) makes the very insightful observation that each policy tool associated with driving or motivating collaboration has its own 'political economy' – an individualised set of agential factors that influence the process.

The interplay between agency and ideas centres on processes of framing (Benford and Snow, 2000) and sensemaking (Weick, 1995), involving the use of 'cognitive short-cuts', abstractions or lenses to conceptualise and understand the environment. Schon (1987, p 4) explains the process of framing as 'depending on our disciplinary backgrounds, organizational roles, past histories, interests, and political/economic perspectives, we frame problematic situations in different ways'. Framing is sometimes difficult to surface or measure, occurring unintentionally but influenced by deep-seated values and ingrained attitudes. It undertakes four main functions: problem identification, causality, prognosis and mobilising. Stone's (1989) insight into problem definition and agenda setting in the public sector emphasises the role of causal ideas and image making. Here images have the effect of attributing blame, responsibility and cause, and individual actors deliberately manipulate or portray them in ways designed to maximise support. Some causal stories place a burden of responsibility on individual people; others empower actors or interests who claim to have the answers, skills or resources to deal with particular problems.

Schon and Rein (1994, p 29) make the particularly important connection between frames and interests, because 'frames are not free-floating but are grounded in the institutions that sponsor them, and policy controversies are disputes among actors who sponsor conflicting frames'. Theatres of collaboration are especially fertile sites for the assembly of people and organisations with different frames. In practice, frame awareness increases the likelihood of conflict and dilemma, because policy debates stem from multiple and conflicting meanings, stories and values about the nature of social phenomena. However, conflict can be channelled constructively to create new and negotiated meanings and realities, and problem resolution depends on an ability to restructure, reconcile or integrate different frames sufficiently to mobilise collective action – to effect a frame restructuring (Rein, 2006). This is no mean task in collaborative situations populated by a diversity of interests and frames. Although frame exposure may appear a rational course of action as a precursor to reaching a workable consensus, Schon and Rein (1994) argue that this is difficult because differentiating between actual and rhetorical frames is problematic, as some courses of action are only consistent with certain frames, and because frames can mutate between different stages of the policy process – especially design and implementation. Perversely, frame articulation and understanding can result in paralysis.

Benford and Snow (2000, p 614) provide a seminal contribution on frames whose purpose is to 'help render events or occurrences meaningful and thereby function to organise experience and guide action'. Core framing tasks are diagnostic, prognostic and motivational, and the credibility of any framing is a function of frame consistency, empirical credibility and credibility of the 'frame articulators' who function as managers of meaning. Key actors in collaboration have the potential to perform this role – operating as 'cognitive filters' by helping and influencing others to interpret the prevailing context. This can be a powerful role and is an expression of Lukes' (1974) third face of power – the ability of certain actors to help shape the perceptions and preferences of others. Framing is a dynamic process involving frame articulation, amplification and punctuation, often linked in strategic processes where actors attempt to 'link their interests and interpretive frames with those of prospective constituents and actual or prospective resource providers' (Benford and Snow, 2000, p 624). Frame processes are central to understanding the shape and course of policy design and implementation, and the role of individual actors. This point is underscored by Emirbayer and Mische (1998, p 966) who argue that agency rests 'in the interpretive processes whereby choices are imagined, evaluated, and contingently reconstructed by actors in ongoing dialogue with unfolding situations'. The formulation and choice of strategic alternatives is driven through interpretation, so enhancing the importance of ideas, narratives and policy paradigms: 'the cognitive templates through which actors interpret the world' (Hay, 2002, p 212).

The discourse of framing theory resonates particularly well with the Advocacy Coalition Framework (ACF) approach to the policy process. Here, a clear role is identified for agency stemming from individual belief systems, values and perceptions, affecting how people acquire and filter information about the world. Sabatier and Jenkins-Smith (1999) refer to the existence of a hierarchical structure of belief systems with deep core beliefs at the apex (relating to human nature, values, social justice and identity); policy core beliefs in the middle (particularly concerning problem identification, cause and seriousness, and value priorities); and finally, secondary aspects which are more local and specific to particular action. The ACF suggests that coalitions are built up around substantial agreement on policy core beliefs, and that conflict between them needs to be mediated by a specific set of actors – policy brokers.

The study of social learning provides a rich source of understanding about how policy actors make sense of, and act within, processes of 'collective puzzling' (Heclo, 1974). Social learning highlights the role of framing and sensemaking referred to earlier – the 'appreciative systems' (Vickers, 1965) that allow individuals to identify some aspects of the situation rather than others, and to judge and value these in particular ways. What induces appreciative systems to change or shift is, however, difficult to explain. Learning is heavily influenced by what we know already – ideas, concepts and theories. It is an interpretive act that is mediated through cognition, communication and perception. Learning with others is particularly important in the public sector within communities of practice (Brown and Duguid, 2000). These are networks of people linked together by training, profession, cause or policy area, and are particularly important in promoting and channelling ideas and constructions of the world.

Although there is a connection between agency and ideas, particularly through processes of framing, interpretation and sensemaking as discussed above, there is also a two-way channel between structure and ideas. Dominant policy paradigms – equality, integration, joined-up government – can have structural expression in terms of institutional and organisational arrangements, and prompt legislative action. Equally, different social, economic and political structures provide the basis for the generation of ideas about how societies and governments should be organised and managed.

Critically, it is important to recognise that this whole system – structure, agency and ideas – is not static and is constantly evolving in a dynamic fashion both in space and time. Policy paradigms emerge and disappear; structural reorganisations are imposed; national governments change; globalisation fosters changed relationships; society is faced with new and immediate challenges; and economic circumstances necessitate difficult choices. Emirbayer and Mische (1998, p 1012) refer to this dynamic as 'relational pragmatics' where actors live simultaneously in the past, present and future, adjusting their patterns of engagement and action accordingly, and laying 'the basis for a richer and more dynamic understanding of the capacity that actors have to mediating the structuring contexts within such action enfolds'.

Boundary spanning and boundary spanners

The 'structure–agency–ideas' model set out above provides a robust framework for exploring the nature and role of boundary spanners in collaboration. The model is predicated on complex relationships and connections between different factors, and critically in the context of public policy practice, is concerned with the implications and management of the boundaries between them. Chapter Two argues that contemporary public management and governance is driven by the need to promote better coordination and integration of public services, to reduce duplication, to make the best use of scarce resources, to meet gaps in service provision, to satisfy unmet needs and to promote citizen-centred and client-focused service delivery models. This requires people and organisations to work together in collaboration to tackle and manage common issues. Fundamentally, this involves boundary spanning.

Boundary spanning

Boundary spanning is stimulated by complex and highly interdependent problems that meander and weave across different types of boundary, some structural and others socially constructed, especially through agency. These cut across the conventional boundaries of organisation, profession, sector and policy. They have cross-scale and cross-level implications: 'leading to substantial complexity in dynamics' (Cash et al, 2006, p 1). As Radin (1996, p 145) explains:

> Government in a complex society, by definition, is characterised by boundaries. Whether as a result of a fragmented political system, differentiation by policy issues, or because of functional imperatives, lines have been drawn that separate organizations from one another.

The institutional structure in the UK has been the subject of frequent and sometimes radical reorganisation in most policy areas in an effort to achieve synchronisation between structures and changing social, political and economic pressures, but boundaries inevitably remain in some form, even in open systems.

Wenger (1998, p 120) refers to boundaries as 'discontinuities' and as 'lines of distinction between inside and outside, membership and non-membership, inclusion and exclusion'. They provide a measure of autonomy for those inside the boundaries, and are often defined by statutory roles, functions and responsibilities. They allow identities to form, accountabilities to be established and resources to be managed independently. The exact position of any organisational boundary is difficult to gauge as it depends on the criteria that are used to define it – typically, the actors involved, social interactions apparent or activities performed. But, the boundaries of public sector organisations are especially unclear as their relationship with civil society frequently alters through negotiation, perception and statutory edict.

In the current public sector context, public organisations are encouraged to have boundaries that are 'sieves, not shells' (Scott, 1998, p 183), and to avoid buffering strategies that are designed to artificially close systems and protect the core competencies of organisations. Arguably, the boundaries that define professional groups are the least able to be penetrated as is evidenced by the challenges involved in promoting inter and multiprofessionality in health and social care. Professions define realities, frame problems, apply normative beliefs, generate rules and create regulatory procedures to clearly demarcate them from others. Entry to professions and the conduct of their members are strictly guarded.

Boundary spanning activities occur in three areas: at the periphery of organisations where the outer membrane allows permeability for organisational actors to look out and others to look in; in the overlaps between agencies where coordinated activity is sustained through personal relationships, joint policies and protocols; and in new spaces between agencies where new structures and relationships are forged involving sharing resources and joint decision making.

Boundary spanning is designed to operate within and manage these interfaces – to blur, breach, dismantle, cross, infiltrate, permeate, bridge or shift boundaries. Boundary spanning is highly complex, particularly when multiple and overlapping boundaries created by different agencies, sectors and professions are involved which often shift in time and space.

Stone's (1997, p 379) view is that 'in a world of continua, boundaries are inherently unstable. Whether they are conceptual, physical, or political, boundaries are border wars waiting to happen. At every boundary, there is a dilemma of classification: who or what belongs on each side?'. She proceeds to argue that particular boundary configurations confer advantages and disadvantages, rewards and penalties to different parties and interests – they imply relationships of power. Collaboration is often about moving boundaries to coalesce around collective purpose, while at the same time maintaining the integrity of existing ones, although, through mergers or integration, new, more permanent boundaries can be created and old boundaries dissolved.

Boundary spanners

Boundary spanners are the individual actors who engage in boundary spanning activities, processes and tasks. However, there is a considerable degree of conceptual confusion about the term and an absence of definitional clarity that must be addressed. An early work by Leifer and Delbecq (1976) generates a range of descriptors for actors operating in collaborative environments, including 'marginal men', 'unifier', 'input transducer' and 'linking pin'. In addition to these, names such as 'foreign affairs person', 'broker', 'cupid', 'boundroid', 'novelty detector', 'gatekeeper', 'networker', 'agent', 'fixer', tactician', 'boundary crosser' and 'collaborator' can also be detected in the literature to refer to actors who engage in boundary spanning activities. The interesting aspect of this highly inventive list is that the names act as metaphors to reflect the dominant role that commentators perceive them to be undertaking.

This book takes up the challenge of defining who the boundary spanners are by dividing them into two broad categories:

• Individuals who have a dedicated job role or responsibility to work in multiorganisational/multisectoral settings, and 'sustain a connection' (Wenger, 1998, p 114) between different interests and practices. Such individuals are relatively few in number compared with the bulk of public sector staff, and can be detected at different levels in the organisational hierarchy. Examples of frontline boundary spanners include people with tasks and functions that straddle service and agency boundaries – for instance, in health and social care, welfare services and community regeneration. Other examples include those posts that are attached to particular types of partnerships and involve coordination and servicing – crime and community safety coordinators, community strategy officers, youth offending coordinators, integrated care managers and health and social care coordinators. A small number of senior posts in the public sector, for example, director of integrated services, might be included in this first group of boundary spanners.

• Practitioners, managers and leaders who undertake boundary spanning activities as part of a mainstream job role. This group is large in number and diverse in function. The argument here is that the type of policy problem facing society is complex and interrelated, and an increasing proportion of jobs demand cross-boundary engagement as an integral and legitimate component of their job specification. The notion of 'collaborative public management' and 'collaborative public managers' coined by O'Leary and Bingham (2009) encapsulates this interpretation. However, if 'we are all boundary spanners now', the question arises as to whether this renders the notion somewhat redundant, or as a possible compromise, should some limit be placed on the proportion of time that a particular actor engages in a boundary spanning activity to warrant him/her being referred to as a boundary spanner?

Following the definition of a boundary spanner into two types, the next question to be addressed concerns the central roles that they respectively undertake. In the context of the conceptual framework outlined earlier in this chapter, and wherever evidence permits, this needs to reflect any significant relationships to structural and institutional factors. These include the extent to which the roles may be enabled or inhibited by different arrangements, the influence of type of policy area, the significance of different stages in the process of collaboration and any differences that might emerge from various types of collaborative form. These contextual factors are examined in a private sector context in Chapter 6 to determine whether there are any parallels with the public sector and to identify possible areas of intersectoral learning.

In addition to an examination of boundary spanning roles, the competencies needed to undertake them are the subject of intensive scrutiny. As well as managing the structure–agency axis, this shifts the focus to the agency–ideas axis, and the processes and attendant competencies that involve framing and the management of multiple policy ideas and their interpretations. It also invites questions about the possible influence that the personality of a boundary spanner might exert, and whether a boundary spanner requires discrete areas of knowledge or experience to discharge their role effectively. Most importantly, the role of the boundary spanner within collaboration that involves managing across and between boundaries created by structure, agency and ideas is likely to generate a range of ambiguities, tensions and paradoxes. What are these, and how does the boundary spanner set about managing them? Are there any particular tools, mechanisms or relational tactics that the boundary spanner uses to manage these, and how effective are they? In addressing these questions, the discussion needs to be alert to any commonalties and contrasts between the two types of boundary spanner under consideration.

Review of main points

- The literature on collaboration is unbalanced – its focuses at a macro and institutional level at the expense of micro-level theorising and modelling that explore individual agency.
- There is considerable support particularly among practitioners for the proposition that the role of individuals is highly influential within the collaborative process.
- The structure–agency framework is a helpful theoretical and practical means of balancing and exploring the relationships between these two forces. However, the debate is highly contested between structuralists, intentionalists and others who advance alternatives to this dichotomy, for example, Giddens (theory of structuration) and Jessop (strategic-relational approach), which focus on the interaction between structure and agency.
- Emirbayer and Mische (1998) choose to examine 'agency' separately and propose an additional way of viewing the structure–agency nexus. The notion of agency is dissected into three components – iteration, projective and practical-evaluative – which variously orientate towards the past, future and present. The double constitution of agency and structure argues that temporal/structural contexts support particular agentic orientations, and these in turn provide different structuring relationships for actors.
- Hay (2002) introduces a further complication into the system by suggesting that 'ideas' have a significant role to play alongside structure and agency.
- The interplay between these components – both within and between – offers a comprehensive and integrated framework for analysing policy design and implementation. Structures can be enabling or constraining, and in the opposite direction, agency supplies learning and knowledge, particularly through experience of the practical consequences of structure, which in turn can influence the design of structure.
- The connection between agency and ideas centres on processes of framing and sensemaking that are prominent in collaborative arenas where multiple interests are assembled. Key actors operate as 'frame articulators', helping to surface, shape, mediate and project different frames that benefit different interests differentially.
- The notion of a 'boundary spanner' is open to much interpretation, but two main types are identified in this book. The first consist of those people who have a dedicated job role to undertake boundary spanning activities, and the second are a much larger group of leaders, managers and practitioners who engage in boundary spanning activities as part of their mainstream job function.

Questions for discussion

1. Consider a policy area/problem with which you are familiar and identify the predominant frames and interests involved.
2. Choose a policy domain/problem and explore the relationships between structure, agency and ideas.
3. How would you define a 'boundary spanner'?

Suggested further reading

Benford, R.D. and Snow, D.A. (2000) 'Framing processes and social movements: an overview and assessment', *Annual Review of Sociology*, vol 26, pp 611–39.

Emirbayer, M. and Mische, A. (1998) 'What is agency?', *American Journal of Sociology*, vol 103, pp 962-1023.

Hay, C. (1995) 'Structure and agency', in G. Stoker and D. Marsh (eds) *Theory and methods in political science*, London: Macmillan.

Schon, D.A. and Rein, M. (eds) (1994) *Frame reflection: Toward the resolution of intractable policy controversies*, New York: Basic Books.

Williams, P. and Sullivan, H. (2009) 'Faces of integration', *International Journal of Integrated Care*, vol 9, no 22, pp 1-13.

FOUR

The role and competencies of boundary spanners

Chapter Two describes the steady proliferation of collaborative working in both UK public policy and further afield. Multiagency models now characterise approaches to the design and delivery of public services in most policy areas, with national government playing a key role in its promotion and development. Boundary spanning activities and processes have paralleled this trend, with boundary spanners now occupying important roles. This chapter explores the nature of the boundary spanners referred to in the previous chapter as 'dedicated' – their role being exclusively grounded within the management, coordination and governance of multiagency and cross-sector arenas. It conducts an in depth examination into the roles boundary spanners play in collaboration, and the competencies they use to discharge these roles effectively.

The boundary spanning role in public sector, multiorganisational environments consists of a number of discrete but interrelated elements (Williams, 2002, 2005). The main ones are reticulist, interpreter/communicator, coordinator and entrepreneur (see Figure 4.1), each having a number of key competencies associated with them. The notion of competency is contested and will be discussed in Chapter 8, but for the present purposes it is understood in the following manner. In order to undertake job roles, individual actors need to possess competencies to equip them to discharge their roles to best effect. The competencies are what the person brings to the job. They may be skills (technical and human), knowledge of particular areas of expertise or accumulated experience of having undertaken this role. Actors also bring personal attributes to bear on their job role. Although these are not considered to be competencies, it is likely that they will influence the manner in which the competencies are discharged. These are considered in the next chapter. Critically, a high degree of connectivity and interplay exists between the various elements and competencies indicating that, in practice, they are used selectively depending on the circumstances presented in terms of context, policy area, form of collaboration, stage in the policy process, issue or problem.

Each of these individual roles is now the subject of detailed exploration and analysis. The discussion is a mixture of material extracted from a review of the literature, interspersed by examples drawn substantially from the author's own research which sought to highlight boundary spanning practice in action. In general, the literature on boundary spanners is limited, diverse and unconsolidated. The approach taken here is interdisciplinary, with material from sociology, organisational studies and psychology assuming particular prominence.

The boundary spanner as reticulist

Figure 4.1: Boundary Spanning Roles

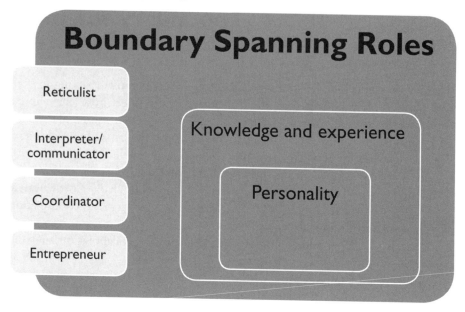

Multiorganisational and cross-sector collaboration evokes interdependencies, interrelationships, connections and networks. It involves a form of organising that is materially different from hierarchies and markets, and demands an understanding of how to manage and govern in this particular type of environment. In response to this challenge, an important element of the boundary spanner's role is that of a reticulist, which appears as a dominant theme in both literature and practice. It is a potentially powerful role because of the boundary spanner's control and manipulation over information and knowledge, and intermediary position at the interface of multiple and overlapping boundaries.

To reticulate is to arrange into a network. Friend et al (1974) refer to the need for reticulist or networking judgements to be made in activating, fashioning, refashioning or creating decision networks to address a particular decision area. These judgements, which are fraught with tension because they are bound up in personal, professional and organisational concerns, depend on the cultivation of reticulist skills, including: an appreciation of problem structure and the political and organisational context within which it is grounded; an understanding of current and future patterns of interdependencies; and a keen awareness of the structure of both formal and informal relationships and roles of the actors involved, together with the costs and benefits of particular actions for each.

A fundamental prerequisite of an effective reticulist is an ability to cultivate a network of personal relationships that, although designed to achieve professional or organisational goals, will be 'guided by other motives at the more personal level such as the desire to be liked or esteemed by his associates' (Friend et al, 1974, p 365). In addition to these, reticulists are expected to deploy political skills which 'must include a sure grasp of modes of behaviour relevant to different types of relationship between agencies and between actors' (Friend et al, 1974, p 367); to appreciate when to engage in bargaining, persuasive or confrontational modes of behaviour; and to adopt a 'mixed scanning' approach (Etzioni, 1967), knowing how to move 'between different levels of strategic and tactical exploration so as to develop an appreciation of how one influences the other' (Friend et al, 1974, p 365). Rhodes (1999) links reticulist skills with the old-fashioned virtues of diplomacy and the arts of negotiation and persuasion.

Reticulist roles

Reticulists are defined as 'individuals who are especially sensitive to and skilled in bridging interests, professions and organizations' (Webb, 1991, p 231), with reticulist roles, in terms of joint opportunities and liaison posts, being of particular value in that 'they give concrete substance to abstract statements of goodwill and foster a sense of shared fate, as well as facilitating communication' (Webb, 1991, p 239). Hosking and Morley (1991) consider that reticulists attempt to influence others in a symbolic fashion by helping to structure and frame situations, through forms of exchange in the relationship, and by negotiation. The negotiated element consists of two components – a cognitive one that focuses on managing complexity and information processing, and a political one that appreciates the differential power relationships between various actors. Ebers (1997) refers to reticulists as 'informational intermediaries' who act as mutually trusted lynchpins to bridge informational asymmetries, reduce communication costs, help establish a common set of goals and facilitate better coordination.

The boundary spanners in the author's research (Williams, 2005) were strategically positioned at the interface between their home organisations and the external environment. At different times this involved being a bridge, a conduit, a filter and a gatekeeper. It entailed intelligence gathering and scanning activities, and was a window on the outside world, radiating and disseminating information. Information processing was at the root of this activity in the mode of Ebers (1997) 'informational intermediary', but Tushman's (1977) notion of a 'gatekeeper' was also apt because the boundary spanners occupied very powerful and often discretionary roles in circulating information. They were able to make potentially key decisions as to whom, why, what and when information was disseminated – mediating the transfer of information to and from the external environment. They were able to draw on the benefits of being a member of an interorganisational network, including being at the leading edge of information, having access to new ideas, gossip and events in other sectors, professions and organisations, and being able to seek support from and influence people in other organisations.

The power of reticulists

Degeling alights on the theme of power with his conceptualisation of reticulists as 'entrepreneurs of power' who are 'concerned with recruiting and building coalitions between strategically located players who are committed to finding new ways forward on specific concerns' (Degeling, 1995, p 297). He suggests that reticulists should command an appreciation of the interstices of power; have an understanding of where coupling, interdependencies and fissures are likely to occur; and be skilled at identifying the strategic points in the leverage exercised. Effective reticulists, he adds, will combine a strong commitment to change through the cultivation of linkages between key individuals with common interests and power, rather than adopting the passive role of organisational representative. Trist (1983) conceptualises networks as non-hierarchical, unbounded social systems that provide rapid channels of communication: 'travelling through social ground rather than between institutional figures' and bringing 'the most unexpected people into relevant contact so nodes and temporary systems are formed which become levers of change' (Trist, 1983, p 280). He labels people who institute networks as 'novelty detectors' and describes these as 'proactive individuals who create new space around themselves', 'who locate and resonate with other individuals whose appreciations are moving in the same direction as theirs' and who 'learn the art of walking through walls' (Trist, 1983, p 280).

Reticulists are 'individuals who engage in networking tasks and employ methods of co-ordination and task integration across organizational boundaries' (Alter and Hage, 1993, p 46); and 'strategically placed individuals' who use their interpersonal skills and relationships to keep pathways open at all levels in the hierarchy (Trevillion, 1991). Challis et al (1988) note that such people are not located at the top of the formal organisational hierarchy, but typically, have good access to it. They are less bound by normal and accepted channels of organisational behaviour and are actively encouraged or allowed to be unconventional. Their position and status within the hierarchy is such that they do not represent an explicit threat to top management, but are tolerated in the expectation that they can deliver solutions to complex problems. Wilson and Charleton (1997, p 51) suggest that reticulists need to be comfortable working within informal decision structures and that the 'skill is to use informal networks, links and alliances to build positive relations between all the different parties', which in turn require good communication and negotiation skills. Finally, reticulists face a fundamental balancing judgement involving who they should network with and how much effort they should devote to it in comparison with managing internally (Meier and O'Toole, 2001).

Undoubtedly, networking is a time-consuming and sometimes exhausting activity, particularly in terms of maintaining contacts and sustaining personal relationships. However, the advantage of being networked often lies in the future and the potential to facilitate rapid and flexible responses to emerging opportunities requiring collaborative action. Existing networks reduce the future transaction costs involved, for example, in responding to frequently launched government initiatives. Equally, government sponsors are keen to derive confidence from the track records of effective local network consortia. However, while recognising the advantages of this front-ended investment in networking, time management is a dilemma for boundary spanners, particularly when balancing the competing demands of intra and interorganisational management. It can be argued that many organisations are fundamentally motivated by self-interest, sometimes questioning the legitimacy of some forms of collaborative activity. Boundary spanners' performance is typically judged in terms of the benefits to the home organisation; hence, care needs to be taken not to neglect intraorganisational roles and responsibilities. There is a danger of being too connected and of suffering from 'network fatigue'!

Network management

Managing in networks often entails working in groups and involves building social capital, shared learning, joint problem solving and negotiation around a whole range of personal, professional and organisational concerns. The creation of synergy requires the dismantling and unpicking of individual actors' ideologies and views, and a subsequent repackaging to co-produce new outcomes. These engagements are based on trust rather than legally bounded authority rules and relationships. Consensus-building frameworks are especially relevant in networked arenas because of their potential to involve all parties in a process of dialogue and mutual action. Collaborative, authentic policy dialogue enhances reciprocity through increased interdependence, builds new relationships and social capital and promotes learning and creativity (Innes and Booher, 2003). The outcomes of consensus are decisions that are high quality, more durable, fair and innovative (Innes and Booher, 1996). Furthermore, the process is viewed as a legitimate outcome in its own right by virtue of the stimulation of new levels of trust, shared knowledge, personal networks and working relationships, all of which might be expected to enable joint action on a more sustained basis into the future through an investment in social capital.

Networking frequently occurs at and around meetings, but is often most effective outside formal decision-making structures, especially in face-to-face conversations. The 'real' business of collaborative working is shaped within the framework of these personal exchanges, when difficulties are shared, aims agreed, problems sorted out, deals struck and promises made – all out of the public gaze. Crucially, this is where collaborative imperatives are translated into the organisational realities of individual participants, and where the agenda and decision making of formal occasions are choreographed and orchestrated in advance.

There is a considerable body of literature (Burt, 1982; Scott, 1991) on the typology and architecture of networks, based on an analysis of the direction, intensity and flow of interactions between 'nodes', measured in terms of physical, social, political or cultural distance. In addition, the metaphor of the network 'broker' is prominent in the literature on managing in networks (Kickert et al, 1997; LGMB, 1997), and Snow and Thomas (1993) identify three such roles: architect, lead operator and caretaker. The role of architect relates to network activation and motivation; the lead operator deals with management processes; and the caretaker focuses on network maintenance, information sharing, nurturing of relationships and so on. It is likely that these different roles will assume prominence at different stages in the development of a network.

The author's research (Williams, 2005) identified a number of the boundary spanners as thick network nodes – 'the Piccadilly Circus of the London Underground' – with significant routes radiating from and through them. At times, this enabled them to take the role of network leader or creator, conducting business in an orchestral-like fashion. At others, their roles were more peripheral but still important to the achievement of overall network goals. Moreover, there was evidence of boundary spanners locking into a number of different networks: at professional, intra and interorganisational levels, or by virtue of their participation in specific collaborative projects and initiatives. There was reference to expanding networks into uncharted areas to extend influence, using other people who were better placed, or perceived to have greater legitimacy, to access information or attempt to wield influence. There was also recognition of the strength of informality and 'weak ties' as a means of increasing commitment and bonding between individual actors. The development of overlapping networks was particularly important in cross-cutting policy areas such as sustainable development, community safety, equality and social inclusion, where there was a need for collective action across different sectors and organisations. One of the most important purposes of networking centres on its contribution to the effective wiring of collaborative agendas into the policy-making processes and frameworks of partnering organisations.

The boundary spanner as interpreter/communicator

The reticulist role is highly dependent on the ability of the boundary spanner to manage difference and communicate effectively in the collaborative arenas in which they operate as agents, intermediaries and gatekeepers. People from a variety of organisational, professional and social backgrounds assemble to pursue mutually beneficial agendas, and it is important to gain an appreciation of these actors because: 'as long as conflicting stakeholders cannot integrate the perspectives of their adversaries into their own rationales, progress in reaching consensus through collaborative effort will be difficult' (Pasquero, 1991, p 56). This demands a continuous investment in time to forge an effective working relationship and a readiness to visualise 'reality' from the perspective of others with an open mind.

Building and sustaining personal relationships

The development of interpersonal relationships is part of a process of exposure, exploration, discovery and understanding of people and the organisations they represent – a search for knowledge about roles, responsibilities, problems, accountabilities, cultures, professional norms and standards, aspirations and underlying values. The quality of this information is invaluable in allowing boundary spanners to identify potential areas of communality and interdependency, and the medium for this process of enquiry and knowledge exchange is the quality and durability of personal relationships. Time is an important element in allowing interpersonal relationships to prosper and understanding to develop. Also, the robustness of these relationships is under constant scrutiny – continually being tested within the highly sensitive and volatile arenas of collaboration.

The value of effective oral, written and presentational communication skills is central to the development of interpersonal relationships. The ability to express oneself and one's position with clarity is critical, as is the choice and use of language. The problem associated with the use and interpretation of 'professional' language and jargon is an area in need of sensitive management in order not to undermine, patronise, mislead or give offence to others. The search for shared meanings is particularly acute in collaborative arenas, and boundary spanners have to become multilingual, particularly in highly technical and professional areas. The use of particular language sometimes suggests connotations of power. Words such as 'strategy' or 'holistic' used insensitively can infer, or are deliberatively designed to promote, superior knowledge in the user. Since many collaborative ventures increasingly involve community representatives and lay people on boards and committees, it becomes particularly important to search for clarity in all forms of communication, as both a means of equal participation in decision making but also as a basis for understanding and consensus seeking. The least effective collaborators are those who have a tendency to hide behind the mask of their professional language and jargon. Conversely, the more effective ones are those who welcome others into their discursive frames through processes of articulation and communication.

The process of communication in the author's research was viewed as a two-way process with information receipt or listening being judged as important as information giving. Listening is very much a willingness or openness to be influenced by the views of other people, as was highlighted by the following comments:

> '"Active listening" that is more than a mechanical function of receiving data but a process that entails "taking on board what people say and adapting your views to what people have told you".'

> 'Listening in a meaningful way.'

'Being open to being influenced and reflecting.'

'Giving time to people to put their views.'

An ability to empathise with others is a further development along the spectrum of building relationships. Trevillion refers to boundary spanners as 'cultural brokers' who have the ability to understand another's organisation and make 'a real effort to empathize with and respect another's values and perspectives' (Trevillion, 1991, p 50). Engel (1994) observes that much interorganisational activity occurs with practitioners working in teams and this needs people to practise empathy, requiring 'a good understanding of their colleague's backgrounds, their professional capabilities and their responsibilities' (Engel, 1994, p 71). He also believes strongly that 'communication underpins and permeates the entire construct of capability for collaboration in a team' (Engel, 1994, p 71), and that empathy is fundamental to this, particularly in relation to imparting information in a way that takes account of differences in professional 'languages' discussed above. Like Engel, Hornby notes the connection with communication and refers to a skill of 'open listening', which she defines as hearing without much interference from preconceived ideas and judgements, and an ability to empathise while maintaining objectivity. Despite the importance of personal relationships, there is a view that collaboration is possible through mutual forms of understanding that fall short of empathy, and need not cross the line between professional and personal relationships, although there are many occasions when this happens to good effect (Van de Ven, 1976).

Without wanting to underplay the importance of empathy, one practical method of reducing its influence is suggested by Nocon's (1989) 'forms of ignorance' in collaborative relations – forms that are referred to as ideological, professional, procedural and personal. In essence, the argument is that if all the 'baggage' of another individual is exposed to complete scrutiny, the barriers to cooperation might be just too difficult to overcome. Hence, the maintenance of a degree of mystery may be the most effective way in achieving areas of consensus.

Rieple et al (2002) see the value of boundary spanners in being able to understand the cultural and linguistic norms of various partners, and to be proficient in translating various languages and behaviours – in some senses to be bi- or multilingual. This ability allows them to be more influential in bypassing organisational roadblocks and being able to access the power holders in respective organisations. The importance of this role is emphasised in a report that advocates the promotion of 'culture breakers' to act as catalysts for cross-cutting behaviour in the civil service. It argues that: 'civil servants need to get better at working across organizational boundaries' and need to change their mindsets from a 'culture of tribal competitiveness to one of partnership' (Cabinet Office, 2000, p 42).

Decision-making frameworks in collaborative arenas are unlikely to be based on the hierarchical imperatives typical of single organisations, but rather proceed more along the lines of consensus to reach mutually agreed decisions among various parties. This form of decision making requires high quality relational and engagement skills that revolve around negotiation, brokering, consensus building and conflict management. Morse (2010, p 244) considers that boundary spanners lever 'relationship capital to enable groups to work through conflict and setbacks', and Wilson and Charlton's practical guide for making partnerships work emphasises the need for boundary spanners to be adept at conflict resolution which is considered inevitable in partnerships because they bring together people from different sectors. They comment:

> It is the ability of individuals to make effective interventions in the management of partnerships that enables the initiative to progress, despite differences of opinion ... [and] technical knowledge about the domain of the partnership is secondary to the personal skills of diplomacy, mediation and negotiation. (Wilson and Charlton, 1997, p 49)

The universal frustration that is often felt about infrequent attendance at formal meetings involving collaborative working underscores the importance attached to building effective personal relationships. This is a constant source of irritation to regular attendees who consider that irregular attendance undermines any investment in, or opportunity to build personal relationships, and signals a general lack of commitment to collaborative working in general.

Power and status

The potential sensitivities involved in working with people from a diverse set of backgrounds demands particular care, especially in an environment where power relationships are contested, distributed and negotiable. These often revolve around 'turf' that refers to the exclusive range of activities and resources that an individual actor has the right to exercise responsibility over including money, staff and professional expertise. Collaborative working often requires a shift in the distribution and configuration of 'turf' among partners, and in effect, boundary spanners trade in the currency of 'turf' that to some may be perceived as a direct threat or with deep suspicion. An effective boundary spanner should be free of the above obsessions and embrace collaborative arenas as opportunities to work with 'like-minded' people to deliver innovative solutions to difficult societal problems, to acquire new knowledge about other organisations and their activities and to enhance personal and career profiles. Bardach takes the view that:

> Empowering individuals with the right problem-orientation, that is, towards service and administration, rather than toward turf, is probably as important as mobilizing individuals with helpful personal characteristics. (Bardach, 1998, p 185)

Boundary spanners need to cultivate an ability to relate to people at all levels in the formal hierarchies of organisations – both top and middle management as well as practitioners at the sharp end of service delivery. This requires a chameleon-like ability to change behaviour to match the expectations of different groups of people in different environments. Discretion and trustworthiness are integral to such relationships. In the author's research (Williams, 2005), there was little doubt that many boundary spanners were permitted to work above their formal status in many organisations because of their potential to lever in extra resources into their organisation. They were allowed additional flexibilities to bypass some bureaucratic processes in pursuit of higher goals. However, there were potential problems of personal isolation, and of being open to the accusation of 'going native'. A local authority community safety coordinator made the point that he was able to forge productive relationships with senior people (above his status) in outside organisations. This suggests that his status was higher in the eyes of people from other organisations than it was in his own, and this was due in no small measure to his overall expertise as a boundary spanner. In an environment where status and power are arguably most acute at the top of organisations, the ability of boundary spanners to mediate and communicate on behalf of their respective organisations up to the top level of others can be very valuable. Messages about what is or is not possible or what a position may be on a specific issue can be relayed between organisations through boundary spanners, often to prepare the ground before more formal exchanges.

Trust: glue or lubricant?

The macro-level literature review discussed in Chapter Two makes reference to three primary modes of social coordination, each with its own distinctive means of exchange relationships – the price mechanism in markets, power and status in hierarchies, and trust in networks. Webb (1991, p 237) captures the consensus in his assertion that:

> Attitudes of mistrust and suspicion are a primary barrier to co-operation between organizations and professional boundaries: collaborative behaviour is hardly conceivable where trusting attitudes are absent.

Boundary spanners therefore have an obligation to undertake their duties through the medium of trust, and a responsibility to take steps to enhance trusting behaviours and attitudes within the arenas within which they perform.

Trust is a complex and contested notion that has attracted a substantial body of interdisciplinary theory (Giddens, 1991; Boon, 1994; Cummings and Bromily, 1996; Lewicki and Bunker, 1996; Lane, 1998; Sydow, 1998; Das and Teng, 2001; Hudson, 2004), and is studied at a number of different levels of analysis: personal, organisational and interorganisational. Newman (1998, p 36) raises a note of caution because it is 'a highly promiscuous concept ... which has become co-opted to a range of different purposes and contexts'. Various models of trust associate the concept with faith, predictability, goodwill and risk taking. Lane (1998) offers a list of common elements in conceptualisations of trust, including:

- an assumption of a degree of interdependence between the trustor and trustee; in other words, it is a 'property of a relationship' (Sydow, 1998, p 44);
- trust provides a way of coping with risk or uncertainty in an exchange relationship; and
- trust is a belief or expectation that the vulnerability resulting from the acceptance of risk will not be taken advantage of by the other party in the relationship.

Lane goes on to suggest that the basis of trust can be derived from three main sources: calculative, value or norm-based and common cognition. Calculative forms of trust are those based on the rational choice model and represent a kind of cost-benefit analysis of taking certain courses of action. Boon (1994, p 88) presents an example of this approach in relation to romantic relationships and, interestingly, there may be parallels with boundary spanning relationships. She defines trust as 'the confident expectation that a partner is intrinsically motivated to take one's own best interests into account when acting – even when incentives might tempt him/her to do otherwise'. She refers to three distinct stages in the development of interpersonal trust – romantic love, evaluative and accommodation (see Table 4.1).

Some models of collaborative working (Gray, 1989; Wilson and Charleton, 1997; Lowndes and Skelcher, 1998) visualise different stages or phases which migrate from loose assemblies of parties coming together to negotiate joint purpose through to more formal periods where the emphasis is more on robust evaluation of self-interest and freedoms to compromise. Boon's model may have some resonance here, linking her stages of trust with the various stages in the process of collaboration. Lewicki and Bunker (1996) embrace Boon's model to help understand trust in professional relationships. Their understanding of trust is very much an explicit calculative and perhaps arithmetical perception resulting in a three-stage model: calculus, knowledge and identification-based.

Moving away from calculative and rational models, value or norm-based trust infers a moral basis or social obligation. Trust is:

> ... an individual's belief or a common belief among a group of individuals that another individual or group (a) makes good-faith efforts to behave in accordance with any commitments both explicit or implicit, (b) is honest in whatever negotiation preceding such commitments, and (c) does not take excessive advantage of another

even when the opportunity is available. (Cummings and Bromily, 1996, p 303)

Table 4.1: A model of trust in romantic relationships

	Stage	Characteristics
1	Romantic Love Stage	Characterised by "a profusion of positive feelings" and "expectations about a partner .... are little more than tentative theories that speculate, in the absence of real data, that the partner's feelings and motives are essentially equivalent to his or her own" (Boon, 1994: 91).
2	Evaluative Stage	Here the parameters of the interdependence are assessed and, with more information, a more realistic agenda crystallizes; a number of criteria guide such an evaluation – dependability, responsiveness (being self-sacrificing), capacity to resolve conflict and faith – "a sense of closure regarding the question of a partner's trustworthiness and the relationship future" (Boon, 1994: 99). It is doubtful, however, whether closure is in practice possible, and a range of issues are raised in circumstances that lead to the failure of trust and where the degree of trust in a relationship falls somewhere between the two extremes of trust and mistrust.
3	Accommodation Stage	"partners must seek mutually acceptable solutions to areas of incompatibility and opposing interests exposed during the preceding stages" (Boon, 1994: 95).

Trust is therefore seen as a belief consisting of the essential ingredients of commitment, honesty and not taking advantage of another. It projects an optimistic view of individual behaviour in contrast to interpretations within economic literature that emphasise competition as the basis of human interaction. A supporting view of the belief-based definitions is provided by Mishra who defines trust as 'one party's willingness to be vulnerable to another party based on the belief that the latter party is (a) competent (b) open (c) concerned and (d) reliable' (Mishra, 1996, p 265). Lastly, the common cognitions view of trust refers to systems of shared meanings of which Sydow (1998) identifies three types: process-based which is rooted in personal relationships and can include technical competence or knowledge; characteristic-based which is related to personal characteristics or qualities; and institutional-based which is founded on traditions or professions.

Bachmann (2001) refers to trust as a mechanism for coping with uncertainty and complexity, and there are theories that position trust at both a personal and system level. Also, Bachmann (2001) is anxious to stress the relationship between trust and control, both being mechanisms for coordinating social interactions. Similarly, Hardy et al (1998) distinguish between real and simulated trust, and attempt to disentangle the two heavily loaded notions of trust and power. They suggest that most functional interpretations of trust 'ignore the fact that power can be hidden behind a façade of "trust" and a rhetoric of "collaboration" and can be used to promote vested interests through the manipulation and capitulation of weaker parties' (Hardy et al, 1998, p 65). Page (2010, p 247) agrees with this observation, and comments that:

> Those who espouse collaboration may do so only for instrumental reasons, to cloak the guileful pursuit of their own interests in the language of public deliberation and stakeholder accountability.

Hardy et al argue that common definitions that relate trust to predictability and goodwill, for instance, do not reflect the true complexity of the notion or define how it can be created. The alternative propounded by these authors refers to trust as a process of communication where 'trust rests on reciprocal communication, and does not involve communication undertaken in order to sustain asymmetrical power relations or to exploit a position of power' (Hardy et al, 1998, p 69). The emergence of forms of shared meaning is considered axiomatic to this conceptualisation and they develop a classification of trust as power-based (or façades) trust and trust-based – manipulation and capitulation and spontaneous and generated. Newell and Swan (2000) submit that different types of trust interrelate in particular ways depending on the motives holding actors together in a network. It is also instructive to note the effect of interpersonal trust between boundary spanners at an institutional level because: 'the trust among them influences the orientation of other organizational members toward the partner organization, thus facilitating interorganizational collaboration' (Tsasis, 2009, p 17).

Lastly, from a practical point of view, there is an important question to be resolved in relation to building and sustaining trust. Vangen and Huxham single out expectation forming and risk taking as the main determinants of a model that envisages a cyclical process because:

> Each time partner's act together they take a risk and form expectations about the intended outcome and the way others will contribute to achieving it. Each time an outcome meets expectations, trusting attitudes are reinforced. The outcome becomes part of the history of the relationship, so increasing the chance that partners will have positive expectations about joint actions in the future. (Vangen and Huxham, 1998, p 8)

This approach resonates with Sydow's cycle of trust which he describes as tentative and consisting of small, resilient and persuasive steps that acknowledge carefully 'the prevailing rules of signification and legitimation' (Sydow, 1998, p 39).

The notion of trust, therefore, is highly complex and the subject of much theorising. However, how much of this material is of practical benefit to boundary spanners is less clear. Images from the author's research (Williams, 2005) generated a variety of interpretations reflected in the literature, although the general consensus was that it underpinned relationship building both at an individual and organisational level and that effective collaborative working could not really be contemplated without sufficient levels of trust between partners. A typical view expressed was:

> '... you cannot have effective working relationships with people you can't trust; a good trusting relationship is where the boundaries between your organisations almost fall away; these artificial boundaries are less important, and it's about how we work together as individuals representing these agencies.' (local authority boundary spanner)

Understandings of trust were dominated by calculative models (Boon, 1994; Lewicki and Bunker, 1996), involving taking small risks and evaluating their effects, valuing reliability and not harming either party. Versions of trust implied a form of reciprocal risk taking involving a process of information sharing, usually about themselves or their organisation that was not generally in the public domain. This was expressed by a boundary spanner in the NHS in the following way: "a lot of what we do is negotiate, trade information, tell things to people behind closed doors – information you would not normally disclose but you consider it is safe to do so – a process of calculated risk". The risk was that if the person being entrusted with this information misused it, then some harm could potentially fall on that person. The process was one of gradual 'exposure' to test out the dependability of a relationship and 'not being stitched up'. In this interpretation, trust involved not being underhand and provided the trustor with security, honesty and respect in such a relationship.

The following account is a personal reflection of the meaning of trust by a boundary spanner in the NHS:

> 'It isn't organisations getting on with one another – it's individuals sitting around a table. It's about trust between individuals – me knowing who to contact, who is going to be an ally and who I need to work on; each individual has his/her own reputation ... I'm someone who says it and does it; I am straight to the point and tell it as it is. People need to be prepared to put the energy into personal relationships – it's about finding people who want to talk and nurturing that relationship – that's the way to influence people ... I spend 5/10 mins before every meeting talking to people about their kids, hairdressers, holidays and what's the gossip in each organisation – it's intimate personal stuff where you expose yourself to risk – trust is if people don't take advantage of you – you have to tell people a lot about yourself – it's doing people favours – honesty and trust are the glue that bind people together.' (NLIAH, 2009, p 10)

In general in the author's research, building trust was seen to happen over time through a process of continual testing, and evaluating the extent to which people could be relied on to deliver on their commitments and promises. If people 'passed' these tests, there was a sense that something more enduring had been created. This was referred to as 'deep trust'. This was particularly the case where levels of trust were evaluated over a period of time, enabling a judgement to be made as to whether 'debts' had been repaid and benefits had been seen to accrue for both parties. Interestingly, trust between people was generally approached in one of two ways: either (a) by assuming people were trustworthy from the outset, or (b) by believing that people were naturally devious and testing whether this proved to be a self-fulfilling prophecy. One person in the author's research described the latter as having a healthy mistrust, and another explained the first position in the following terms:

> 'I trust most people and go in with a positive and not suspicious attitude – most people can be relied upon … there is a need to recognise the philosophy of benevolent intent – most people are not trying to catch you out – most people are honest and well intentioned … I trust people until they prove to the contrary. I give them a chance to hang themselves.'

A masterclass workshop (NLIAH, 2009) involving a set of boundary spanners from the health and social care sector deliberated on the challenges of building trust, and generated a list of practical ways in which it might be encouraged, including:

- through a better understanding of people's roles and motivations;
- by meeting/socialising with people outside working hours;
- by engaging with people outside their work role/context;
- by making the first overture to say sorry if trust is broken;
- through networking;
- delivering on promises;
- sticking with people during difficult times;
- handing delivery failure (breaking trust) in an open and transparent fashion;
- being honest and thoughtful when having to renege on a promise or harm someone;
- 'playing fair' – being open, honest and transparent.

A number of boundary spanners interviewed in the author's research reflected on the inherent superficiality or fragility of trust-based relationships. They recounted bitter experiences of situations where vicious downward spirals of distrust were precipitated by events often out of the direct control of the actors concerned. Interventions by national government, the results of public inquiries into scandals or failures of public agencies, and divisive performance management frameworks were all considered likely candidates to destabilise painstakingly crafted local collaborations. For instance, the issue of delayed discharge of patients or 'bed-blocking' was cited as an example that severely tested relationships between health and social care agencies, often resulting in mutual recriminations and accusations of ineffective action. In a highly charged local political environment and on topics of pressing public interest, boundary spanners sometimes find it difficult to maintain confidence in the goodwill or trust of their colleagues in partnering organisations. On occasions, the 'untrustworthy' behaviour of one actor can lead to all people in a particular organisation being 'tarred with the same brush'. As Boon (1994) suggests in her model of trust building, although trust can be repaired when broken, it is difficult to return to the levels that originally defined it, as the criteria for evaluation will be that much stiffer.

There were also a number of references to 'the partnership game' and the suggestion that, in order to be effective in a collaborative environment, it was necessary to play by a different set of rules, including using trust as the medium of interpersonal relationships. Therefore, there was a question mark over the genuineness of people promoting trusting relationships, and the belief that it was simply a tactic to influence others in the absence of alternative forms of power. Also, when representatives of a particular organisation at partnership meetings frequently change, trust is often difficult to maintain. Finally, the author's research identified other interpretations of trust referred to in the literature, such as value-based (Cummings and Bromily, 1996), reflected in, for example, a marked commitment to a particular user group such as those suffering mental illness, and technical and professional-based trust (Sydow, 1998), implicit in most public service professions.

The boundary spanner as coordinator

A role element that emerges from the work of boundary spanners relates to coordinating and organising the process of collaboration. There can be little doubt that the planning, coordination, servicing and administration of multiagency collaborations make very heavy demands on boundary spanners, particularly in terms of their time. The logistics inherent in these tasks are complicated by the range of actors involved and the need to ensure that each is treated fairly and inclusively through effective means of communication, information sharing and decision-making processes. Maintaining an efficient and up-to-date list of contacts in disparate organisations, arranging mutually convenient meetings, collecting, storing and disseminating information, producing briefings for, and minutes of, meetings, assembling and monitoring work programmes, progress chasing, liaising with a range of stakeholders and interests and producing publicity – the list seems endless, especially for those boundary spanners who have dedicated coordination posts for particular initiatives, partnerships or programmes. Unfortunately, in many situations, insufficient resources are allocated to these tasks in terms of back-up administration, and boundary spanners are faced with considerable pressures of time management and prioritisation. Boundary spanners are called on to support and facilitate the often lengthy decision-making process that accompanies collaborative working – the informal meetings and conversations, the negotiations and the investment in social capital that underpin the formal machinery of collaboration.

The experience of some boundary spanners suggests that the wide range of expectations that often accompany 'coordination posts' affords them opportunities to enhance their influence and demonstrate their value in tasks that might conventionally be viewed as 'above their status'. For instance, a manager of a multiagency health and social care initiative in South Wales indicated that her role had not been solely confined to basic 'housekeeping', but had spilled over into strategy preparation, monitoring, project management, research and providing technical support for different workstreams (NLIAH, 2009). Arguably, these opportunities would not be available in more defined and conventional job roles and posts, and such experience often proves invaluable in subsequent career progression. In terms of competencies, they lie very much in being able to develop good working relationships with a range of people in different organisations, effective communication and well-developed networking skills. A point made earlier in this chapter is that being at the centre of a communication/information highway can be both rewarding and potentially powerful.

The boundary spanner as entrepreneur

The entrepreneurial element of the boundary spanner's role reflects a view that many current public policy problems are not readily amenable to traditional approaches, but rather demand the application of new ideas, creativity, lateral thinking and a rejection of conventional practices. As a consequence, Morse (2010) suggests that boundary spanners are needed to play a catalytic role to visualise potential public value through collaboration. Also, unprecedented restrictions in the availability of financial resources places a premium on being able to devise and deliver innovative solutions, often incorporating practices from the private sector and resulting from 'blue skies' thinking. Degeling (1995, p 297) considers that people employed to undertake this role need to be 'committed to finding new ways forward on specific concerns'; Challis et al (1988) use the term 'risk takers'; and Hornby and Atkins(2000, p 159) focus on the importance of flexibility and a 'readiness to explore new ideas and methods of practice'.

Leadbeater and Goss (1998) draw attention to the urgent need to recruit 'civic entrepreneurs' to the public sector to reflect a refocusing of the debate from a narrow obsession about the size and structure of the state, to the promotion of the 'capacities and skills it needs to learn and change swiftly' in dealing with complex public policy problems (p 14). They profile civic entrepreneurs as 'often creative, lateral-thinking rule breakers' who 'frequently combine a capacity for visionary thinking with an appetite for opportunism' (p 15). These operators either innovate new products or services themselves or 'create the space for others' to do so. Moreover, they possess an armoury of both political and managerial skills, which, when absorbed in experimentation and innovation, are used to support risk taking.

Policy entrepreneurs

Bryson and Crosby (2005, p 156) refer to the role of policy entrepreneurs as 'catalysts of systemic change' who are 'inventive, energetic, and persistent in overcoming systemic barriers', who can be involved at any stage of the policy change cycle, who attend to most on-cycle decision-making processes but must understand off-cycle ones, who manage ideas, particularly in relation to the framing of problem causes and explanations, who analyse and manage the multiple interests that are often associated with public problems and who help to design or re-engineer appropriate structures to sustain desired changes. Critically, policy entrepreneurs are considered to require effective political skills, experience of bargaining and negotiation and an appreciation of the different demands of the policy process, from policy formulation, through delivery and finally to evaluation. Cobb and Elder (1981) consider that policy entrepreneurs orchestrate the flow of people, problems, and solutions; and Eyestone (1978) distinguishes between two types: the initiator who is responsible for shepherding an idea to the point where it commands active attention from decision makers, and the broker who builds coalitions of policy makers to ensure the passage of that idea through the difficult terrain of institutional processes. The job of brokering involves 'processes of translation, coordination, and alignment between perspectives. It requires enough legitimacy to influence the development of practice, mobilize attention and address conflicting interests' (Wenger, 1998, p 109). Ambivalence is an occupational hazard of brokering because of the need to balance two opposing forces: 'being pulled in to becoming full members and rejected by intruders', and this involves 'yielding enough distance to bring a different perspective, but also enough legitimacy to be listened to' (Wenger, 1998, p 110).

The following example illustrates a boundary spanner discharging a brokering role in relation to a Sure Start programme. It highlights both the time-consuming and rather tortuous nature of the process as it often involves a 'merry-go-round' of meetings before a final solution can be agreed. Here, the boundary spanner helped the parties understand each other's issues and perspectives, and to search for a solution that was mutually beneficial to all concerned:

> 'Two hospital trusts with children's services were in competition with each other for Sure Start resources. I worked between the trusts to develop a single proposal. One trust had a reasonable proposal but the other was over the top. I negotiated a compromise by meeting them separately and together and getting them to agree a single integrated proposal with clearly defined roles and responsibilities for each trust. The role I was able to play was that of "honest broker" to achieve a

result where there was something in it for both.' (Williams, 2005, p 169)

Public entrepreneurs

Roberts and King (1996) provide a seminal contribution on the notion of 'public entrepreneurs' whom they describe as people who 'introduce, translate and implement an innovative idea into public practice' (p 10). They argue that an individual's identity as a public entrepreneur derives from a unique set of skills, knowledge, values, motivation and personality, some of which depend on innate characteristics and others that are the result of learned behaviour. Particularly important attributes include effective problem-solving skills, whole systems thinking, good communication skills, a risk-taking ability, being focused and tenacious and being comfortable with 'difference'. The importance of managing 'meaning' is highlighted because of the differential framing of policy problems, and an appreciation of power and politics within the process of innovation is underlined. Roberts and King go so far as to suggest that 'policy entrepreneurs appear to have a unique identity with certain innate personality characteristics' (p 157), namely, being highly intuitive, critical analytical thinkers, instigators of constructive social action, well-integrated personalities, highly evolved, developed egos, high level of leadership potential, high level of managerial potential, and finally, ending this impressive list, average or above-average creative potential.

DeLeon evokes the image of public entrepreneurs as innovators, where innovations are not necessarily new but can be a creative repackaging of existing ingredients, and risk takers who 'have keen ears to hear opportunity knocking' (DeLeon, 1996, p 497). She further develops this image by references to such people as 'derring-do, Robin Hoods of the bureaucracy', 'catalysts who bring together problems and solutions that otherwise would bubble chaotically in the convection currents of modern policy streams' (DeLeon, 1996, p 498), and 'loners or mavericks, sometimes ... regarded with the suspicion commonly accorded "outsiders" or "aliens"' (DeLeon, 1996, p 498).

However, one view suggests that it is unwise to allow such entrepreneurs unbounded freedom, and rather, it is important to exercise a restraining influence to ensure that 'anarchic zones are encysted within a bureaucratic or organizational matrix' (DeLeon, 1996, p 505). This potentially creates some tensions, and DeLeon's solution involves advocating a protected zone of autonomy, to buffer the entrepreneurial or anarchic activity from the rest of the organisation; however, it could equally be argued that a strategy of integration into the organisational mainstream is a more appropriate and sustainable approach.

Coupling problems, policies and politics

Kingdon (1984) likens the prevailing policy terrain to a kind of 'primeval soup' in which windows of opportunity, some predictable and others unpredictable, bubble up and require the coupling of problems, policies and politics. He refers to the notion of policy entrepreneurs, whose primary function is 'to play a major part in the coupling at the open policy window, attaching solutions to problems, overcoming the constraints of redrafting proposals, and taking advantage of politically propitious events' (Kingdon, 1984, p 174). The idea is that policy entrepreneurs lie in wait for windows to open, with ready-prepared recipes – they are 'ready to paddle, and their readiness, combined with their sense for riding the wave and using the forces beyond their control, contribute to success' (Kingdon, 1984, p 190). The defining characteristics of these policy entrepreneurs include the claim to be heard by virtue of expertise, an ability to speak for others or the occupation of an authoritative decision-making position, a competency in negotiating skills and well-developed political connections.

As policy entrepreneurs, boundary spanners both advocate their proposals as part of a softening up process, and act as brokers to negotiate successful couplings between the necessary stakeholders; they are associated with creativity because of the free form of the process; they quite often bend problems to solutions (and therefore goals which are too tightly defined can be restrictive); and have 'excellent antennae, read the windows extremely well, and move at the right moment' (Kingdon, 1984, p 192).

Mintrom comments on 'policy entrepreneurs' who engage in: 'identifying problems, networking in policy circles, shaping the terms of policy debates, and building coalitions to support policy change' (Mintrom, 2000, p 57). Investing significant time in networking enables boundary spanners to appreciate the different 'worldviews' of other stakeholders and build credibility. The profile of effective policy entrepreneurs suggests that they must be creative and insightful, socially perceptive, able to mix in a variety of social and political settings, able to argue persuasively, be strategic team builders and be prepared to lead by example (Mintrom, 2000). A key message is that creativity and innovation must be coupled with an appreciation of how and when to convert solutions into practice. Further, although technical expertise and legitimacy are important, other competencies, centring on political awareness and networking, must be brought to bear on the task to ensure successful implementation.

The following two examples taken from the author's research (Williams, 2005) illustrate perfectly the classic role of the 'policy entrepreneur' identified by Kingdon (1984) and Mintrom (2000), where skilled actors are able to couple solutions to problems, and are often ahead of the game with ready-made solutions prepared in anticipation of future political openings, resource opportunities or unlocking 'policy windows'.

'It is about knowing when the situation is right to do something, and knowing when it is better left. It is around judgement. Often I come across something, and think we really need to do something about this; but for whatever reason, I don't think we should do it now, and it is better left. However, what you do is to have it ready, like in true Blue Peter style [this is one that I have prepared earlier], and keep up with what is happening so that you can actually predict when the time is right. We did this last year in relation to carers' services. Now with the Harold Shipman trial, it will be about single handed GPs.'

'It started with a meeting, where for both prison healthcare and discipline staff and myself, it represented both a physical and organisational crossing of boundaries. The meeting served to open a door on a whole range of unresolved issues and untapped potential, which could improve the care upon admission and discharge from prison of an extremely vulnerable group. Furthermore it was an opportunity to improve the prison's potential to deal more appropriately with mental health problems themselves as opposed to the current arrangements, which can encourage referral to hospital services inappropriately. What had not been anticipated at the time of this meeting was the announcement of resource from the National Assembly for the development of prison in-reach services, which did follow some two months later. The programme eventually put together would serve to provide the foundations upon which these services could be developed. Both during and after the incident I had a great sense that real improvements would follow this initiative.' (Williams, 2005, p 171)

Oborn et al's (2011, p 340) research, which looks at the role of a single policy entrepreneur in the London health service, suggests that agency in Kingdon's model needs to be extended: 'not simply in coupling but in shaping the context, and process of the policy development', which they refer to as a translational role. The policy entrepreneur studied in this research was observed to mesh 'windows' in a dynamic process of stakeholder engagement, resulting in a refinement of the policy context. In particular, he invested considerable time in recruiting and working with the 'right' actors across local and national networks, displaying high quality interpersonal skills to build and sustain effective relationships, and aligning different interests to a unified vision and common set of goals. Readiness, connectivity and flexibility were found to be the hallmarks of the effective policy entrepreneur's role.

Conclusion

This chapter has explored four main, but inherently connected boundary role elements: reticulist, interpreter/communicator, coordinator and entrepreneur Each of these role elements is considered to have a number of key competencies associated with their practice (see Table 4.2).

Table 4.2: Roles and competencies

Role	Dominant images	Main competencies
Reticulist	Informational intermediary, gatekeeper, entrepreneur of power	Networking, political sensitivity, diplomacy, bargaining, negotiation, persuasion
Interpreter/communicator	Culture breaker, frame articulator	Interpersonal, listening, empathising, communication, sensemaking, trust building, conflict management
Coordinator	Liaison person, organiser	Planning, coordination, servicing, administration, information management, monitoring, communication
Entrepreneur	Initiator, broker, catalyst	Brokering, innovation, whole systems thinking, flexibility, lateral thinking, opportunistic

The reticulist role stresses the importance of understanding and managing relationships and interdependencies. An eclectic range of competencies is considered necessary to discharge this role – personal in relation to developing and maintaining network links; cognitive to understand complexity and the linkages between interests, professions, organisations and other factors; strategic and tactical; managerial in order to operate within networks; and political to manage relationships between differential power holders using diplomacy, influencing and promoting consensus-seeking behaviour. Particular prominence is given to the ability to manage and process information of many types, and to use that effectively through formal and informal channels of communication. Sullivan and Skelcher (2002) consider reticulists should have the following skills and attributes: a critical appreciation of environment and problems/opportunities presented, understanding different organisational contexts, knowing the role and playing it, communication, prescience, networking, negotiating, conflict resolution and risk taking.

Boundary spanners are archetypical networkers operating in the social interstices of organisational space. They represent thick nodes radiating connections both within their own organisation and to and from others in a web-like or reticular fashion. These connections are part of a rich information highway in which boundary spanners occupy a pivotal role as intermediaries able to filter, direct, subvert, dilute and channel the nature and flow of information which span multiple communication boundaries. As a consequence of this position and using Castells (2000, p 502) reference to 'switchers connecting the networks', and Goldsmith and Eggers (2004, p 169) 'connectors' who 'span several very different worlds, bringing people together from disparate environments', boundary spanners occupy very powerful and influential positions, often far removed from their formal status and position in the organisation. Boundary spanners have to earn the legitimacy, autonomy and freedom to act outside some normal organisational rules and conventions.

The boundary spanner as interpreter/communicator centres on appreciating the cultures, motivations, gazes and practices of a wide range of actors, professionals, organisations and sectors populating collaborative environments. They liaise, gatekeep and collaborate with individuals representing different and sometimes changing interests. This role needs a firm foundation in an individual's ability to foster and sustain effective interpersonal relationships mediated through trust – interpersonal ties that provide the infrastructure on which to build collaborative relationships (Tsasis, 2009). The skills of communication, listening, empathy, negotiation, consensus building and conflict resolution are considered to be valuable commodities in this context. The heart of the role involves understanding and valuing difference that require an appreciation of the particular sensitivities involved within interpersonal relationships, and the careful judgements that are needed to manage the intensity of these, together with the implications of redistributed power relationships. The consequences of dysfunctional interpersonal relationships are protracted and ineffective collaborative working, with low levels of cooperation and high costs of lack of coordination.

The entrepreneurial element reflects the imperatives of innovation, creativity and new ideas in the formulation of effective solutions to complex problems. Opportunism and risk taking, not always associated with the public sector, are essential parts of this role, to allow boundary spanners to initiate and broker practical solutions between different parties and coalitions. Coupling, windows of opportunity and political opportunism are apt metaphors for a process that is as much about personal relationships, networks, negotiation and bargaining as it is about technical possibilities. Civic and public entrepreneurs are encouraged to embrace some of the values and disciplines of their colleagues in the private sector. Experimentation is encouraged, informed by best practice and evidenced in a recent trend towards the use of initiatives and pilot projects.

It needs to be emphasised that, although it is possible to unpick individual elements from the boundary spanner's role, there is a high degree of interplay between them and in the deployment of the associated competencies. Although particular circumstances may demand that special attention is given to one element – reticulist or entrepreneur – the research assembled in this chapter suggests that the role elements are not generally discharged independently of one other, but are used in various combinations in response to given challenges and circumstances. The consequence of this is that a range of individual competencies are required to be used in support of a number of different role elements. This requires boundary spanners to appreciate what types of intervention are required, to be selective in terms of how they behave and what 'tools' to use, and to be able to switch effectively in the highly dynamic environment of collaboration. There is clearly a complex interplay between the different boundary spanning roles and competencies, and a degree of synergy is needed to combine them to best effect.

Review of main points

- The role of dedicated boundary spanners operating within public sector collaborations involves four main elements: reticulist, interpreter/communicator, coordinator and entrepreneur. They have particular competencies associated with them, and there is a high degree of connectivity and interplay between the role elements and competencies.
- The reticulist role concentrates on the management of relationships and interdependencies within a network mode of governance. It highlights the importance of networking and network management, diplomacy, communication, negotiation and influencing without formal power. Reticulists are key conductors of information – receiving, channelling and directing it to best effect. They are referred to as 'informational intermediaries' and 'gatekeepers' and often work through informal rather than formal channels.
- The interpreter/communicator function centres on appreciating the diversity of actors and their backgrounds and being able to liaise with and connect with these different and changing interests. At the heart of this role is the ability to build and sustain effective intepersonal relationships using skills of communication, listening, empathy, negotiation, conflict management and consensus seeking. Trust is paramount in these processes although there are many interpretations of this notion.
- The collaborative process needs coordination, planning and servicing. These are time-consuming responsibilities but are very important to ensure the smooth running of any collaboration.
- The boundary spanner as entrepreneur focuses on the importance of developing new solutions to complex problems evidencing creativity, opportunism and innovation. The job of the civic, policy and public entrepreneur is not just a technical one relating to ideas and resources, but also a personal and political one involving building coalitions and brokering deals among disparate interests. It is a catalytic role to ensure the effective coupling of problems, policies and politics using a range of particular skills including problem solving, whole systems thinking, communication, risk taking and managing meanings.

Questions for discussion

1. Think about an effective boundary spanner you are familiar with. Identify the roles that he/she plays, and the main competencies that are used to undertake them. Give examples where possible.
2. Is any boundary spanning role more important than the others, and do boundary spanners undertake other significant roles not considered in this chapter?
3. Trust is often seen as pivotal to building and sustaining effective collaboration between people and organisations, but what is it? What steps would you take to develop trust in collaboration? What happens when trust is broken, and how might this be repaired? Can you still work with people in other agencies that you don't trust?

4. Think of examples where a boundary spanner combines the individual role elements to tackle a particular challenge.

5. Does the role of the boundary spanner alter significantly in different policy areas or in different types of collaborative structure?

6. What sources of power do boundary spanners draw on, and how do they use them during the course of collaborative working?

7. How does a boundary spanner go about designing and delivering an innovative project/programme? Give examples.

8. What practical steps are needed to build and sustain interpersonal relationships?

Suggested further reading

Ebers, M. (1997) 'Explaining inter-organizational network formation', in M. Ebers (ed) *The formation of inter-organizational networks*, Oxford: Oxford University Press, pp 3-40.

Hornby, S. and Atkins, J. (2000) Collaborative Care: Interprofessional, Interagency and Interpersonal Oxford: Blackwell Science

Hosking, D.-M. and Morley, I.E. (1991) *A social psychology of organizing*, London: Harvester Wheatsheaf.

Hudson, B. (2004) 'Trust: towards conceptual clarification', *Australian Journal of Political Science*, vol 39, no 1, pp 75–87.

Kickert, W.J.M., Klijn, E.-H. and Koppenjan, J.F.M. (1997) *Managing complex networks*, London: Sage Publications.

Kingdon, J.W. (1984) Agendas, Alternatives, and Public Policies New York: Little, Brown

Williams, P. (2002) 'The competent boundary spanner', *Public Administration*, vol 80, no 1, pp 103-24.

FIVE

Challenges in the boundary spanning role

The last chapter explored the boundary spanning role in some depth together with the main competencies required to undertake it effectively. This chapter develops and extends this discussion by focusing on a couple of important questions that are prompted by this analysis, and by investigating the problematic nature inherent in the boundary spanning role. The questions relate to, first, the issue of substance and what, if any, specialised areas of knowledge, expertise and experience are required by boundary spanners to complement or underpin the skills and abilities previously discussed; and second, the extent to which personality influences the manner in which boundary spanners discharge their role. In other words, is there a certain type of person who may be particularly suitable for this type of post? Following this discussion, the chapter proceeds to examine the many challenges that accompany this role which are manifested in the form of tensions, paradoxes and ambiguities.

Does the work of boundary spanners require specialised knowledge, expertise and experience?

Professionals normally acquire their legitimacy through the possession of a discrete repository of knowledge and expertise that in turn is codified and protected by professional bodies. Can boundary spanners make a claim to a special area of knowledge, and if so, what is it? One view is that a key area of expertise and knowledge lies in an understanding of the context in which boundary spanners operate – the configuration and distribution of roles, responsibilities, cultures, operating systems and accountabilities of individuals and agencies working in a particular collaborative domain. An appreciation of the multiple motivations underpinning the drive to collaborate is critical as is their interplay and dynamics. Posner (2009, p 238) makes the point that: 'public programmes work through implementation regimes featuring actors with mixed motives that have incentives to both co-operate and defect from new public policy initiatives'. The challenge for boundary spanners is to appreciate the values and intent of different actors, and to understand how to manufacture the appropriate incentives to mobilise collective action.

This is a picture of complexity and interdependence and the value of boundary spanners lies in their ability to appreciate and analyse the connections, links and interrelationships in this system, as illustrated in the following example (Williams, 2005, p 201).

'It is important to be able to understand the whole. This is about exposure, getting out and about, spending time with different groups and teams, and talking to people. I am very nosy and inquisitive. It's about asking people questions about what they're doing and why. It is having a genuine interest in others. This is absolutely important in partnership working and helps me to engage with them. It gives me extra knowledge, an opportunity for making linkages, and an opportunity for getting back to them to say, I've got this scheme or pot of money, what can we do with this? Most of my time is doing this kind of scanning and trying to work out linkages and emerging themes. Different people are saying the same thing, so add them together and come up with something and then reflect that back in a kind of iterative process. Sometimes I suggest it; other times I let them suggest it. I look for win-win solutions for everyone and help other people see the whole and linkages. I make connections partners haven't spotted, and feedback the linkages and connections in various permutations.'

Capra (1997) refers to the need for 'contextual' thinking that appreciates the whole system and the interactions between the constituent elements, evoking what Wildavsky referred to as far back as 1979 as a situation where interdependence among policies increases faster than knowledge itself. The consequence of such complexity is the creation and persistence of ambiguity, tension and uncertainty – in many ways, sources of excitement and vibrancy in which effective boundary spanners need to demonstrate a propensity to thrive within. Ambiguity materialises in many ways, including the nature of the problem faced; the amount, status and reliability of information available; the multiple and often conflicting interpretations of problem structure and solutions; the differences in value orientation; unclear, multiple and conflicting aspirations; lack of causal explanations; problematical evaluatory frameworks and systems of accountability; and differences in culture and language (Weick, 1995).

One of the main sources for understanding the connectivity and relationships within collaborative arenas is accumulated, 'on-the-job' interorganisational and intersectoral experience (see Table 5.1).

The frequent exposure to other boundary spanners and representatives of partner agencies enables boundary spanners to assemble a store of knowledge and understanding about different viewpoints, constraints, cultures and working practices. A record of employment in different types of organisation and sectors can be very helpful because experience of different organisational cultures, ways of working, roles and responsibilities and past networks – expressed as 'insider knowledge' – is invaluable for understanding the motivations, mindsets and behaviours of colleagues in partner agencies. It can also be the basis on which to formulate complementary agendas and promote relationships between the interests of different organisations, and be a highly effective method of accumulating network contacts, based on established trust of sufficient quality to enable possible future collaboration, albeit within a different set of organisational relationships and accountabilities.

Table 5.1: Collaborative knowledge and experience

Knowledge for collaboration
Organisational behaviour – structures, models, roles, dynamics, cultures and methods of working
Intersectoral knowledge – organisational and professional cultures, funding and resourcing regimes, decision-making processes, management styles and approaches and accountability and performance management frameworks
Collaborative motivations and drivers, statutory and governance systems
Management and organisational studies – nature and dynamics of working in teams and groups
Political theory – notions of trust, power, political elites, governance
Psychology – knowledge of human behaviour and motivation
Experience of collaboration
Experience of working with people from a diversity of backgrounds, personalities, professions and disciplines: people with different 'gazes' on the world, different assumptions, agendas and beliefs, and inculcated with different sets of values through processes of professional and other socialisation; experience of working in different roles, including representative and free-standing positions; and experience of relating to people at different levels in the organisational hierarchy
Experience of working in, and with, different types of groups and teams
Experience of working for different sectors to understand the nature and character of potential partners. This helps build empathy and detailed 'inside' knowledge
Experience of different organisational types and models including experience of different organisational structures, cultures, languages and accountability frameworks

The advantages of interorganisational and intersectoral movement can be valuable at an organisational and systemic level. The movement of actors with different competencies and experiences is beneficial in terms of innovation, knowledge, perspective and enhanced network potential. However, it is not without problems and risks. For individuals, host organisations are not always receptive to 'outsiders', and problems of organisational acculturation and other barriers can devalue learning potential; and, at an organisational level, the outward movement of key personnel can be potentially destabilising in the short term, resulting in a leaching of intellectual and experiential capital.

For boundary spanners, although there is often a strong rhetoric surrounding the desirability of movement between different sectors, prevailing institutional, employment and other barriers are still restrictive. These include terms and conditions of service, pension rights, leave entitlement, availability of flexible working, life cycle factors relating to family responsibilities and the congruence and transferability of different forms of academic or professional accreditation. On the question of the need to be knowledgeable in areas of expertise or possession of a suitable professional qualification, one view is that boundary spanners might benefit from 'trans-disciplinary knowledge' as a form of passport of legitimacy to engage with people in other organisations (see Table 5.1). Harnessing the power of knowledge is still very important in the realms of public policy despite frequent attacks on the primacy of professionalism, paternalism and objectivity. This position supports the view that, although collaborative working focuses on process and styles of working, there must be a substantive content to the exchanges, and these inevitably require technical knowledge and understanding. An opposing viewpoint is that boundary spanners need to be 'a jack of all trades' because it is unlikely than any single person can claim to be an expert in so many diverse professional areas of expertise that frequently coalesce within the theatres of collaboration. The possession of suitable knowledge and experience are fine in themselves but rather superfluous if the holders are not able to utilise them effectively. Hence, the ability to interpret, manipulate and analyse information is an essential requirement for boundary spanners. This is often expressed as: 'being able to think laterally', 'taking a holistic view', 'understanding the big picture' and 'strategic thinking'. Whether these abilities are rooted in experience or a function of a particular cognitive style is less clear.

Does personality influence the role of boundary spanners?

An occasional theme in the literature on boundary spanners relates to personality and personal attributes. The question is whether effective boundary spanning can in some way be linked to particular personality traits in the actors involved. The references in the literature fall broadly into three categories. First, those that link boundary spanners to extrovert personalities including being outgoing, sociable, friendly, people-orientated and cheerful. Second, those that reflect a moral soundness such as respect, openness and honesty; and finally, those characteristics that emphasise commitment, persistence and hard work.

Examples of these in relation to research on networking within community regeneration initiatives suggest that important personal characteristics include being 'honest, committed, energetic, trustworthy, open, friendly, and charismatic' (Skelcher et al, 1996, p 16); 'outgoing, lateral thinking, able to cover cross-cultural boundaries, inclusive and accepting' (LGMB, 1997, p 10); and 'open and honest' (Wilson and Charleton, 1997, p 51). Fairtlough (1994) lists the strengths of a boundary spanner as diplomacy, tact, dispassionate analysis, passionate sincerity and scrupulous honesty, and suggests that this may be an impossible string of virtues! In a similar vein, Sarason and Lorentz (1998, p 107) consider that these people need to be 'paragons of virtue' or 'secular angels' because they need to be 'likable, outgoing, but not pushy, tactful, inquiring but not intrusive, a listener'. Another researcher refers to the 'need to be able to practice self-discipline, self-restraint, punctuality and courtesy' (Engel, 1994, p 71); Beresford and Trevillion (1995) consider that collaborative values are characterised by honesty, commitment and reliability; and, Kingdon (1984) in his analysis of policy entrepreneurs, believes that personal tenacity and persistence are necessary to be successful in the job. Finally, DeLeon derives a set of personal characteristics for public entrepreneurs that are markedly different in nature to those described above. She suspects an association with egotism, selfishness, waywardness, domination and opportunism, attributes which might appear to have vice-like connotations but are 'the extremes of qualities that are functional for their role as innovators' (DeLeon, 1996, p 508). During the course of many interviews in the author's research (Williams, 2005), numerous references were made to the personality of practising boundary spanners, in the form of personal attributes or traits (see Table 5.2). Respondents inferred that these played a part in the way in which boundary spanners approached their job roles and the effectiveness with which they were able to discharge their competencies. For instance, one boundary spanner was described as:

Table 5.2: Desirable personal characteristics of boundary spanners

Personal attributes	Description
Respect for others and their views	Appreciating, comprehending and accommodating diversity and difference in people's perspectives and opinions. The key word here was respect, which did not mean agreement but valuing other people's right to their own views. It was considered important also to look for opportunities to demonstrate this respectfulness, and to be tolerant of others' positions on various matters. Innate curiosity about the 'bigger picture' was thought to be an invaluable personal attribute.
Honest, straight and trustworthy	Evidenced by being open in dealings with people, not being underhand or devious, or going behind their back.
Approachable	This was about people who were accessible and not 'standoffish'; sometimes amusing, talkative and interesting.
Diplomatic	Actors with well-honed political antennae who were careful in the use of language.
Positive and enthusiastic	Constantly championed and extolled the virtues and benefits of partnership working.
Confident and calm	People who exude good judgement and were firm where necessary.

Source: Williams (2005)

'Being a nice person, who had the knack of pulling things together and drawing people's attention to it; and whose personality and the way she went about things, helped get things done.'

The most effective boundary spanners were considered to be those with an easy and inviting personality, particularly people able to divest themselves of their organisational and professional demeanours, and blind to the trappings of status and similar conventions.

It was pointed out that boundary spanners were expected to perform and behave appropriately in a wide variety of formal and informal arenas including committee meetings, working groups, seminars, conferences, public meetings and council meetings. This required, it was argued, an engaging and flexible personality that could adapt freely to any particular social or professional situation. People who were committed to working in teams were considered to be valuable, and individuals who were unwilling or unable to perform appropriately in this type of environment were judged unlikely to flourish or succeed. To some extent, the interviewees painted a picture of a group of people who, because of the non-hierarchical nature of the operating environment in which they worked, where power was more contested and negotiated, needed to influence the course of events, in part through their individual competencies but also through the force of their personality. Many interviewees held firm views that a person's personality was an important factor in collaborative arenas, and they were able to nominate particular individuals whom they considered and observed to be excellent role models to support this assertion. These individuals were considered to possess personal attributes that were valuable in collaborative settings, and contrasted with those whose personality was an impediment to their effectiveness in this type of environment.

During the course of the interviews, the boundary spanners in a case study were asked to think about, but not name, an ineffective exponent of their art with whom they were familiar, and to give reasons for their selection. It became apparent on analysis that, in almost every case, they selected and described one particular individual, and of the many reasons given, aspects of personality were at the forefront. The list of unhelpful characteristics attributed to this individual included: extreme narrow-mindedness, inability to look outside their own remit, lack of preparedness to listen to other people's perspectives and views, wanting credit for everything, intransigence and rigidity, fearing the loss of power, confrontational and aggressive approach, failure to keep people informed, constantly operating in 'organisational representative mode', seeing problems rather than solutions and self-interest.

Interestingly, by common consent, the most effective boundary spanner was a woman, and the least effective (described above) was a man. This inevitably invites some speculation as to the possible significance of gender. The author's view, which is supported by the literature (Cockburn, 1991; Alvesson and Billing, 1997; Belbin, 2001), is that a number of competencies such as building effective interpersonal relationships, listening, empathising and being facilitative and empowering in style tend to be associated with female approaches to management, and it is these that are particularly relevant in collaborative arenas. However, even though the most effective boundary spanner in the survey group was a woman and the least effective was a man, other respondents of both sexes demonstrated the competencies needed for collaborative working. There was no evidence to indicate that gender was an issue in the discharge of boundary spanning roles – those competencies that were essentially relational in nature and associated with female styles of management were found to be as appropriate for male as well as female boundary spanners.

As is clearly represented above, there is often a 'tendency to attribute the consequences of people's action to people's dispositional attributes or personality bias' (Brunas-Wagstaff, 1998, p 94), but there is not a consensus on this viewpoint. On the one hand, personality psychologists assume that people are different because of differing characteristics, personalities or temperaments. Trait theories of personality are typical of this school of thought where traits are 'relatively enduring descriptive characteristics of a person' and usually conceived as 'predispositions to behaviour having cross-situational consistency' (Eysenck, 1994, p 40). As well as being descriptive, traits are sometimes used 'as explanations of the actor's behaviour, in which they are viewed as causal or generative mechanisms' (Hampson, 1994, p 25). There is some consensus among multi-trait theorists on the basic structure of personality and reference is made to the so-called 'Big Five' personality factors with their particular bundles of illustrative traits. However, there are many differing views on the relative importance of individual factors, even though there is the presumption shared by most that the factors are stable over time. In particular, traits are seen 'in terms of temperaments or underlying predispositions to behave in characteristic ways' (Brunas-Wagstaff, 1998, p 63), and can be used to predict behaviour across different situations.

It is at this point that problems arise. Apart from the accusations of subjectivity and arbitrariness, personality factors have been found to be poor predictors of behaviour. Psychologists who suggest that behaviour can be predicted from a knowledge of the situation, challenge the assumption that actions arise from stable internal dynamics, processes or predispositions existing independently. These so-called 'situationalists' argue that, 'behaviour can be explained entirely in terms of regularities in external events or situations' (Brunas-Wagstaff, 1998, p 80). Needless to say, there is a middle position adopted by supporters of the interactionalist school who maintain that both dispositional and situational variables have an impact on determining behaviour.

A second approach to the explanation of individual differences in behaviour is associated with cognitive psychology that sees 'individuals as information processors and thus individual differences are described in terms of different processes or strategies which we use to solve various problems' (Brunas-Wagstaff, 1998, p 84). Theories of causal attribution and cognitive style (preferred ways of using abilities or thinking processes) fall within this school of thought. Also, there are theories which attempt to make connections between thinking styles and the way we organise our behaviour around personal goals, from the fundamental and abstract, to biological, social and cultural, and even to those which determine our second-by-second behavioural choices. There is psychological evidence to suggest that some goals are internalised and automatic and have the effect of energising behaviour in an implicit fashion. In summary, because people have different goals, 'many individual differences in behaviour and thought may be explained in terms of goal differences rather than differences in temperament or personality' (Brunas–Wagstaff, 1998, p 131).

The importance of this discussion on the influence of personality is that it raises the question of how far it is possible to train and develop people in particular competencies, and how far behaviour is limited by personality characteristics. If it is a matter of personality, there is not much you can do about it! The author's general view is that an actor's personal attributes or traits are likely to influence the manner in which he/she undertakes their boundary spanning role, and as Taylor (2000, p 41) infers: 'this cannot be engineered, but it is possible to increase the likelihood that the right people will be in the right place at the right time'.

Tensions and ambiguities in the boundary spanning role

The boundary spanner works in a world of complexity and diversity, populated by a range of stakeholders and interests from different agencies, professions and sectors. Searching for collaborative solutions to difficult policy issues is demanding. This requires the use of different competencies and careful judgements as to how and when to intervene to best effect. However, in the course of this engagement, the boundary spanner is faced with a range of tensions, ambiguities and paradoxes that even the most proficient find taxing. These include:

- managing in and across multiple modes of governance
- blurred personal and professional relationships
- dilemmas of multiple accountabilities
- appreciating multiple framing processes.

Managing in and across multiple modes of governance

Ferlie and Pettigrew (1996) suggest that in many areas of public policy, actors face the challenge of managing in mixed modes of management – networks, hierarchies and markets – and effective boundary spanners need to appreciate when and how to switch between these different modes. However, Machado and Burns (1998) indicate that this is fraught with potential difficulties because of the zones of incongruence and tension that are created at the junctures and interfaces of the different modes of organising. They argue:

> At these points or zones, there is potential ambiguity, confusion and conflict – agents and processes may clash. That is, the different modes or rationalities of organising embody structural sources of tension and conflict. (Machado and Burns, 1998, p 357)

The collision, confusion and blurring of markets, bureaucracies and networks are difficult to reconcile, often resulting in increased transaction costs. Boundary spanners are a source of mediation in this environment, with their ability to bridge and negotiate across different modes of organising. The:

> Successful mediators or liaison actors are those who possess attributes and orientations intermediate to the units they bridge as well as command important skills and essential technical competence. It is also important that they enjoy high status and influence in the various organizational units that they are mediating. (Machado and Burns, 1998, p 372)

Such people are also able to influence between modes through discourse and the management of meaning around collaboration and a new set of rules and norms. Machado and Burns (1998) suggest that these people operating in networks can get away with practices that would be inappropriate within bureaucratic orders.

A report by the Local Government Management Board (LGMB, 1997, p 10) refers to the role of 'special' people in networks 'bringing unlikely partners together, in breaking through red tape, and seeing things in a different way', and who are skilled in communication and coalition building. The challenges facing effective networkers include: finding the right balance between formality and informality within a predominantly bureaucratic environment; being able to tolerate the 'messiness' of networking; and nurturing a 'habit' or culture of networking in the face of conventional organisational rigidities. This is particularly the case with communication patterns within organisations that are embedded in systems that are 'constituted by networks of graded relationships' and speak 'the language of hierarchical discourse' (Stohl, 1995, p 110). Gilchrist (2000, p 271) identifies community workers as good examples of networkers because they:

> Perform a covert role in "networking the networks", providing the boundary-spanning links and identifying the beacons, barriers and bridges which enable others to navigate across unfamiliar and hazardous terrain. They spin and mend relationships across the web, putting individuals and organizations in touch with one another, helping them to communicate effectively and generally facilitating those links made difficult by organizational procedures, cultural misunderstandings or fear.

Blurred personal and professional relationships

Support relationships in personal and professional relationships are not without dilemma because boundary spanners:

> … must be adept at breaking down boundaries between themselves
> and recipients to listen empathetically and build trust; they also need
> to enforce boundaries to protect themselves from enmeshment with
> the recipient's problems. (Bacharach et al, 2000, p 706)

This is a delicate balancing act between inclusion and separation, dependence and autonomy. Hornby highlights the relational competencies of boundary spanners through the notion of 'reciprocity', which is manifested 'in respect and concern for the individual, giving value to mutual understanding and the building of mutual trust' (Hornby, 1993, p 160). This involves exchanging information about approach, province and domain, a recognition and appreciation of others' skills and consideration of feeling and a willingness to work on trans-boundary difficulties.

Some research suggests that the quality and frequency of exposure between reticulists leads to the blurring of the boundaries between professional and personal relationships. Van de Ven (1976, p 31) submits that:

> The greater the length of time and degree of intimacy in the personal
> relationship … the more similar their attitudes, values, and goals; the
> greater their mutual trust of one another; and, as a result, the greater
> their predisposition to help one another out by committing their
> organization to an interorganizational relationship.

In a similar vein: 'networking is characterised by personal relationships and social, informal exchanges', 'it is important for participants to have the opportunity to get to know each other socially' and 'problems and potential conflicts are frequently ironed out in the context of long-term friendships and relationships of trust' (LGMB, 1997, p 10). This process of social bonding can change the reliance on inter-role relationships to that of interpersonal relationships, may assist in a deeper understanding of the cultures of respective organisations and the constraints that may apply in any potential cooperation and 'partially mitigates … professional role orientations, and … provides an alternative avenue for role specialists to resolve their conflicts' (Ring and van de Ven, 1994, p 109).

In the author's research (Williams, 2005), there was a recognition that, although strictly professional relationships could exist as the basis for networking, the inherent social component of networking and more personal relationships increased the potential, quality and richness of the interchange. Examples of this school of thought included:

> 'It is difficult to remain wholly professional because you will exchange
> confidences; this is part of relationship building and a support
> mechanism.'

'You have to act out your formal roles and behaviour in formal situations, but not in informal encounters where you can admit to being fallible and vulnerable.'

'We are all human beings and we can't have professional relationships without it being personal in one way or another.'

The overall point being made was that networking was not a round of constant socialising, but implied 'giving something of yourself' in relationship building such as information or comments on family matters, hobbies, political controversies of the day, work problems and opinions of other people. Being able to establish shared views on politics or a common interest in a particular sport was seen to help cement personal relationships, inducing a form of vulnerability that required a considerable degree of trust from both parties. The ability to offer comments on the competence and performance of other key players without fear of compromise was also highly valued.

An alternative view suggests a downside to 'informality or reliance on personal and social relationships' (LGMB, 1997, p 11). The tensions between the cultivation of personal relationships and accountability to the 'home' organisation are fraught with difficulty. An over-reliance on social and personal relationships is inherently unstable, given the fact that people often move between posts and employers, and more significantly, friends sometimes have the habit of becoming enemies! Finally, personalised ways of working can be very exclusive, giving rise to 'cliques' of various kinds. If the 'right' stakeholders are not involved, this has the potential of undermining collaborative effort. There is always a balance to be struck between the formal and informal modes of working, and there is a 'need to situate personal relationships within a context of clear and inclusive ground-rules and flexible but transparent structures' (LGMB, 1997, p 11).

Boundary spanners are often exposed and marginalised in their own organisations – the subjects of 'uprootedness' (Wenger, 1998) – and in frequent need of external support, comfort and succor from individuals in similar situations. They face the problem of not always following conventional career paths within their home organisational structures, and are perceived to be different – even thought of as 'having gone native'. Therefore, networks of boundary spanners are able to act as sources of peer group advice, personal support and constructive criticism.

Dilemmas of multiple accountabilities

A significant area of debate concerns the perceived loss of control and accountability in network governance as opposed to that in hierarchies and markets. This stems from a lack of transparency in the policy-making process, dispersed and unclear lines of accountability, insufficient democratic legitimacy and a general 'leakage in the channels of authority' (Bardach and Lesser, 1996, p 198), and Agranoff and McGuire (2001, p 310) pose the dilemma that: 'with no single authority, everyone is somewhat in charge, thus everyone is somewhat responsible; all network participants appear to be accountable, but none is absolutely accountable'. These problems are exacerbated by the demands of multiple accountabilities listed in Box 5.1.

> ## Box 5.1: Sources of accountability
>
> 1. Accountability to their home or employing organisation; contractual liability requiring actors to operate within its organisational parameters and promote its interests
> 2. Accountability to a collaborative as member, partner or board representative (may be formal or informal)
> 3. Accountability to professional bodies
> 4. Accountability to citizens, the public, service users or to value systems such as the public service ethos
> 5. Accountability to self – personal value systems and beliefs

In helping to resolve these dilemmas and acknowledging that the application of principal–agent relationships are difficult to apply in collaborative contexts, Agranoff and McGuire (2001) suggest that accountability in networks should move away from notions of hierarchical accountability more to a focus on effectiveness and performance, and Bardach and Lesser (1996) differentiate between two faces of accountability. They refer to 'accountability to' something which is typical of bureaucratic chains of command and control structures, and 'accountability for' something which relates to outcomes or performance, the latter being a more appropriate form of accountability system for collaborative situations, and may include ideals associated with responsibility, public value and democracy. This is not to suggest that accountability for collaborative activity should be sidelined or in some way 'watered down', but new ways of holding collaboratives to account need to be devised. Outcomes and performance are critical both for 'home' organisations and the collaboration as a whole, and these need to be framed within an integrated structure of democratic and stakeholder accountability.

The tensions inherent in the management of multiple accountabilities are brought into sharp focus by the concept of some individuals as 'tempered radicals' (Meyerson and Scully, 1995) who are committed at the same time to their own organisation and/or profession, but also to a cause, community or ideology that is different from or even at odds with the prevailing culture, beliefs and values of that organisation. Wright (2009) argues that boundary spanners claim to be distinct in terms of both the structural and knowledge dimensions of organisational interaction, while emphasising inclusiveness at the political and interpersonal levels. The problems faced by such individuals centre on managing forms of ambivalence. Tempered radicals can speak the languages of multiple constituencies; they have to steer a course between assimilation and separatism; are opportunistic in relation to available resources and shifting power alliances; and take advantage of the fact that they are 'outsiders within'. They can access the:

Knowledge and insight of the insider with the critical attitude of the outsider … [and] whilst insider status provides access to opportunities for change, outsider status provides the detachment to recognise that there even is an issue or problem to work on. (Meyerson and Scully, 1995, p 5)

The author's own research (Williams, 2005) indicated that boundary spanners recognised the first call on their accountability was to their employing organisation, that they were not free agents but remunerated to advance the interests of those organisations. However, it was felt that in discharging this primary accountability, they needed to recognise the value and legitimacy of other sources of accountability that stemmed from engaging collaboratively with other agencies and actors. For instance, a poor partner was perceived to be one who dogmatically ploughed a representative furrow in collaborative arenas and, irritatingly had to 'report back' everything to their home organisation. Conversely, the more effective ones were those who were empowered, within certain negotiated parameters, to engage constructively with other partners. Such people would have a feel for what may or may not be acceptable to their home organisations and were ready to engage constructively with other partners. They would have the judgement and skills to calculate which decisions needed reference back to their home organisation, perhaps matters of policy or 'big issues', and those that could be safely assumed to be in its interest. They could give clear signals of what may or may not be acceptable to their organisations. Consequently, understanding the parameters and constraints of each partner was considered to be highly important.

The matters of accountability and responsibility are by no means clear-cut, and considerable sensitivities and potential conflicts abound. The effective boundary spanner needs to be very much aware of the differential accountabilities of each member of a collaborative group and to be sympathetic to any problems of managing these in relation to the work of the collaboration. The degree of empowerment, or the extent to which individual partners are mandated to commit themselves or their organisation to collaborative decisions, varies considerably between organisations. Typically, in multiagency, multisectoral collaborations, accountability varies widely in form and length – political and managerial in local authorities, non-elected boards in the NHS, unrepresentative management committees in the voluntary sector and company boards in the private sector.

In practice, although 'representative' positions have to be articulated in formal collaborative occasions, there is considerable scope in private discussions to understand different positions and working parameters. This emphasises the value of networking and of working outside the formal structure and machinery of collaboration where a greater accountability to the group can be fostered. Accountability in one collaboration in the author's research was described by one boundary spanner in the following way:

> '... we make sure that people are clear about lines of accountability and reporting back ... it does not constrain what happens in the partnership group ... we accept mutual constraints, understand each other's difficulties and attempt to manage them ... some things I can't bend on and it is important that others understand why ... you need to focus on what you can and cannot do ... there may be public and private positions which relates to trust.'

In some cases, the question of accountability can be blurred with variable levels of commitment to working in collaboration. In others, a feeling of belonging and of being treated as an equal partner is a powerful bond that stretches conventional organisational allegiances. The degree of accountability or commitment to a collaboration can vary with the extent to which a group has developed and gelled into a team. Collective responsibility is more likely to emanate from groups that work well together and have invested in the process as well as the tasks. A youth offending manager in the author's research commented on this point as follows:

> 'My main role is to represent my organisation but increasingly you can align yourself with a particular concern or issues. You can take things back to your own organisation even if it contradicts the organisation's view. Our views have definitely changed over time since working with the police and local authority on the drugs and alcohol team and the Crime Reduction Partnership. It gives us a wider perspective, a more rounded picture of the criminal justice area and where all other players fit into that.'

A measure of a poor boundary spanner, in the opinion of a director of a voluntary services agency, was someone who never departed from a representative role and was always looking at issues from a single perspective:

> 'People don't like this type of person. When you go to a meeting, you should go as yourself and give something of yourself, so that others know you as a person, not as an organisational representative.'

The process of building relationships was considered to be very difficult if someone was constantly locked into a representative mode, and an overly representative disposition could inhibit innovation and creativity, particularly in the search for solutions to complex problems. However, it was considered alternatively, that by distancing themselves from their host organisations, boundary spanners risked losing credibility, and it was better to be open and honest about the parameters of collaboration working and accountabilities. The key to being persuasive may well rest in an ability to convey different messages to different audiences simultaneously.

Appreciating multiple framing processes

Boundary spanners operate in a highly complex, diverse and contested environment where 'reality' is framed in different ways, as discussed in Chapter Three. Collaborative arenas are characterised by actors and interests from a range of backgrounds, cultures, agencies and sectors, increasing the likelihood of disparities in the ways in which 'reality' is framed and enhancing the potential for conflict. Framing is important in the way actors interpret the challenges facing them, and the manner in which they attempt to resolve them, particularly through cooperative strategies. Benford and Snow (2000) suggest that particular actors operate as 'frame articulators' and function as managers of meaning within strategic processes, and this is a role often performed by boundary spanners. The task is to help clarify and understand the ways in which key stakeholders interpret collaborative realities, and assist in the process of shaping, molding and reframing possibilities and preferences in pursuit of shared agendas (Sullivan and Williams, 2009; Williams and Sullivan, 2009).

Some frames remain implicit and little understood, and the boundary spanner can assist in surfacing these on behalf of individual stakeholders. Others are closely associated with professional, sectoral or organisational interests and need to be articulated and communicated to others in an effective and jargon-free manner. Frame articulation needs sensitive management as too much elaboration or ill-timed articulation can potentially lead to problematical encounters.

Framing is fundamentally important in the context of the many different interpretations that are attributed to the notion of collaboration itself, as discussed in Chapter Two. Terms such as 'partnership', 'cooperation', 'integration', 'coordination' and 'collaboration' are very familiar in this policy field but have no universally understood meaning, and indicate meanings of different intensity, intent, purpose and outcome. This can be confusing, particularly in the context of joint action. There is, then, a considerable onus on boundary spanners to help surface and articulate these different understandings as a prelude to securing ownership of, and direction to, collaborative purposes.

Clearly, it is important to establish just how far different actors are prepared to proceed along the collaborative continuum – how much power and authority they are prepared to cede. There is little point in preparing strategies for an integrated service if one or more of the interested parties will go no further than cooperating or coordinating! However, frame articulation is a delicate business because too much clarity risks exposing the true motivations of recalcitrant actors and stymie possible future collaboration.

An example of the multiple interpretations of a policy concept is highlighted in Box 5.2 in relation to the notion of a 'locality model' that was used as a means of securing integration in health and social care. Here, stakeholders in the same partnership emphasised the polysemous nature of the 'locality model': putting the needs of the service user at the centre of the design and delivery of services; understanding local needs and linking to communities; making the most cost-effective use of scarce resources; keeping people out of hospital and developing primary and community services to support them; and coordinating health and social care services at a local level.

One immediate implication of these differences in interpretation was securing consensus on what constituted the most appropriate size of population for the locality. The local NHS trust adopted a cost-effective use of resources approach – a larger size of population being more efficient particularly in the engagement specialist secondary care interests such as consultants and specialist nurses/ therapists, whereas other interests favoured a lower number because it was particularly keen to focus on a small population in order to engage GP practices in thinking about organising and delivering their services across a wider area.

Box 5.2: Multiple interpretations of the locality model

Interpretations of the locality model

'It is a delivery mechanism based on geography and population size; it focuses services around a certain population that enable service providers to deliver population-sensitive services and to deliver and link different models of care that are sensitive to the needs of that population.' (NHS director)

'It means different things to different people, and can be manifested in unknown ways; to me it is about the efficient and effective use of services and a vehicle to deliver the chronic condition management agenda; but it can be used to deliver other health and social care outcomes.' (NHS senior manager)

'It is a multidisciplinary team within a geographically defined area linked to a number of general practitioners' practices.' (social services director)

'It's about fewer people in hospital beds and keeping more people at home, and a greater involvement of social services.' (GP)

'It's getting a balance between economies of scale, but being not too big as to not have a local feel; efficient and effective use of services but with a user focus which allows their ownership and involvement.' (NHS trust head of service)

'To coordinate the management arrangements and resources in one locality; to create an alignment between people serving the same population through effective clinical and managerial leadership resulting in a re-shaping in the use of resources.' (NHS local health board chief executive)

Source: NLIAH (2009)

Research in the context of the preparation of community strategies in Wales (Sullivan and Williams, 2009) discovered that different stakeholders understood this statutory duty differently, and the coexistence of different interpretations had serious practical implications for delivery. Five broad frames were identified – as rational planning, civic renewal, network governance, multilevel governance and learning – but there was evidence of both within as well as between-frame differences. Community strategy coordinators, as boundary spanners, were instrumental in guiding and servicing community strategy partnerships, and in the main reflected the frames of the most powerful interests rather than directed them. Professional interests tended to support a rational approach whereas voluntary sector interests championed the ambitions of civic renewal. Although dominant frames could be identified in particular areas, there was a tendency to embrace most if not all of the frames in some way, storing up huge difficulties at the point of implementation. This example clearly indicates the centrality of framing processes within collaborative arenas and the consequent responsibility that falls on boundary spanners to manage them purposively.

Conclusion

This chapter has posed and explored two particular questions relating to the boundary spanner's role. First, whether the job requires access to specialised repositories of knowledge, expertise and experience as is the case with most professionals, and second, whether a boundary spanner's personality influences his/her effectiveness. In answer to the first question, while not necessarily being discrete, in-depth knowledge of the nature and parameters of the context can be seen to be particularly valuable, as is intersectoral and interorganisational experience. In relation to the second question, opinions differ, although a generous catalogue of helpful personal attributes are cited in the literature, and practitioners often believe certain personal characteristics to be essential.

This chapter also presented considerable evidence on the problematic nature of the boundary spanning role, evidenced in the tensions, paradoxes and ambiguities inherent in managing in and across multiple modes of governance; blurred personal and professional relationships; the dilemmas of multiple accountabilities; and appreciating multiple framing processes. Although reticulist behaviour has many positive benefits, it is fraught with difficulties at the 'zones of incongruence', requiring sensitive handling to manage through the fog of formal/informal situations, personal/professional relationships and the competing demands of multiple accountabilities of varying importance.

Managing interpersonal relationships is a particularly delicate process requiring careful judgements about their intensity, and an acute appreciation of the implications of redistributed power relationships. The consequences of dysfunctional interpersonal relationships are protracted and ineffective collaborative working, with low levels of cooperation and high costs of lack of coordination. Other areas of difficulty and tension include managing without power and balancing the opposing forces of cooperation and competition, and these are discussed in the final chapter.

Review of main points

- Boundary spanners can claim to embrace specialised areas of knowledge, expertise and experience. Key knowledge areas relate particularly to the context within which they operate – roles, responsibilities, motivations, cultures and accountability frameworks. The ability to understand interdependence and relationships is especially relevant, and an additional source of support can be gathered from interorganisational and intersectoral experience – working in different types of organisation, in different policy areas, in different sectors and within different teams.
- The question of whether an effective boundary spanner is somehow influenced by particular personality traits is a contested one. However, there are many examples of helpful personal attributes cited in the literature including being extrovert, honesty, respectful, trusting, open, sociable, diplomatic and persistent.
- The boundary spanner is faced with a range of tensions, ambiguities and paradoxes in the course of their work, including managing in and across multiple modes of governance; blurred personal and professional relationships; dilemmas of multiple accountabilities; and appreciating multiple framing processes.
- Boundary spanners need to know how and when to switch between different modes of governance, but face tensions because of the incongruencies that exist at the interfaces between them.
- The interface between personal and professional relationships is often blurred, causing the boundary spanner problems in differentiating between them. This has implications for processes of listening, empathy and trust. Although well-developed interpersonal relationships have the potential to release enhanced cooperative behaviour, they can be fragile and unstable.
- The boundary spanner faces a range of tensions and ambiguities stemming from different, and sometimes conflicting, sources of accountability. These require sensitive management and constant attention.
- Problems, issues and solutions are the subject of implicit and explicit framing processes by the different interests represented in collaboration. The boundary spanner needs to be acutely aware of these and assist in the process of shaping, molding and aligning these to achieve collaborative advantage.

Questions for discussion

1. How do boundary spanners manage multiple and sometimes conflicting accountabilities?
2. Are boundary spanners born or bred?
3. What forms of knowledge do boundary spanners need to demonstrate about collaborative working?
4. Discuss the assertion that an effective boundary spanner has to possess a specific set of personality characteristics.

5. Give some examples of multiple framing processes within forms of collaboration you are familiar with. How can boundary spanners manage framing differences between stakeholders in a particular collaboration?
6. Discuss the problems associated with personal and professional relationships, and outline the most effective mechanisms for dealing with them.
7. Is collaborative working constructed around a scaffolding of interpersonal relationships? If so, what are the implications of this?

Suggested further reading

Agranoff, R. and McGuire, M. (2001) 'Big questions in public network management research', *Journal of Public Administration Research and Theory*, vol 3, pp 295-326.

Bacharach, S.B. Bamberger, P. and McKinney, V. (2000) 'Boundary management tactics and logics in action: the case of peer-support providers', *Administrative Science Quarterly*, vol 45, no 4, pp 704-36.

Benford, R.D. and Snow, D.A. (2000) 'Framing processes and social movements: an overview and assessment', *Annual Review of Sociology*, vol 26, pp 611-39.

Fairtlough, G. (1994) *Creative compartments*, London: Adamantine Press.

Machado, N. and Burns, T.R. (1998) 'Complex social organization: multiple organizing modes, structural incongruence, and mechanism of integration', *Public Administration*, vol 76, pp 355-86.

Meyerson, D.E. and Scully, M.A. (1995) 'Tempered radicalism and the politics of ambivalence and change', *Organization Science*, vol 6, no 5, pp 585-600.

Sarason, S.B. and Lorentz, E.M. (1998) *Crossing boundaries: Collaboration, coordination and the redefinition of resources*, San Francisco, CA: Jossey-Bass.

SIX

Learning from the private sector

The previous two chapters have explored the nature and role of boundary spanners in a public sector context. In contrast, this chapter shifts the focus to the private sector to examine whether there are any practical or theoretical lessons and learning from the activities of boundary spanners in this sphere of management and governance which may be of interest to the public sector. Moreover, it looks at public–private partnerships (PPPs) for additional insights and perspectives into the work of boundary spanners.

Early perspectives

The early literature from organisational theory on boundary spanning was set primarily within a private sector context. Here, the boundary spanning function is considered to be one of managing the interface between organisations and their environments. Katz and Kahn (1966) suggest that this involves a process of exporting goods, services and ideas from an organization, and of importing staff and raw materials into it; Adams (1976) and Aldrich and Herker (1977) identify two main roles in this function, an information-processing or transmitter role involving filtering and facilitation, and an external representation or gatekeeping function which includes resource acquisition and political/social legitimacy; Aldrich (1979, p 249) views it as a process of 'buffering, moderating and influencing external events'; and finally, Thompson (1967) suggests that it involves controlling threats from the environment. Tushman and Scanlan (1981b, p 290) focus on issues of communication across boundaries caused by differences in 'idiosyncratic languages and coding systems' and 'local conceptual frameworks' resulting in bias and distortion of information. Aldrich and Herker (1977) argue that the nature of the environment has a direct influence on the need for boundary spanning roles in organisations. Organisations positioned within heterogeneous and dynamic environments, and involved in mediating technology, are considered more likely to warrant the creation of boundary spanning roles.

References are made to the potentially powerful position of boundary spanners because of their access to information and control over its dissemination, and to their enhanced status acquired through their exposure to the external environment. In view of the multiple roles boundary spanners are expected to discharge, this can be seen as a source of stress and conflict, although alternatively some argue that it might 'serve as resources for status enhancement and role performance' and 'enrich the personality and self-conception of boundary spanners, offering them a diversity of experience closed off to other members' (Aldrich, 1979, p 262). There is a suggestion in this literature that boundary spanning is seen as a job for 'special people', who are variously described as 'organizational representative' (Brown, 1983), 'organizational liaison' (Tushman, 1977, p 592) 'foreign affairs person' (Evan, 1971) and 'internal communication stars' (Tushman and Scanlan, 1981a, p 84), and that their role is important to the success of their organisations and can be a catalyst for innovation and structural change (Aldrich and Herker, 1977). Katz and Tushman (1983) discovered that boundary spanning supervisors provided an important leadership and training function for junior staff through their ability to act as socialising agents and network builders, and Tushman and Scanlan (1981b) suggest that the antecedents of boundary role status are technical competence and a background and skills to communicate with external areas.

Cooperative strategies

However, this literature is limited, and does not do justice to the activities of businesses and companies whose motivations are not solely fixated on protecting and managing their organisations and their external environments, but actively involve seeking cooperative strategies, both as a means of enhancing the qualities that afford competitive advantage, and to strengthen their individual corporate strategies. Forms of cooperation are realised through strategic partnerships, alliances, joint ventures, consortia, networks and many other forms of business relationships.

Companies have increasingly looked to cooperate because of the limitations of coping successfully on their own in a turbulent world where markets have become global and conditions of high economic uncertainty prevail, because technologies are changing and again have become global and because of rapid technological change which requires significant investment to develop products with shortening life cycles. Aiken and Hage (1968, p 915) cut to the chase and assert that: 'organizations go into joint ventures because of the need for resources, notably, money, skill and manpower', and Kogut (1988) refers to three motivations driving the formation of joint ventures: the search for lower transaction costs, to improve a firm's strategic position and as an opportunity for organisational learning. Broadly speaking, there are two main rationales underpinning cooperative strategies between firms. The first relates to the advantages of gaining access to competencies or resources from other companies, particularly those that are perceived to be complementary. The second focuses on learning and innovation where potential partners feel deficient in particular areas and look to access learning and knowledge from others better placed.

Although cooperation rather than competition is the preferred route for organisations wishing to achieve their objectives in this form, it is important to remember that competitive advantage is still the overall rationale. There are many risks associated with these approaches, especially in terms of alliances that aim to shape or manipulate markets, and the risks associated with being taken advantage of by partners through opportunistic behaviours and failure to reciprocate. This leads to a further important point which is central to the book, in that whereas economic arguments for cooperative strategies may well be necessary, they are not always sufficient and there must be a political motive perceived by a firm's decision makers for the adoption of such an approach. The role of agency becomes highly influential in the course of partner selection, form of cooperation and alliance management. Porter and Fuller (1986) identify a number of criteria for choosing an alliance partner, including the possession of the desired source of competitive advantage, complementary or balanced contribution, compatible view of international strategy, low risk of becoming a competitor and high organisational compatibility. These mainly relate to achieving a strategic fit between partners, but equally important is the extent of cultural compatibility or difference. Culture has the potential to have an impact on the implementation of cooperative strategies. It can be a barrier particularly where there are significant national cultural differences or differences in approaches to management. These may have an impact on the form of cooperative strategy, and the processes leading to the agreements to cooperate, and can give rise to operational problems. Conversely, cultural diversity can be perceived as a resource through the creation of opportunities to use the competencies and knowledge from each partner's culture. Managing cultural diversity is highly problematic and strategies range across a spectrum, from domination to integration. Integration looks to create a new synergy from the best of each partner, whereas segregation aims to preserve distance to avoid conflict and minimise the time involved in cultural management. Strategies to manage intercultural alliances can be pitched at a personal or team level, with communication being paramount.

Alliance managers and management

The management of alliances, joint ventures, partnerships and other forms of cooperative strategies are often vested in dedicated individuals (the boundary spanners), operating individually or sometimes within defined alliance management units (see Table 6.1). The key functions of such a dedicated strategic alliance capability include improving knowledge management, increasing external visibility, providing internal coordination and helping to eliminate accountability and intervention problems (Dyer et al, 2001). In the context of managing multiple alliances, Doz and Hamel (1998) refer to the role of the network manager as offering a focal point for communication and exchange, a watchdog for free riders, a central repository of information and member performance, and finally, a maintainer of behaviour norms. Child et al (2005) point to the importance of 'intercultural boundary spanners' within international joint ventures needing to bridge two different organisations or two or more people from different cultures.

A number of references are made to the existence of different stages in the alliance management life cycle with different roles requiring different alliance staff (dealmaker, launch manager, alliance chief, alliance operating staff and corporate alliance manager). Bamford et al (2003, p 186), for instance, assert that 'an alliance lifestyle has seven distinct stages. The skill sets required from an alliance manager are different in each one of those stages – a visionary is called for at one stage and a facilitator at another'. Yoshino and Rangan (1995) identify five tasks that are critical to the job of being an alliance manager: establishing the right tone, particularly in relation to trust; monitoring the contributions and obligations of partners; recognising the importance of information flows; reassessing strategic viability; and focusing on internal relationships through being seen as a champion, fostering organisational understanding, maintaining links at all levels and managing internal demands and expectations.

Particular attention is focused on the social aspects of alliance management and the pivotal role of personal relationships. Hutt et al (2000) refer to the social network of a strategic alliance and the need for boundary spanning to occur at multiple levels: top management, middle management and operational personnel. They emphasise the importance of interpersonal relationships being superimposed over a formal structure, and being able to expedite communication, conflict resolution and learning, build trust, speed decision making and uncover new possibilities for partnership working. Communication is seen to be especially influential because it helps to produce a shared interpretation of goals and agreement on roles and norms. The role of personal relationships is a theme picked up by Adobor (2006), and he suggests that although alliances often proceed through early, growth and maturity stages, the benefits of personal relationships are mostly realised in the early stages, and the dysfunctions of personal ties are more likely in later stages. He provides a balanced view of the advantages and disadvantages of personal ties. The main advantages include speeding up the alliance formation process, reducing relational risk, building and strengthening trust and helping to reduce uncertainty, as against the disadvantages of conflict of interest, pursuit of self-interest and escalating commitment to a course of action, the fate of an alliance being tied to personal relationships, and the possibility of increased agency and transaction costs of the relationship.

Relational capital – the accumulation of trust, respect and friendship built up between individuals – is, in the opinion of Kale et al (2000, p 221), important for the performance of alliances in general, but particularly for those based on learning, because strong relational capital 'can facilitate exchange and transfer of information and know-how across the alliance interface'. Tacit learning, which relies on close contact between partners, is especially dependent on stocks of relational capital. Kale et al (2000) also suggest that relational capital is helpful in managing the tensions that exist between partnering firms that strive to learn from others, but in a way that does not risk losing their own core proprietary assets through opportunistic behaviour from partners.

The development of trust is central to the maintenance of effective interpersonal relationships, and Perrone et al (2003, p 435) make the interesting point that boundary spanners should be given space to develop this. They argue that:

> Boundary spanners with greater autonomy to manage interorganizational relations are better able to cultivate trust from their counterparts. Freed

from the constraint of strictly adhering to rigid rules and requirements of their own organizations, boundary–spanning agents have greater latitude in upholding commitments to partner organizations and fulfilling the positive expectations of their representatives.

The critical point here is that trust is considered to be meaningful if it is allowed to develop as a result of a person's free will rather than an expectation of a job role. However, Zaheer et al (1998) believe that interorganisational trust is more important than interpersonal trust in driving exchange performance between firms and managing negotiation and conflict. But, in the context of the structure–agency debate, they conclude that interpersonal trust may also matter through its institutionalising effects on interorganisational trust.

The life of boundary spanning agents within collaborative settings is invariably the subject of considerable tension and ambiguity because of the problems associated with balancing competition with cooperation; of resolving the accountability issues between alliances and the respective partners; and because of the challenges faced by unhelpful managerial mindsets, the tyranny of details and complex systemic issues (Yoshino and Rangan, 1995). In particular, managing without power does not come naturally to many actors used to operating within business organisations, and as Mohr and Speckman (1994, p 148) comment: 'such a wilful abdication of control (and autonomy) does not come easily but appears to be a necessary managerial requirement for the future'.

Managing in this type of environment can be seen to require a particular set of skills and abilities. Bamford et al (2003) refer to the following skills in alliance management: threshold (self-confidence, inspiring others, innovative, respectful); distinguishing (depth and breadth of internal and external networks, trust); high performance (credibility, articulating mutual benefits); and Child et al (2005) consider the following to be the most important: effective communication, adaptability, ability to function in fluid conditions and to cope with ambiguity and personal stress, capacity to work in and manage teams of diverse membership, relationship and negotiation skills, ability to work with people over whom they have no direct authority and capacity to build trust. Yoshino and Rangan (1995) suggest that alliance managers are ambassadors, intermediaries and 'point men', with well-developed personal networks, and credibility with other managers at all levels. Also, their value does not just lie in the management of the process but in their knowledge of their own business, its strategy, its functional areas and the structure and economics of the industry. The interesting question to pose is whether these skills and competencies are similar to those required within organisations, or unique to alliance management.

Wright (2009) identifies a small group of people operating within some organisations whose roles have considerable resonance with alliance managers. He refers to these as 'internal boundary spanners' (Wright, 2009) because they discharge job responsibilities that cut across departmental, divisional or professional boundaries. This reflects the breakdown of classical hierarchical structures in many

Table 6.1: Profile of alliance managers

Roles and functions	<ul><li>Knowledge management</li><li>Internal coordination</li><li>External visibility</li><li>Communication hub</li><li>Information management</li><li>Intercultural management</li><li>Performance monitoring</li></ul>
Main images	<ul><li>Champion</li><li>Point man</li><li>Ambassador</li><li>Intermediary</li></ul>
Competencies	Interpersonal relationships, building trust, communication, conflict management, learning, team working, negotiation
Personal characteristics	Self-confidence, inspiring others, respectful, credible, adaptability
Tensions	<ul><li>Balancing competition and cooperation</li><li>Managing accountabilities</li><li>Coping with complexity</li><li>Managing without power</li><li>Switching between different management approaches</li></ul>

organisations, the trend towards cross-functional working and more networked forms of management. Wright (2009) discusses the ambiguous identities that such people face as a consequence of being both organisational 'insiders' and 'outsiders'. In practice, his research suggests that these people worked through their identities across four boundary dimensions: structural, knowledge, political and interpersonal. The image of the boundary spanner was expressed most clearly in relation to structure because of the freedom they were allowed to operate outside normal lines of reporting and authority, and being able to cross departmental, hierarchical, geographical and divisional boundaries. In terms of knowledge, the research found that this group of people adopted the role of 'esoteric expert' underpinned by a claim to possess 'exclusive knowledge and skills beyond the grasp of normal managers' (Wright, 2009, p 320). As a counterbalance to the promotion of 'distinctiveness' through the dimensions of structure and knowledge, 'inclusiveness' was promoted through interpersonal relationships and access to the centres of organisational power.

Boundary spanners in public–private partnerships

Public–private partnerships (PPPs) represent a particular form of collaborative governance that has steadily grown in popularity in a number of countries including the US, Australia and parts of Europe including the UK (Greve and Hodge, 2010). They are designed as a mechanism to lever in more financial resources and private sector disciplines into the public sector, and have been used to construct large and long-term infrastructure contracts in the realms of health, schools, defence, prisons and transport. However, the model has more recently begun to be used for delivering and managing some public services. PPPs are manifested in a number of different forms, and since their introduction in the UK, their attraction has crossed the political divide. Their main expression has been through the private finance initiative (PFI) introduced by a Conservative government, but the model has been subsequently embraced by New Labour, albeit for somewhat different reasons. There have been vigorous political and academic debates about the potential of PPPs, particularly in relation to their long-term financial implications (Pollock et al, 2007), and the human and industrial relations repercussions of staff moving from the public sector to PPP projects. The latter has been the source of much acrimony, especially among trades unions.

There are a number of significant organisational and managerial challenges involved in PPPs. Perhaps the foremost of these is their level of complexity, focus on contracting and the legal and financial arrangements. These require a huge investment in negotiation which is made more difficult by the number of actors involved in the process, the multiple forms of accountability stemming from different parties and the fundamental differences in purpose and value base emanating from public sector and private sector interests (Klijn and Teisman, 2003). However, although it is recognised that designing and managing PPPs is a considerable and different proposition from managing conventional public services, little mention is made in the literature on the role and necessary competencies of boundary spanners. Fischbacher and Beaumont (2003, p 176) highlight the importance of the process in PPPs, and suggest that given the complexity of the technical and human resources issues involved, 'training may be an essential precursor' to any project, as well as the development 'of skills in managing the process'.

The exception to the lack of focus on individual actors is contained in the work of Noble and Jones (2006) and Jones and Noble (2008), which represents the most comprehensive exploration of the role and behaviour of boundary spanners in PPPs. They distinguish between the roles of 'project champions' (senior managers who create the conditions for partnership working), and the boundary spanning managers who are deeply involved in day-to-day management, and suggest that the key challenge is to devise mechanisms to cope with the fact that: 'their routine is jolted from normal intra-organizational life to the more complex world of inter-organizational relations' (Noble and Jones, 2006, p 914). Boundary spanners are seen as making sense of any challenge by labelling PPPs as threats or opportunities judged on the basis of different forms of distance – autonomy, cultural and cautionary. Autonomy refers to an awareness of the need for partnership; cultural distance relates to the different values, concerns, objectives and accountabilities of agencies from different sectors; and cautionary distance centres on levels of risk involved in working with unknown partners in terms of reliability and trust.

Noble and Jones (2006) proceed to argue that PPPs progress through a number of distinct stages in their lifetime – pre-contract, trawling, sizing up and structuring

– each having a different focus, and consequent set of boundary spanning challenges. The implementation of PPPs is identified as a particularly challenged part of the exercise, which in turn is heavily dependent on trusting, committed and respectful interpersonal relationships. Working to debureaucratise PPP processes is a favoured tactic of boundary spanners, but managing the consequent tension between a formal approach and one based on tacit and informal agreements requires a delicate balancing act. Interestingly, Noble and Jones conclude that managing in a PPP environment is different to that in single agency settings, particularly in relation to the absence of hierarchical power structures, and as a consequence, requiring a different managerial style and mindset.

Contrasts and comparisons with the public sector

The public and private sectors represent quite different rationales and values, and these often become blurred in arrangements that involve organisations from either sector working together. In the private sector, although firms may embark on a course of partnership, it can be argued that their core purpose of competitive advantage is 'cloaked' behind the notion of cooperation, and the danger of opportunistic behaviour requires eternal vigilance. Similarly in the public sector, although public organisations invariably espouse the virtues of working together to realise 'public value', this again masks motivations that can be grounded in achieving power, status, image and resources. Hence, the role of the boundary spanner operating in either context is fraught with managing the multiple and often conflicting motivations of different interests. Given that 'true' motivations are often unstated, the boundary spanner is forced to work informally, primarily through interpersonal relationships.

There is a high degree of compatibility in the roles of the boundary spanners in the two sectors. The reticulist or network role emerges strongly in both – the notion of the boundary spanner as a focal point with internal and external communication being especially important. The coordination and organising role is a central part of the working lives of both, with information and knowledge management being key resources, and the emphasis placed on interpersonal relationships is consistently highlighted in both contexts. The success of collaboration is as much about relational capital, trust and cultural appreciation as it is about strategic fit.

There is recognition in the alliance literature that management in this mode is different to that within single organisations, and consequently requires a different set of skills. In particular, these relate directly to working with others who are different – hence, the need for conflict resolution, communication, interpersonal and cultural awareness skills. The private sector literature makes reference to the life cycle or stages of alliances and the need for boundary spanners to major on particular aspects within each stage, requiring the use of different skills. There are some parallels here with Lowndes and Skelcher's (1998) life cycle model developed in relation to urban regeneration projects, and the differences in modes of governance at different stages. Both imply a high degree of flexibility and multiskilling on behalf of boundary spanners to be able to switch between different stages, to adapt to the particular requirements of them and to deploy the right skills for the various tasks in hand. It may be, of course, that dedicated boundary spanners are not charged with operating across all stages and that senior managers and leaders have a role in some, particularly the formative stages. The next chapter undertakes a detailed examination of the role of these particular actors.

The literature on boundary spanners in the private sector emphasises the importance of learning far more than the comparable public sector material. Perhaps this is more a reflection of the value of learning and knowledge management in alliances and joint ventures, and the need to design explicit strategies for both. Acute sensibilities abound in transferring learning and knowledge, and absorptive capacities of firms have to be fit for purpose. The alliance managers or boundary spanners have a key role to play here, both in promoting transfer but also in cataloguing and monitoring flows of information, data and knowledge. Another aspect of the boundary spanner's function in the private sector that emerges is the pivotal role that they play in relation to mediating the interface between the internal organisation and the joint venture, alliance or whatever form of cooperative relationship is being managed. There are parallels here with the public sector, but the creation of alliance management functions and units to deal with this and broader matters tends to be more sophisticated and better resourced. Critically, there is evidence to suggest that investment in alliance management capabilities pays dividends in terms of greater performance. Public sector counterparts need to reflect on this finding when considering whether or not to invest in similar capabilities.

The experience of both private and public sector boundary spanners is that their lives are fraught with many tensions that stem from sometimes opposing calls on their allegiance from home organisations or alliances, the difficulties of operating without the benefit of formal power over capital, staff or other resources which comes with organisational status, and balancing the complexities of multiple motivations, some of which may be cooperative and others, competitive.

Review of main points

- Early perspectives on boundary spanners in the organisational studies literature considered their role to be more about protection rather than collaboration – as managing the interface between their organisation and the external environment, as gatekeeper, information processor and liaison person.
- Boundary spanners in the private sector are those involved in alliance, joint venture and strategic alliance management. Sometimes they act alone, and at other times within dedicated units. Their key roles involve internal and external communication, knowledge management, bridging cultures and performance management.
- Interpersonal relationships, trust and transparency are very important here as the basis of building relational capital. A particular set of skills is required which includes conflict management, adaptability, team management and communication.
- The job of the boundary spanner in this context is replete with ambiguities and dilemmas stemming from issues of accountability, balancing cooperation with competition, avoiding opportunistic behaviours and managing without power.
- Boundary spanners in both private and public sectors share much in common in terms of their functions and roles – networking, organising, coordination, communication and the development of interpersonal relationships is important to both.
- The notion of the differing demands of the alliance life cycle, the management between parent firm and alliance and the creation of dedicated alliance capability functions have valuable lessons for the public sector.
- Boundary spanners working in PPPs face a distinct set of managerial and organisational challenges.

Questions for discussion

1. Compare and contrast boundary spanners working in different contexts.
2. Is it possible for boundary spanners to move effectively between contexts?
3. Design an alliance management unit for a new venture. What functions would it undertake and how would it be staffed? What steps would be taken to communicate between the partners and their parent firms, and how would learning and knowledge management be organised?
4. How might boundary spanners minimise the potential for competition and opportunistic behaviour in cooperative strategies?
5. What are the main challenges for boundary spanners working in PPPs, and which competencies do they need to deal with them effectively?

Suggested further reading

Aldrich, H.A. (1979) *Organizations and environments*, Englewood Cliffs, NJ: Prentice Hall.

Bamford, J.D., Gomes-Casseres, B. and Robinson, M.S. (2003) *Mastering alliance strategy*, San Francisco, CA: Jossey-Bass.

Child, J., Faulkner, D. and Tallman, S. (2005) *Cooperative strategy: Managing alliances, networks, and joint ventures*, Oxford: Oxford University Press.

Jones, R. and Noble, G. (2008) 'Managing the implementation of public–private partnerships', *Public Money and Management*, April, pp 109-14.

Noble, G. and Jones, R. (2006) 'The role of boundary-spanning managers in the establishment of public–private partnerships', *Public Administration*, vol 84, no 4, pp 891-917.

Tushman, M.L. and Scanlan, T.J. (1981) 'Characteristics and external orientation of boundary spanning individuals', *Academy of Management Journal*, vol 24, no 1, pp 83-98.

Yoshino, M.Y. and Rangan, U.S. (1995) *Strategic alliances: An entrepreneurial approach to globalization*, Boston, MA: Harvard Business School Press.

SEVEN

We are all boundary spanners now?

Introduction

The interrelated, multilevel and interdependent nature of the policy environment, the characteristics of many societal problems and the spread of new types of governance have stimulated new forms of public management. In particular, the discernible shift towards network governance has embraced managerialism but in a way that has superseded the efficiency and customer orientation principles implicit in new public management: 'to take on the challenge of working across boundaries and to take up the goal of holistic working' (Stoker, 2004, p 14). Network governance is multilayered, characterised by a diverse range of horizontal relations, and consists of a complex architecture of institutions drawn from across all areas of civil society – public, private and third sectors. The consequence of this trend for public management is that many public managers have now begun to develop dual, but highly connected, roles. The first relates to their traditional role of intraorganisational management, and the second concerns their involvement in forms of collaborative management with a variety of other actors from different sectors, professions and organisations. This is driven, not just by external forces that seek to deliver greater efficiency, effectiveness and synergy across public services, but also by an acceptance that single organisational objectives cannot be achieved without the cooperation of other agents. For example, the manager of a mental health rehabilitation service appreciates that meeting the multiple and complex needs of many clients is dependent on coordinated interventions from a number of professionals and carers – occupational therapists, nursing staff, psychiatrists, support staff and voluntary sector groups. So in order to achieve their business aims in a mainstream job role, public managers have to become boundary spanners – not in a wholly dedicated fashion as discussed in earlier chapters, but through a combination of intra and interorganisational management. This chapter examines the nature of this boundary spanning role, how it is discharged, what particular competencies and capacities are needed, and whether this form of management creates any special challenges.

As with public managers and for similar reasons, it is now common practice for leaders of most public organisations to be heavily involved in forms of cooperation, coordination and collaboration with other agencies both within and between sectors. This is necessary to both achieve the objectives of their own organisations, and to contribute to shared policy and societal purposes. Therefore, many leaders play a key role in the leadership of their own organisations, and contribute to leadership for collaboration as a boundary spanner. Chief executives, directors and heads of service of local authorities, health agencies, police authorities and other public agencies are heavily engaged in a range of voluntary and mandated forms of collaboration across all policy areas. A significant proportion of their time is devoted to the collaboration agenda. However, while a great deal is known about leadership in single organisations, considerably less is understood about exactly what constitutes leadership for collaboration. This chapter aims to address this relatively underdeveloped aspect of leadership through a critical evaluation of the literature, interspersed with perspectives from the author's own research. But first, the focus is on public managers as boundary spanners.

Public managers as boundary spanners

Network management and policy network approaches (Kickert et al, 1997; Goldsmith and Eggers, 2004; Koppenjan and Klijn, 2004; Agranoff, 2007) capture much of what is required of boundary spanning public managers. The literature on network management acknowledges the interdependencies between public, private and third sector actors in the design and delivery of public policy, and reflects a realism that 'government is unable unilaterally to control the complexities and pluralistic diversity which are fundamental characteristics of modern societies' (Kickert et al, 1997, p 4). Network approaches involve tackling complex problems through cooperative action, and critically, they are premised to some extent on a style of management that is different from that in classical organisations based on intraorganisational forms of management, although Agranoff (2007, p 124) sits on the fence and suggests that: 'management in the collaborarchy is thus simultaneously similar to and different from management in hierarchical organizations'. Network management can be seen as inherently interorganisational and intersectoral, and network managers have pivotal boundary spanning roles to discharge.

The roles and functions of network management are well documented (Kickert et al, 1997; Agranoff, 2004, 2007; Goldsmith and Eggers, 2004; Koppenjan and Klijn, 2004) and include structuring and intervening in networks; activating and facilitating networks; promoting interaction between network actors; and building consensus and joint problem solving. By general consensus, the 'quality and skills of network managers constitute a crucial precondition for success' (Kickert et al, 1997, p 58), particularly managing complexity, negotiation and mediation, tactical and strategic appreciation and reticulist competence. Provan and Kenis (2008) relate network-level competencies to network governance types. They discuss three main types: shared governance, involving a small number of participants, which are highly decentralised with equal participation from members; lead organisation, where one organisation takes a lead role on behalf of a moderate number of others, brokering deals and centralising decision making; and network administrative organisations, where a separate entity, individual or unit, is responsible for the management and affairs of others. They argue that, on the basis of the nature of the tasks performed and of the external challenges faced, more coordination skills are necessary to deal with highly interdependent situations, and more skills in relation to conflict resolution, communication, lobbying, external funding and building external legitimacy are needed to manage particularly in the latter two types of network governance models.

Although there is a growing repository of research and literature on network management, Herranz (2008) detects a lack of consensus on its nature stemming from its 'metaphoric elasticity', and that it underemphasises key sectoral differences. He suggests that there is a continuum of public management approaches to networks along a passive to active axis that emphasises different roles and competencies for network managers, permutations of which are relevant in

Table 7.1: Network management roles and behaviours

Type of governance	Type of management behaviour	Role of network manager
Public/bureaucratic	Hierarchical-based directive administration and/or active coordination	Coordination through authoritative and procedural mechanisms not social and relational incentives; similar skills to those below but 'more of the' AND/OR direct management through operational levers (activation, framing, mobilising and synthesising); high levels of administration; use of discretion to combine social, procedural and incentive mechanisms
Private/ entrepreneurial	Contingent coordination and/or active coordination	Active coordination; managing perceptions and interactions of participants; managers use opportunistic directive influence but scope is limited and contingent on network interests and resources AND/OR direct management through operational levers (activation, framing, mobilising and synthesising); high levels of administration; use of discretion to combine social, procedural and incentive mechanisms
Third sector/ community-based	Reactive facilitation and/or contingent coordination	Facilitative with emphasis on managing social interactions rather than procedural mechanisms AND/OR active coordination; managing perceptions and interactions of participants; managers use opportunistic directive influence but scope is limited and contingent on network interests and resources

Source: Based on Herranz (2008)

particular sectors, as illustrated in Table 7.1. Rethemeyer (2005) contrasts the 'facilitator' role of network managers in passive models with the 'maestro' role in the more active models – 'conducting both the horizontal relationships he/she makes and the vertical relationships imposed by institutional and constitutional structures' (2005, p 119). The types of governance included in this framework do not reflect multisectoral variations which present challenges stemming from goal incongruence, imprecise oversight, miscommunication, fragmented coordination, data deficits, capacity shortages and relationship instability. So-called heterarchic networks are characterised by dispersed authority, highly interdependent relationships, a blurring of sectoral boundaries and sometimes divergent value systems and purposes.

One of the main reasons why the network manager's job is so difficult is that the nature of the challenges faced involve dealing with different sources of uncertainty (Koppenjan and Klijn, 2004) – substantive uncertainty revolving around information and knowledge of the problem, complicated by differential framing processes; strategic uncertainties arising from the process and the presence of different actors with different perceptions, values, aims and behaviours; and institutional uncertainties stemming from the wide variety of agencies involved of different types, levels, cultures and sectors. In addition to sources of uncertainty are network tensions (Provan and Kenis, 2008), including efficiency and inclusiveness – getting on with the task in hand as opposed to building longer-term potential through trust and social capital; internal versus external legitimacy, in other words, pursuing self-interest and individualistic agendas as opposed to collectivist purposes; and flexibility versus stability. Although networks embrace flexibility, looseness, informality and opportunism, the most effective mechanism for longer-term stability is the creation of a more formal hierarchy. More fundamentally, Newman (2000) considers that the shift towards partnership and collaboration is limited because of the inherent contradictions in the discourse alluding to a false unity between inter and intraorganisational collaboration. She suggests that the partnership values of equality of power, shared values and common agendas inevitably clash with the political realities of different interests and divergent goals.

The problems of implementation in collaboration present collaborative public managers with particularly complex challenges. Thompson's (1967) notion of different types of interdependence between organisations (sequential, reciprocal and pooled) highlights the influence that structure has on shaping the type of interventions that are required by actors. O'Toole (2009) makes a number of observations about the situation facing public managers at the implementation stage of collaboration: that they can never assume support but must build it; that they cannot rely on hierarchical institutional arrangements to secure agreements beyond their own formal jurisdictions; that they have to develop a new infrastructure of communication; and that the tasks are not about controlling and directing, but about manoeuvring and influencing the decision points of many agencies. The tactics he suggests should be deployed to promote effective implementation centre on manufacturing 'collaborative glue' through building and re-enforcing common purpose, and facilitating cooperation through different forms of exchange to cement the various parties together.

The notion of a collaborative public manager (O'Leary and Bingham, 2009) is one that seeks to build in boundary spanning capabilities rather than bolt them on to an existing set of intraorganisationally focused duties. This may be easier said that done in practice because of the tensions and ambiguities of simultaneously working as managers with direct accountabilities to single agencies, and as agents within mechanisms of collaboration. O'Leary and Bingham (2009) maintain that the consequences of this division of responsibilities are the tensions and paradoxes of managing in two modes of governance – hierarchical and network. This involves working with autonomy and interdependence; being participative and authoritarian; balancing advocacy and enquiry; and being able to manage conflict using effective bargaining and negotiation skills. This argument is premised on there being clear differences in the two modes of governance.

A counterview is that managing within single agencies – particularly those that are highly differentiated by profession and purpose – may also respond to collaborative management, and indeed, some aspects or stages of collaborative governance may need directive approaches. Simply switching between different modes may not be a straightforward management strategy. Nevertheless, assuming that managing in different contexts is materially different, the logic is that: 'a different type of practice and new capacities are needed' (Bingham et al, 2008, p 274), and Table 7.2 lists a range of skill sets generated by different researchers. These highlight a range of positive personal traits relating to interpersonal competence; skills particularly around mediation, negotiation and conflict resolution; and behaviours associated with strategic thinking and facilitating collaborative groups.

Table 7.2: Competencies for collaborative public managers

Goldsmith and Eggers (2004)	Bingham et al (2008)	Agranoff (2004)
• Big picture thinking • Coaching • Mediation • Negotiation • Risk analysis • Ability to tackle unconventional problems • Strategic thinking • Interpersonal communications • Team building	• Network design • Structuring governance for the collaborative group • Negotiating ethically • Facilitating meetings • Managing conflict • Engaging the public • Designing evaluatory frameworks	• Balancing accountabilities • Sharing administrative burden • Orchestrating the agenda • Recognising expertise • Creativity • Patience and interpersonal skills • Sensitivity to roles and responsibilities • Incentivise collaboration

Source: Adapted from Goldsmith and Eggers (2004), Bingham et al (2008) and Agranoff (2004)

The public manager as boundary spanner needs to be proficient in network management to operate effectively in collaboration. The precise nature of the network management role varies with type of governance, sector and stage in the policy process, and the competencies required to operate within them also differ in type and intensity. Although a range of competencies is identified as suitable for network management, 'the "softer" skills of listening, inclusivity, sharing and generosity of spirit' (Ling, 2000, p 99) are considered to resonate with the particular needs of this form of governance. In addition, Goldsmith and Eggers (2004, p 165) underscore a central theme permeating this chapter when they assert that 'managing a network model also requires attitudes and behaviours not commonly developed as part of the typical public manager's experience'. They also refer to the fact that the role is fraught with tensions and challenges emanating from sources of uncertainty, complexity, modes of governance and different accountabilities. They contend that the job is very difficult because:

> Managing within this environment requires flexibility and adaptability, knowing when to listen and when to lead, and understanding the need for change and flexibility while still managing for high levels of performance against agreed-upon metrics. It demands a combination of tacit knowledge and strong bridge-building and boundary-spanning skills. The network manager must manage partnership relationships, formulate feedback loops to get results, and monitor performance across the public and private sectors – all at the same time. (Goldsmith and Eggers, 2004, p 65)

In many ways, the skill sets required of public managers in their network governance role and the problematic nature of the challenges faced closely resemble those of the dedicated boundary spanners discussed in an earlier chapter. Perhaps a key difference is that public managers have more power by virtue of their status in the organisational hierarchy and formal control of resources such as money and people. These, together with the legitimacy that flows from proven professional or specialist expertise and the limitations of organisational accountability, sometimes conspire to dampen the appetite for collaboration, and instead promote more directive management approaches.

Leaders as boundary spanners

Only comparatively recently have some researchers and academics turned their attention to leadership in collaborative contexts, but still this field of study remains neglected. The purpose of the following discussion is to redress this imbalance, to explore the nature of leadership for collaboration and to focus in particular on the roles, competencies and challenges for leaders involved in collaborative leadership practices as boundary spanners. This is not a straightforward task because:

... the literature on leadership in the social sciences and elsewhere ... looms before us as a vast, complex body of human thought and effort that ... ultimately plays out as rather confused and inconclusive. (Rainey, 2003, p 289)

It is voluminous, diverse, interdisciplinary, expanding and contested; it attracts interest from many different areas of social, political, economic, organisational and religious life; and its relevance transcends different levels of governance. Finally, it is the subject of considerable definitional dissensus, although a very early attempt highlights a number of common elements: 'leadership may be considered as the process [act] of influencing the activities of an organized group in its efforts toward goal setting and goal achievement' (Stogdill, 1950, p 3).

The approach taken below to understanding leadership for collaboration involves the interrogation of different models or theories of leadership. Parry and Bryman (2006) advance a framework based on approaches that have dominated various eras over the last half-century (see Table 7.3), and this presents a useful starting point for this enquiry.

Table 7.3: Leadership theories

Theory	Dominant period	Main characteristics
Trait	Up to 1940s	Leaders have physical traits, individual abilities and personality characteristics which distinguish them from non-leaders
Style	1940 to 1960s	Focus moves from traits to behaviours; two dominant behavioural styles: consideration for subordinates/initiating styles; emphasis on training rather selecting leaders
Contingency	Late 1960s to early 1980s	Situational factors affect leadership effectiveness
New leadership	1980s>	Leaders as managers of meaning – leaders as transformational, charismatic, visionary and transactional
Dispersed leadership	1990s>	Leadership is not 'heroic' but widely dispersed in an organisation; aims to nuture leadership capacity in individuals and teams
Collaborative leadership	2000s>	Leadership reflects context which is interdependent, diverse and collaborative; demands styles which are facilitative and empowering; catalytic and connective

Source: Adapted from Parry and Bryman (2006) and Palmer and Hardy (2002)

It's the leader's traits and personal attributes

Trait approaches are based on identifying the personal characteristics and qualities of leaders as opposed to those of non–leaders. It assumes that leaders are born rather than can be nurtured, but there is little evidence to support the notion that leaders are born with special traits that non–leaders lack, and inconsistent evidence concerning the importance of cited traits devalues the legitimacy of this approach. Van Wart (2003, p 216) comments that: 'without situational specificity, the endless list of traits offers little prescriptive assistance and descriptively becomes little more than a laundry list'. The question arises as to whether traditional leadership approaches such as this and others discussed below have any value or relevance for contemporary collaborative environments, although Kellerman and Webster (2001, p 493) counsel that: 'sometimes the so-called old ways do work'.

However, trait approaches appear unlikely to offer much explanatory potential within collaborative arenas, especially in the light of the inconclusiveness of research evidence, although new leadership theories and some models of collaborative leadership discussed later frequently make reference to the desirability of particular personality characteristics or traits (Linden, 2002). Morse (2008), for instance, prefers the notion of personal attribute rather than trait because trait denotes something that is generic, fixed and incapable of change, whereas a personal attribute is 'a characteristic quality, but not necessarily one that is hard wired or fixed' (Morse, 2008, p 85). This resonates with van Wart's (2005) interpretation of a trait, which although stable by adulthood, is still amenable to improvement through training and education.

It's a matter of style

The style approach moves the focus from the personal characteristics of leaders to their observable leadership behaviours. Two underlying behavioural styles characterise this type of leadership: one, a consideration for subordinates, and two, initiating styles where leaders tell subordinates what to do and how to do it. Critics of this approach argue that there is a lack of attention given to the impact of a situation on leadership effectiveness, that it is difficult to establish causal interpretations and that there is an unwarranted focus on the behaviour of formal leaders rather than on informal leadership processes.

Bardach (1998) compares the virtues of two contrasting styles – facilitative and advocacy – in his treatise of interagency working. He suggests that facilitative styles are appropriate in situations where stakeholders are particularly sensitive about their 'resource contributions and political vulnerabilities' and are suspicious of positional top-down leadership. A facilitative style is diplomatic, inclusive, consensual, neutral, and brings together actors in an open and equal process. In contrast, an advocacy style might be more appropriate where reaching consensus is unrealistic, and where the leader is prepared to face down certain interests in pursuit of a strongly held view about a particular course of action.

Hambleton et al (2001) embrace the style approach in their research on urban partnerships. They develop a three-fold typology of leadership styles – designed and focused, implied and fragmented, and emergent and formative – and argue that these styles are influenced primarily by the policy environment, partnership arrangements, personal characteristics and relationship with followers. In terms of personal characteristics and attributes, their research findings suggest that leadership in collaborative settings is most effective when it is clear, accountable and pragmatic, and based on a particular style or styles such as broker or negotiator. Conversely, it is least effective when it is opaque and precarious. These researchers also conclude that 'strong' leadership' is not appropriate in these environments because of the need to be collaborative, to build consensus and not 'to be suspected of taking over' (Hambleton et al, 2001, p 13).

It may be that different styles are more appropriate to different stages of the life cycle of a partnership. For instance, Lowndes and Skelcher (1998) argue that although multiorganisational partnerships have a particular affinity with network modes of governance, at different stages of the partnership life cycle, hierarchical and market relationships can predominate. Arguably, different leadership styles need to mirror these distinct, but in practice, blurred stages.

It's what the situation demands

Advocates of contingency approaches to leadership place situational factors at the centre of any understanding, and seek to establish the factors that might modify the effectiveness of different leadership approaches, such as the nature of the work undertaken, the characteristics of the followers or the nature of the external environment. Leadership in this approach demands adaptation and flexibility to ever-changing situations and contexts. The main criticisms of this approach centre on the problems associated with how to measure 'the situation', concerns over identifying causal patterns, a lack of guidance in any of the theories as to how leaders might deal with conflicting situation factors (Parry and Bryman, 2006), and similar to the style approach, the exclusion of informal leadership processes.

However, if it is accepted that collaborative settings present a number of key features that set it apart from other environments, contingency models, with their focus on the effect that situational factors have on the different leadership approaches, may appear to have some value. The relationship between leaders and followers seems to be particularly fundamental where 'followers' may be situated in a number of different organisations subject to different operating rules and accountabilities, and where the web of power relationships is distributed in subtle and complicated forms that are most certainly not hierarchical. Contingency approaches support flexible and adaptive approaches to leadership, and given the very wide range of the manifestations of collaboration – information sharing, joint working, coordination, strategic partnerships, alliances and mergers – and their deployment over different policy areas, this approach appears to be attractive.

It's managing meaning

A number of leadership approaches can loosely be bundled under the banner of 'new leadership' – charismatic, transformational, transactional and visionary. Although there are significant differences between them, they share a view of leaders as managers of meaning, articulating organisational realties through visions, missions and core values. The transformational approach, for instance, is based on a close relationship between leaders and followers, centring on a leader's ability to inspire others to a higher moral conduct through strategies which focus on vision, inculcating meaning through communication, building trust and having self-respect for everything. Typical transformational behaviours include being charismatic, offering support, guidance and encouragement, providing intellectual stimulation and supplying inspirational motivation through visions, values and symbols.

New leadership approaches highlight the importance of visions, but 'little is known about what the essential properties of a vision are, or how to craft a vision that has either charismatic or transformational effects' (Boal and Hooijberg, 2001, p 527). Visions can have a cognitive component that focuses on outcomes and the means of achieving them, and an affective component that makes a direct appeal to a follower's personal values and beliefs.

Charismatic leadership is a function of leader traits and behaviour, the situational context and the needs of the followers. Typically, charismatic leaders are believed to exhibit high self-confidence and a conviction in their own beliefs; articulate ideological goals for subordinates; appeal to hopes and ideals of followers; use role modelling when they can; communicate high expectations; and arouse motives related to an organisation's mission. This form of leadership is dependent on the follower's trust in the correctness of the leader's beliefs and the similarity of the follower's beliefs to the leader's beliefs; there is often an unquestioning acceptance of the leader by followers, sometimes affection for that leader and a willing obedience to the leader; and it relies on cementing an emotional involvement of followers to the mission of the organisation as a means of heightening performance. These are challenging prerequisites for public sector leaders operating in volatile and difficult environments, many responsible for large organisations consisting of a range of professional groupings, and made more complex by the blurred boundaries between executive and political leadership roles.

New leadership approaches, with their focus on 'meaning', have considerable relevance for collaborative settings. Indeed, a number of researchers who refer directly to collaborative leadership highlight the importance of leaders being managers of meaning: 'creating and communicating shared meaning' (Crosby and Bryson, 2005b, p 191) and 'conceptualizers, providers of reasoning and context' (Feyerherm, 1994, p 268). Negotiating common and shared purpose is also seen as a fundamental building block of successful collaborative working, and the role of visioning and the articulation of key values as mechanisms to achieve this figure prominently, particularly in the context of multiagency community initiatives.

However, crafting visions to achieve a catalytic effect and to provide a coherent focus for collective action is a notoriously difficult proposition in the public sector. Problems relate to whose visions they are, and whether they are credible, attainable and acceptable to a wide range of stakeholders.

Javidan and Waldman (2003, p 239) conclude that:

> While charismatic leadership is more or less similarly conceived in the public sector, it may not necessarily produce the types of performance or motivational results that are typically associated with it in private-sector organizations.

The proposition here is that this form of leadership is constrained by a risk averse and volatile political and bureaucratic context, and that it may be more appropriate to situations where structures are non-bureaucratic, or in situations characterised by high degrees of turbulence and uncertainty where followers may be more receptive to charismatic visions. Many forms of collaboration would fit these criteria.

Along with the other approaches discussed above, new leadership models have been the subject of a number of criticisms that include:

- over-emphasising the notion of the 'heroic' leader;
- having an undue focus on leaders at the top of organisations, assuming that leadership is the exclusive preserve of this elite, and an added preoccupation with those who are perceived to be successful;
- assuming that leadership is enacted by the leaders at the apex of their organisations in a unidirectional and hierarchical fashion;
- making a clear demarcation between 'leaders' and 'followers';
- according little attention to informal leadership processes.

It should be spread around

Distributed (Brown and Gioia, 2002) shared or dispersed leadership (Pearce and Conger, 2003) approaches reject the notion of heroic leaders and a focus on top management, and instead emphasise the need to turn followers into leaders through the development of leadership processes and skills in others. In the field of education, Spillane (2006, p 26) points out that 'expecting one person to single-handedly lead efforts to improve instruction in a complex organization such as a school is impractical', and the reality is that multiple leaders typically perform leadership work, both formally and informally. A distributed perspective on leadership highlights leadership as the product of interactions between leaders, followers and their situation.

Distributed leadership is seen as a widely dispersed activity that is not necessarily the sole responsibility of formally appointed leaders. It is multidirectional, multilevel, dynamic, relational, often occurs within the arenas of teams and work groups and presumes that expertise is spread across the many rather than the few (Thorpe et al, 2008). Hosking and Morley (1991) note that this view of leadership stands in sharp contrast to traditional approaches where leaders are emphasised rather than leadership processes, where leadership is understood as a means of manipulating non-leaders to pursue organisational goals. They define leadership as 'a more or less skilful process of organizing, achieved through negotiation, to achieve acceptable influence over the description and handling of issues between groups' (1991, p 240). Those people who make contributions of this kind are seen as leaders, and skilful leadership is the product of focused attention on the cognitive and political qualities of three major leadership processes – networking, negotiation and enabling.

Gronn (2002) suggests that distributed leadership addresses the limitations of the traditional leadership–followship dichotomy, which fails to accommodate new patterns of interdependence and coordination in the workplace, and the dissatisfaction with the individualism inherent in charismatic and transformational approaches. Distributed leadership is defined in terms of the influence attributed voluntarily by organisational members to other individuals, an aggregate of separate individuals to small sets of individuals acting in concert or larger pluralistic member organisational units. The influence may be direct experience, through first-hand experience or vicarious experience – reputed, presumed or imagined. Importantly, the individuals or units to whom influence is attributed potentially include all organisational members, not just those with formal role descriptions.

Gronn (2002) argues that a variety of structural relations and institutionalised practices are established in an attempt to regularise distributed leadership, such as spontaneous collaboration, intuitive working relations, new structures designed to pool distributed capacities such as task forces and conjoint agencies where individual agents unilaterally transfer the right of control over their actions in the expectation of achieving benefits, and a framework is provided to secure a coincidence of effort, goals and resources. Spillane's (2006) research in schools suggests that the distribution of leadership is dependent on leadership function, subject matter, type of school and school size, and furthermore, leadership responsibilities can be organised by design, default or crisis. This form of leadership is also not directly related to individual performance but to collective achievement created through shared responsibility, teamwork, mutual learning and shared understanding (Fletcher and Kaufer, 2003).

Models of distributed, shared or dispersed leadership clearly resonate well with the demands of a collaborative setting, particularly their non-hierarchical nature where a number of different actors have legitimate power, both formal and informal leaders have key roles, actors are the subject of different and multiple accountabilities, knowledge and expertise are widely distributed, the focus of much collaborative activity takes place in cross-functional/agency groups, and negotiation and consensus-seeking strategies are paramount in the quest for common purpose.

However, the seductive appeal of distributed forms of leadership masks a number of problems. First, there is a view that while this approach to leadership is easily subscribed to, particularly in the spirit of delegation, empowerment and increased responsibility that infuse contemporary approaches to public management, it is less easy to deliver in practice. Second, formal leaders, who are required to both disperse authority and act hierarchically, face an ever-present dilemma of balancing control with autonomy. Dispersing leadership functions means handing over power to others, but what if things go wrong? What if this is abused, used ineffectively or the processes involved are too time-consuming and performance suffers? What control do formal leaders retain and what are the effects of taking back leadership functions? Child and Heavens (2003, p 314) suggest that formal leaders should maintain 'a judicious combination of control, in the form of guidance and resources, and the autonomy required to motivate knowledge-generators and encourage the free flow of information'. Lastly, to introduce a dispersed model of leadership into an organisation that has been structured around traditional models certainly requires 'strong' leadership at the outset and a significant investment in resources for training and support. Sustainable change cannot be achieved overnight.

There is a suggestion among some commentators (Spillane, 2006) that distributed leadership can perhaps coexist with, and be used beneficially, to explore top-down and hierarchical approaches. In collaborative environments, agencies working together will often have different views on the appropriateness of different leadership models and will themselves have a range of models in their own organisations. For instance, the police are often dominated by strong authoritarian and hierarchical leadership structures, the voluntary sector may be more collegial in approach and the public sector led along bureaucratic lines. Collaboration, therefore, often involves agencies with traditions of different leadership approaches attempting to devise a new collaborative methodology. There will be inevitable tension and incongruence between incompatible approaches that may have subsequent implications for joint accountabilities and governance. The process of collaboration itself may invite a different emphasis at different stages, and the nature of the challenges faced can be influential. The delivery phase of any policy can be highly problematical, and experience suggests that more directive and hierarchical leadership approaches can be more effective than those where responsibilities are less clearly structured.

It may be overly simplistic to accept distributed leadership as the answer for collaboration, and as Spillane (2006, p 23) notes:

> While collaborative leadership is by definition distributed, all distributed leadership is not necessarily collaborative. Indeed, a distributed perspective allows for leadership that can be more collaborative or less collaborative, depending on the situation.

It's leading collaboratively

There is an emerging literature that can be loosely grouped under the banner of 'collaborative leadership' that applies equally to both intra- and interorganisational contexts. It seeks to reflect the increasing interdependence and connectivity in public governance and management and counter the limitations of traditional hierarchical approaches to leadership. For instance, Lipman-Blumen's (1996) so-called 'connective leadership' rejects individualistic, competitive, manipulative and charismatic leadership strategies in favour of an approach that addresses the tensions between two antithetical forces – interdependence and diversity. Connective leadership is based on three general categories or sets of behaviours used by individuals to achieve their objectives: a direct set, closely related to various forms of diversity and expressions of individualism; a relational set, which emphasises identification with others; and an instrumental set, which provides a source of ethically rooted action to harmonise the contradictory forces of diversity and interdependence.

The metaphor of a highly networked society is reflected in Saint-Onge and Armstrong's (2004) notion of a 'conductive' organisation where leadership is a critical component of its structural capital – a core competency expressed by leaders through five main capabilities: detecting patterns, responding with speed, creating partnerships, generating capabilities and infusing meaning. Leadership in these circumstances requires brokerage to link actors, problems and solutions, and Mandell (1990) identifies three types of broker: the 'orchestra leader' who can envisage the final outcome; the 'laissez-faire' leader who brings parties together but has no interest in the outcome; and the 'film producer' who is very involved in the process and is anxious to keep others engaged.

Allen et al's (1998) model of 'collaborative/reciprocal' leadership promotes a fundamental change in the practice of leadership, both transforming the role of 'followers' and revolutionising the design of organisations. The collective leadership process is based on the view that: 'depending on the need, situation, and requirements, different people assume the leadership role and everyone has leadership potential' (Allen et al, 1998, p 576). Leadership is vested in groups and communities rather than individuals, and the role of formal leaders is shifted to 'that of facilitators, supporters, consultants, and sometimes teachers' (Allen et al, 1998, p 580). The principles underpinning this approach to leadership are:

- Structuring a learning environment: including open communication, mutual trust, sharing ideas and promoting continuous self-development and reflection.
- Supporting relationships and interconnectedness: which concentrate on building effective interpersonal relationships based on trust and mutual responsibility.
- Fostering shared power: through the distribution of decision making, accountability and responsibility.
- Practising stewardship and service: by ensuring that other people's needs are being met and not exercising power, privileged and control.

- Valuing diversity and inclusiveness: through trust, respect and empathy.
- Committing to self-development: involving personal transformation.

Denis et al (2001), referring to their notion of 'collective leadership' in pluralistic organisations, also favour an approach where leadership is shared by members of a 'leadership constellation' playing different roles and providing different contributions in a dynamic and changing fashion, acknowledging, however, that this can often be a fragile arrangement because of the problems of 'uncoupling' at a strategic, organisational or personal level.

Slater (2005), undertaking research in education, found that there was strong support for the view that 'working collaboratively requires principals to develop new skills, behaviours and knowledge', and rejected the assumption that 'individuals who have worked in conventional or traditional ways in schools will know how to collaborate effectively' (Slater, 2005, pp 330-1).

She draws particular attention to the emotional nature of collaborative leadership because, far from being a peaceful rational process, it is: 'fraught with discomfort, ambiguity and uncertainty' (Slater, 2005, p 331). Slater concludes with the view that 'collaboration requires leaders to develop a new compendium of skills and adapt new "mind-sets" and "ways of being"' (p 332). Finally, Marion and Uhl-Bien (2001) apply complexity thinking to propose the notion of 'complex leadership' based on the application of five core leadership roles including: fostering network construction through the cultivation of interdependencies; catalysing this network building in a bottom-up fashion through delegation, encouragement and empowerment strategies; becoming leadership 'tags' by providing a symbol, ideal or flag around which others rally around; dropping seeds of emergence by encouraging creativity, experimentation and innovation; and lastly, through systematic thinking and the encouragement of the 'bigger picture'.

This stream of literature makes use of terms such as collaborative, connected, collective and complex. It is anti-heroic, dispersed and predicated on a particular set of skills and principles. However, it raises a couple of questions in particular. Is it a distinct leadership approach or a variant of an existing perspective such as distributed leadership? And to what extent can it be relevant to both intra and interorganisational situations when the context and challenges in each are likely to be different?

Leadership in interorganisational contexts

It is possible to discern a comparatively recent and emerging body of literature that is set specifically within the context of inter and multiorganisational settings (Peck and Dickinson, 2008), although both Connelly (2007) and Chrislip and Larson (1994) point out that it remains substantially underdeveloped in comparison with other forms of leadership. Crosby and Bryson (2010, p 227) capture leadership for collaboration under the banner of 'public integrative leadership' that rather ambitiously involves:

Aligning initial conditions, processes and practices, structures and governance mechanisms, contingencies and constraints, and outcomes and accountabilities such that good things happen in a sustained way over time.

In other words, bringing people together from a range of organisations and sectors, and working across boundaries to create public value. Chrislip and Larson (1994) note that collaborative settings are invariably populated by 'wicked issues' – a problem type where neither the problem nor the solution is definable (Grint, 2005). Consequently, they argue that interorganisational leadership needs to be based on four principles: inspiring commitment and action, leading as a peer problem solver, building broad-based involvement and sustaining hope and participation. This form of leadership foregrounds the process where the leadership role 'is to convene, energize, facilitate, and sustain this process' (Chrislip and Larson, 1994, p 146).

Crosby and Bryson (2005a, p 360) have been advocating a distinctive approach to leadership for collaboration for over a decade as a means of 'developing regimes of mutual gain'. They promote a leadership framework which articulates visionary, political and ethical dimensions, and which is influenced by work on policy entrepreneurship, advocacy coalitions and agenda setting. The framework is grounded in the realities of an interdependent world of diverse stakeholders and shared power arrangements, emphasises the widespread use of deliberative forums to share meanings, resolve conflicts and negotiate the best way forward, highlights the importance of an integrated approach to strategic management and policy change and promotes the exercise of eight main leadership capabilities: personal, team, organisational, visionary, political, ethical, entrepreneurial and contextual. The emphasis on a shared and inclusive approach to leadership is underscored in the comments of a leader responsible for an integrated health and social care service (NLIAH, 2009):

'You can't tell people what to do; you must find out what their views are. You have to explore and understand other people's perspectives and have the confidence in the ability to work together, and not to try and impose vertical lines of management in a network type of arrangement.'

Feyerherm (1994) explores three leadership behaviours that are most likely to result in convergence between different groups working within interorganisational systems. First, surfacing or illuminating assumptions and beliefs, referring to either one's own or others' interpretations to create more information about different views and to extend the possibilities for joint action. However, surfacing assumptions does not necessarily mean that changes will occur in interpretive schemes. Second, by creating alternatives involving problem-solving behaviours coupled with supporting, bridging and facilitating to generate new frameworks and social consensus. Lastly, initiating collective action to form structures and develop and present proposals. This research emphasises the importance of leaders as managers of meaning. Page (2010) highlights the sense-giving thread underpinning effective 'integrative' leaders and the main leadership tactics involved in leading collaborative governance initiatives: framing the agenda, convening stakeholders and structuring deliberations. The leadership role centres on influencing the focus of the collaboration, the participants involved and the processes of collaborative governance, although the overall effectiveness will be influenced by different interpretations of the stakeholders and the results achieved. The constructionist lens applied to leadership is manifested in Ospina and Foldy's (2010) concentration on the 'space' between leaders and followers, and their subsequent identification of five leadership practices which are necessary to create the fertile conditions in which to assemble diverse groups to engage in collaboration: promoting cognitive shifts which relate to reframing issues around collective interests; naming and shaping identity to engender commitment and ownership to new collaborative forms; engaging dialogue about and valuing difference; creating equitable governance mechanisms; and weaving multiple worlds together through interpersonal relationships. The key to success is seen to be building bridges between diverse interests to minimise power inequalities, recognising the strategic value of 'difference'.

Leadership that brings groups together is the centrepiece of Pittinsky's (2009) notion of 'intergroup leadership'. He maintains that in situations where leaders are forced to tackle problems that are outside their formal authority and responsibility – such as 'wicked issues' – the crux of the leadership challenge is to bring subgroups together in such a way that a balance is achieved between maintaining their internal cohesion, but also acknowledging the potential for external conflict caused by intergroup diversity. He refers to the need to create positive intergroup activities 'that move intergroup relations past mere tolerance to willing, active co-existence and co-operation' (Pittinsky, 2009, p xviii). In practice, this means creating superordinate identities associated with shared purpose and new collaborative forms, but not dissolving subgroup identities. Collaborative value lies in both diversity and unity. One particular problem facing leaders in collaborative settings is that, in contrast to intraorganisational situations, leaders are not in a position to directly influence the composition of collaborative groups. This is usually within the gift of participating agencies that nominate, delegate or authorise named individuals to represent their agency. It can be a matter of 'luck' whether group members are able to work together, and particular groups present variable challenges to leaders in terms of cohesiveness and effectiveness. In single agencies, leaders have markedly more control over recruitment and selection to teams and groups.

Luke (1998) refers to the concept of catalytic leadership for interorganisational settings that require leaders to have certain foundational skills. First, an ability to think and act strategically, involving systemic thinking to reveal interconnections and strategic leverage points, to frame and reframe issues, to define outcomes and to assess stakeholder interests. Second, the need for interpersonal skills to facilitate a productive working group or network, requiring the application of facilitation, negotiation and mediation skills; and lastly, the need for an underlying character which is not synonymous with personality, but is evidenced by a passion for results, a sense of connectedness and relatedness, exemplary personal integrity and strong ethical conduct. This resonates with the view expressed by a leader involved in the provision of integrated children's disability services (NLIAH, 2009) in her comment that: 'leadership needs to be more facilitative – to be more persuasive, influencing and supportive, rather than based on "you will do this"'.

Linden (2002) uses the term 'collaborative leadership' and sees this expressed through four qualities in collaborative leaders: being resolute, focused and driven especially about collaboration; having a strong but measured ego; being inclusive and preferring to 'pull' rather than 'push'; and finally, having a collaborative mindset which focuses on seeing connections to something larger. The challenge for the collaborative leader is to apply these qualities to key tasks which essentially focus on the process of collaboration including helping to identify shared purposes, demonstrating a desire to search for shared solutions, identifying the right people, highlighting the importance of an open and credible process founded on trust and championing initiatives.

An example of aspects of Linden's model is expressed through the approach adopted by a director of voluntary services in her role of chair of a multiagency welfare partnership providing health, financial and employment services for people claiming incapacity benefits involving representatives from the Department for Work and Pensions, local authority, local health board, local NHS trust, and voluntary sector (NLIAH, 2009):

> Her approach was based on developing an inclusive collaborative culture based on the premise that every stakeholder had something to offer. She promoted mutual respect and listened intelligently. Meetings were characterised by plentiful discussion, task–orientation and frequent summing up of people's/group's positions. She balanced agenda setting with agenda sharing; believed that greater ownership and commitment to action and outcomes were achieved if agendas were set together, and clearly understood the roles and responsibilities of every partner. Motivation was provided by repeatedly emphasising the outcomes of a collaborative approach for a vulnerable set of service users.

Kanter (1997) offers a profile of 'cosmopolitan leaders' who must be integrators, who can look beyond obvious differences among organisations, sectors, disciplines, functions or cultures; diplomats who can resolve conflict and influence people to work together; cross-fertilisers, to bring the best from one place to another; and deep thinkers who are smart enough to see new possibilities and to conceptualise them. Kanter (2009) is also a subscriber to 'intergroup' leadership that is designed to make productive use of difference by motivating and mobilising different groups to work together – the essence of collaborative working. The core leadership skills here involve convenorship; building an overarching goal or motivational framework; focusing on the future; providing opportunities for intergroup working; and fostering a culture of inclusiveness based on strong interpersonal relationships and emotional integration. The reality of promoting intergroup collaboration is exceedingly difficult to achieve in practice because of the many structural, institutional and professional barriers and boundaries that emphasise uniqueness and independence. Negotiating those boundaries (both real and artificial) in pursuit of common purpose and promoting the benefits of interdependence are core leadership tasks.

In Huxham and Vangen's (2005) theory of collaborative advantage, notions of informal, emergent and shared leadership are considered to be relevant, where structure, processes and participants provide the framework for 'contextual leadership'. Enacting this form of leadership to achieve collaborative advantage is seen to depend on embracing the 'right' kind of members, empowering members to enable participation, involving and supporting all members and mobilising members to make things happen.

Alexander et al (2001) outline a case for collaborative leadership within the setting of community health partnerships which:

> Possesses distinctive characteristics that call for a type of leadership (and that produce leadership dilemmas) unrecognised or rarely discussed in the collaborative leadership literature. (Alexander et al, 2001, p 160)

Collaborative leadership is viewed in terms of five distinctive leadership themes: systems thinking, vision-based leadership, collateral leadership (which is not quite the same as distributed leadership because broad-based leadership supports, but does not substitute for, leadership expressed by formally designated leaders), power sharing and process-based leadership. The practicalities of 'boundary spanning leadership' are addressed by Ernst and Yip (2009) in their discussion of the tactics that are available to manage the boundaries between different groups. They refer to suspending, which involves creating neutral spaces where interaction can take place between people rather than groups; reframing, where attempts are made to unite people under a new superordinate identity; nesting, to preserve intergroup differentiation within the framework of common purpose; and finally, weaving, to loosen social group identities by cross-cutting work group roles with social group identities. This can also foster creativity and increase the potential for future collaboration.

Conclusion

The leadership literature plays out as very confusing, with a galaxy of seemingly plausible approaches on offer – 'great man' theories based on individual traits, contingency models that reflect responses to different situations, transformational approaches that stress 'managing meaning', dispersed and shared models that are intent on turning followers into leaders and collaborative models that reject hierarchical approaches premised on sovereign sources of power in favour of models that are more facilitative and inclusive in tone, and equally applicable to both intra and interorganisational settings. It may be that Van Wart's (2003) notion of 'multifaceted' leadership is the most appropriate description of this phenomenon in collaborative settings to reflect a whole variety of approaches deployed at different times by different leaders in response to different settings and challenges. So, we must inevitably accept multiple perspectives of leadership in multisectoral partnerships (Armistead et al, 2007) – leadership that is based around three strategies: first person, which relates to the traits and behaviours of the actors involved; second person, focusing on their interactions between groups; and third person, based on structures, systems and processes.

However, the emerging literature on leadership for collaboration – specifically in the context of multiagency and cross-sector arenas – does begin to emphasise certain roles, behaviours and desirable competencies for leaders as boundary spanners. The dominant role concerns the process of collaboration. This involves convenorship, assembling the relevant interests and stakeholders together, and building a common collaborative culture based on an appreciation of interdependence and common purpose. The leader as integrator is key to the success of this role – working across professional and organisational boundaries, and building bridges between multiple constituencies through a focus on visions, shared goals and solving problems. Managing meaning and an acute appreciation of the different frames of multiple interests are central to a leader's ability to build common purpose and collective action.

The skills that leaders need in these roles occur at a personal and group level. Building and sustaining high quality interpersonal relationships between a diverse set of stakeholders, fostering trust and managing complex, shifting and subtle power relationships are critically important. Promoting effective, transparent and inclusive group working is an essential part of the job with negotiation, mediation and conflict resolution skills often in demand. The leader's role is catalytic and facilitative, and leadership activities are generally dispersed and shared at different levels and between appropriate stakeholders. Underpinning these roles and skills is the need for boundary spanning leaders to be what Kanter (1997) refers to as 'deep thinkers' to reflect the complexities of the job and the strategic competence that is required to be successful. One example of a leader demonstrating a profile similar to the one described above is set within the context of a multiagency project designed to reconfigure local health and social care services involving a large number of diverse stakeholders across a wide geographical area (NLIAH, 2009). The chief executive described his approach to leadership for collaboration in the following manner:

'I have to put time into it, especially to keep people herded together. I try to keep people focused and on board, with a constant emphasis on the vision and the citizen. I share views as well as sharing. I value others, and encourage them to participate and to be involved. I am facilitative in style, work across interfaces, and my personal style is consistent across intra and inter-organisational settings. I look to align with others, to look for their perspectives. I then elaborate their interests and seek to align with our overall objectives.'

A number of colleagues of this chief executive also commented on the personal attributes of this actor – being respectful, humble, personable, calm, humorous and charismatic. However, the literature in general is ambiguous about whether particular personal attributes are essential requirements for this job. Linden (2002) and Luke (1998) certainly refer to the importance of particular qualities and aspects of personality, but Bardach (1998) sees leadership holding interagency collaboration together, not through the personal talents of individual leaders, but through their roles in a system of strategic, integrative and creative interactions.

As with other types of boundary spanner already discussed, the leader as boundary spanner is faced with dealing with a number of paradoxes and dilemmas. Connelly et al (2008) capture a number of these, including the paradox of knowing when to lead and when to follow; the dilemma of balancing the forces of independence and interdependence; the tension of inclusivity and ineffectiveness – all set against the background of a realistic assessment of the costs and benefits of collaboration formed at the outset. Paradox and complexity are facts of collaborative life and leading across boundaries confront challenges that seriously test the competence and stamina of boundary spanning leaders.

The question of whether leadership in collaboration is materially different from leadership in hierarchical/single agencies is difficult to resolve. Luke (1998) certainly perceives a sharp contrast between traditional and collaborative styles of leadership. Traditional approaches evoke hierarchy, followship, taking charge, direction setting, being heroic and providing answers, whereas in contrast, collaborative approaches emphasise convenorship and facilitation of the process, being catalytic and accepting solutions although having a stake. Alexander et al (2001) also clearly differentiate between leadership within traditional organisations linked to formal hierarchical authority, and leadership in partnerships mainly because even formally designated leaders here only hold tenuous authority. Silvia and McGuire (2010) attempt to answer the question through their research study which uses 'integrative leadership' as the notion of leadership for collaboration. Van Wart's (2005) list of leadership behaviours, grouped into people, task and organisation-orientated behaviours, are used to compare collaborations and single agencies. In general, they conclude that there is a difference with a clear emphasis on people-orientated behaviours in collaborative situations. These are evidenced in behaviours such as sharing roles, creating trust, sharing information, treating others as equal and encouraging support. Task-orientated behaviours appear to dominate more within single agencies. However, the authors concede that more empirical research needs to be undertaken in this area to enable more definitive conclusions to be reached.

Review of main points

- The prevailing public policy landscape has witnessed the spread of new forms of governance that emphasise collaboration – networks, alliances and partnerships. This is partly as a result of the multilevel, complex and interdependent nature of policy issues that cannot be resolved by single agencies acting alone. These new forms of governance have stimulated different approaches to management including network management and collaborative public management.

- The consequence of this trend is that a large proportion of public managers and leaders are now engaged in cross-boundary activity as an integral part of their mainstream job roles – they represent a particular class of boundary spanner.

- The literature and research on network management and collaborative public management offer two complementary perspectives on the role of public managers as boundary spanners.

- In the network management literature, the role of the network manager demands boundary spanning skills, such as managing complexity, negotiation and mediation, reticulist competency and interpersonal skills. Dealing with sources of uncertainty about problems, processes and structures are central to this job role.

- The collaborative public management perspective alights on the particular problem of managing the tensions and ambiguities arising from working as managers with direct accountability to single organisations (hierarchical) as well as agents within collaborative governance (network).

- This requires actors to switch between different modes of governance – the latter form which must be underpinned by a different type of management practice, skills and capacities, including strategic thinking, mediation and negotiation, team building, facilitation and orchestration and managing accountabilities.

- A counter-argument is that 'collaborative management' is also important within single organisation management.

- Understanding the nature of boundary spanning leadership is hampered by the relative paucity of research on this topic coupled with a highly complex, confusing, voluminous and contested literature on leadership in general.

- A range of theories, models, approaches and perspectives are advanced about leadership based on traits, style, contingency and meaning. These approaches have been the subject of some criticism because of their over-emphasis on heroic individuals, leading from the top and not acknowledging the contribution of informal leaders.

- Distributed and shared models redress this balance and advocate the dispersal of leadership activities throughout an organisation, particularly within teams and groups. This style is embraced by more recent literature that similarly rejects hierarchical models in favour of those that are described as collective, reciprocal, conductive and networked.

- Leaders in this context – both within and between organisations – adopt more facilitative styles based on interpersonal relationships, team building, sharing power and valuing diversity.
- A stream of literature which can be packaged directly under the banner of leadership within intersectoral and interorganisational settings emphasise a common set of themes, including building and sustaining interpersonal relationships; building collaborative cultures with multiple constituencies based on trust and reciprocity; managing complexity and strategic interdependence; fostering creativity and innovation; and coping with dilemmas and paradox.
- However, clarity around a single model of leadership for collaboration remains elusive and one may have to acknowledge its multifaceted nature with different approaches being relevant and legitimate at different times for different circumstances. Leadership is the subject of the subjective interpretations of different actors.

Questions for discussion

1. 'We are all boundary spanners now.' Discuss this assertion in relation to your assessment of public management in the future.
2. How realistic/ethical is it for leaders to alter their styles of leadership – for example, from being directive within their own agency, and facilitative and empowering when operating in collaborative settings? What are the tensions and ambiguities in this approach and how are they best resolved?
3. Which leadership theory(ies) best describes leadership for collaboration, and why?
4. Is leadership in single organisations different from that in multiorganisational, cross-sector collaborations, and if so, how?
5. What are the capacities and capabilities necessary to be an effective leader managing across boundaries?
6. The case for a different set of skills and behaviours in collaborative settings to those necessary within organisations is over claimed. Explore this position.
7. Is it the structures, processes and institutions of collaborative governance that define the nature of leadership possibilities, or is it how individual leaders frame and enact leadership that matters?
8. Compare and contrast the skills and competencies required to be a dedicated boundary spanner with those of collaborative public managers and leaders.
9. Think of a collaborative public manager or collaborative public leader you consider to be effective in this role. Explain why you have come to this conclusion, what the skills and behaviours that he/she displays, and provide some practical examples to evidence your choice.
10. What are the implications of collaborative public managers and leaders on the importance of professionalism within public services?

Suggested further reading

Agranoff, R. and McGuire, M. (2003) *Collaborative public management: New strategies for local government*, Washington, DC: Georgetown University Press.

Allen, K.E., Bordas, J., Hickman, G.R., Matusak, L.R., Sorenson, G.J. and Whitmire, K.J. (1998) 'Leadership in the 21st century', in G.R. Hickman (ed) *Leading organizations: Perspectives for a new era*, London: Sage Publications, pp 572-80.

Chrislip, D.D. and Larson, C.E. (1994) *Collaborative leadership*, San Francisco, CA: Jossey-Bass.

Crosby, B.C. and Bryson, J.M. (2005) *Leadership for the common good: Tackling public problems in a shared-power world*, San Francisco, CA: Jossey-Bass.

Koliba, C., Meek, J.W. and Zia, A. (2011) *Governance networks in public administration and public policy*, London: CRC Press.

Luke, J.S. (1998) *Catalytic leadership: Strategies for an interconnected world*, San Francisco, CA: Jossey-Bass.

O'Leary, R. and Bingham, L.B. (2009) *The collaborative public manager*, Washington, DC: Georgetown University Press.

Parry, K.W. and Bryman, A. (2006) 'Leadership in organizations', in S.R. Clegg, C. Hardy, T.B. Lawrence and W. Nord (eds) *The SAGE handbook of organization studies*, London: Sage Publications.

Spillane, J.P. (2006) *Distributed leadership*, San Francisco, CA: Jossey-Bass.

EIGHT

Implications for policy and practice

Why does it matter?

A host of reasons have been advanced in this book to explain the steady and continuing growth of collaborative working across the UK public policy landscape, including the interdependence and complexity of problems; the fragmentation of organisational and institutional arrangements; and the blurring of the boundaries between different levels and sectors of governance. Cross-boundary working has emerged as a central plank in local and national government policy approaches, and there is every likelihood that this will continue in the future, albeit in different forms. A considerable amount of managerial and organisational resources are devoted to collaborative activity in an effort to reap the benefits of this form of working and to secure real improvements in the quality of lives of citizens and service users. However, as has already been intimated, the rewards of collaborative working are not always readily apparent – they are difficult to measure, they often take time, and the problematic nature of this form of working solely tests the resilience of even the most hardened advocates of collaboration. In relation to health and social care, Powell et al (2004, p 314) conclude that: 'research that brings together rigorous and systematic evidence of the outcomes, causality and costs of partnerships has yet to be conducted'.

Clearly, in these circumstances, it is critically important to understand 'what works' and what needs to be done to design and deliver the most effective and sustainable forms of collaboration. Although policy makers and practitioners can learn through experience and practice, there is a role for robust and high quality theory and research to inform the policy community. The mantra of 'evidence-based' policy making has been prominent for the last decade, although in reality its rhetoric often outweighs its impact on the ground. Coote et al (2004) conclude that evaluation and research have had only a marginal impact on policy design and practice in general, and Weiss (1998) reflects that it is comparatively rare for research to have a direct influence on policy decisions. The difficulties of realising evidence-based policy making revolve around the timeliness of research, the relationship between researchers and policy makers, the political convenience or contestability of the findings, the appreciation of research methodologies and the effectiveness of dissemination techniques. Van de Ven (2007) makes a strong case for cementing a better relationship between academia and practice through a process of 'engaged scholarship' which aims to build bridges between theory and practice using more effective approaches to research design, implementation and communication.

Building capacity and capabilities

Chapter Three aimed to position the nature and role of boundary spanners within the general framework of the structure–agency (and ideas) debate. Various positions and perspectives were outlined on this heavily contested question, and it is beyond the scope of this book to work through and develop the implications of the idealised model offered in full. Rather, it unapologetically presents an agentially orientated narrative and focus, partly as an antidote to the current emphasis that has been placed on the importance and role of structural factors. It provides a wealth of material on the roles, skills and behaviours of boundary spanners – leaders, managers and practitioners – active within collaborative arenas. It should follow that a greater understanding of what boundary spanners do and how they do it will contribute to more effective collaborative outcomes. Also, it should follow that improved policy intelligence about this set of actors will be used to build appropriate capacities and capabilities into the design and delivery of collaborative processes. Supportive collaborative cultures need to be constructed to facilitate the roles of agents intent on securing collaborative advantage, and organisational structures and arrangements need to be designed in ways to promote and not inhibit cross-boundary activity. Coterminosity of boundaries, unified performance management frameworks, common planning frameworks and clear accountability arrangements are examples of mechanisms that can be used to assist collaboration. But at the end of the day, it is people who have to operate within them to support their leadership and management practice, and the thrust of this book is that this involves critical decisions in relation to their education, training and development.

Managing learning and knowledge collaboratively

In order to assimilate and use the key lessons and messages that emerge from a better understanding of the nature and role of boundary spanners, the public policy community has to ensure that appropriate learning and knowledge mechanisms are in place. Although in many ways learning and knowledge management represent the very essence of collaboration, arguably they are rarely accorded sufficient priority within collaborative management and governance. People and organisations come together to learn with and from each other about the management and resolution of difficult issues. The combined and diversified competencies of this collective resource are critical to understanding complex problems and enabling the design of innovative solutions. Boundary spanners are important in both the design and facilitation of this process, but their role is made easier by institutional and other structures that encourage, facilitate and sustain cross-boundary activity.

Learning and knowledge management are often assumed to happen spontaneously, an unplanned by-product of people and organisations coming together, rather than being the subject of explicit and planned strategies. These are very complex and interrelated phenomena, and need fertile conditions in which to prosper. It is critical to negotiate and secure clarity of intent, role and purpose for the contribution of learning and knowledge management within the overall purposes of a particular collaboration – the form of learning, and whether it concerns service development or governance and management processes. For instance, Lane (2003) makes a distinction between operational learning, that simply requires single loop and error-correcting learning, with conceptual learning, which challenges 'taken-for-granted' assumptions such as models of health or policy approach, and which are most likely to face actors operating in collaborative environments.

A differentiation should also be made between exploratory and exploitative learning (Jansen et al, 2009), the former being directed towards generating new knowledge, insights and innovation, in contrast to the latter which concerns incremental improvement of existing skills, knowledge and systems. Exploratory learning fundamentally involves more risk, experimentation and new ideas that challenge the existing status quo, whereas exploitative learning is about refinement, efficiency, extension of existing competencies and service models. A key issue is where the learning is expected to take place – at the individual, group, organisation or network level?

The implications of the distinction that is made between types of knowledge – tacit and explicit – are particularly important in collaborative settings. Explicit knowledge is something that can easily be codified and communicated, whereas tacit knowledge is more complicated (Ray et al, 2004), not easy to capture, translate or transfer (Palmer and Hardy, 2000), and does not readily move between different cultures (Schein, 1997; de Long and Fahey, 2000), professions and agencies, which is precisely what faces many collaborations. Tacit knowledge-orientated activities are best encouraged through socialisation between different groups of people and the cultivation of trusting relationships. This helps to build social capital, encourages openness and transparency, identifies areas of interdependency and common purpose and enhances joint communication. However, the time-consuming and costly nature of this process should not be underestimated (Inkpen, 2000). Particular structures, processes and carriers facilitate different forms of knowledge conversion and management, as illustrated in Figure 8.1. These require different roles and behaviours to be undertaken by boundary spanners.

Carlisle (2004) also offers a framework for sharing and assessing knowledge across different types of boundary: syntactic, which is relatively straightforward and involves information processing to transfer knowledge; semantic, which is more difficult to overcome, involving tacit knowledge and requiring translation and interpretation; and lastly, pragmatic, which is even more problematic because it demands transformation. Boundary spanners are likely to be important in the process of translating knowledge because of the existence of different meanings and the preponderance of tacit knowledge, and the need to assist with the creation of shared meanings. Similarly, a transformation of knowledge needs constructive dialogue and an acute awareness of the power implications of knowledge to facilitate new understandings, and again boundary spanners can be key facilitators in this process.

Figure 8.1: Methods of knowledge conversion in collaboration

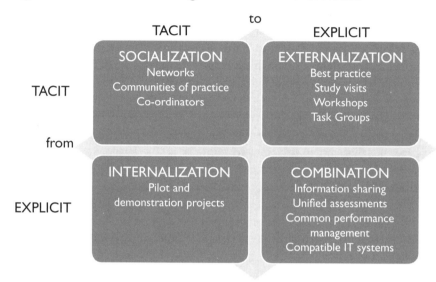

Source: Adapted from Nonaka (1994)

Knowledge transfer across boundaries is 'sticky' and 'leaky' (Carlisle, 2004) as above, and effective learning is problematic, not only in the absence of clarity of purpose, but also where insufficient attention is paid to building collaborative capacities, abilities and cultures. It is important to raise the levels of absorptive capacity among collaborating agencies in terms of receptivity, time, resources, attitudes, competence, skills, previous knowledge and experiences. As is suggested in Figure 8.1, particular structures and organisational configurations can help the flow of knowledge and learning – for instance, cross-functional teams, tolerance of experimentation and risk through demonstration and pilot projects, promotion of networks and communities of practice and the collection and dissemination of best practice. Although bringing people together in groups and teams is seen as a productive strategy to encourage learning and knowledge sharing, there are many issues to managing these processes arising from the ownership and control of knowledge, and the identity of social and professional groups. Collective learning can be inhibited by the amount of 'social distance' between groups, and, although it appears logical to aim to 'reduce cognitive distance in order to achieve a sufficient alignment of mental categories' (Nooteboom, 2008, p 610), a fine balance may be necessary between the cognitive proximity needed to engender mutual understanding and collaboration, and cognitive distance necessary to promote innovation and creativity.

Unless sufficient attention is placed on learning and knowledge management issues in collaboration, the lessons for policy and practice on the role and activities of boundary spanners are unlikely to be fully realised.

Implications for developing and training boundary spanners

A key area of discussion arising from the exploration of the role and activities of boundary spanners relates to their training and development. It has been argued that this group of actors is influential in shaping and delivering collaborative action, and is in some ways unique in terms of the group's particular roles and associated competencies. So what does that mean in terms of human resource strategies for their education, development, learning and training? There is no professional body that promotes, regulates and accredits boundary spanners, nor any clearly defined or accredited training, development or education pathways for individuals wanting to practise in this specific realm of public policy. In an otherwise highly professionalised public service, there is an important paradox here that was aptly summarised by a probation service manager in the author's research (Williams, 2005). He commented that:

> 'You have to be trained to be a probation worker on which I spend 30 to 40 per cent of my time. No training is required to work in partnership to which I now devote 60 to 70 per cent of my time!'

Another respondent offered a possible explanation for this state of affairs. He suggested that: 'partnership working is where management development was 10 years ago. People get into it without training and development'. This follows the view that it was commonplace in many public agencies for people to acquire managerial positions primarily by virtue of being proficient in a particular area of expertise or profession. However, climbing a career ladder arguably requires less technical expertise and more managerial abilities, and this was not always recognised by employers or given sufficient weight in recruitment. This issue has now been identified and addressed and management development is an integral component of effective human resources across public and private organisations. Management development opportunities of various types are now commonplace in organisational training and development programmes, and these are delivered by a range of providers, including higher education establishments, external consultancies, in-house training units and others that are sector-specific.

This treatise on boundary spanners suggests that there are, perhaps, parallels with the position and profile of management development some years ago. The thrust of the discussion in this book suggests that effective management within collaborative arenas requires the acquisition and utilisation of particular competencies, and although some of these may be relevant for other modes of organising, collaborative management is not simply an extension of intraorganisational management. This point is underlined by Mandell (1999, p 5), who argues that: 'collaborations require the use of different management styles and policy instruments than are used in more traditional public policy efforts'. Geddes (1998, p 148) reaches a similar conclusion in his work on local partnerships in Europe, and makes the point that:

> Those involved in partnership require a specific set of skills to manage complex projects and promote communication and understanding between partners. If local partnerships are to attract and retain suitable staff, consideration also needs to be given to the implications of partnership for the career patterns and training of managers and staff.

Jupp (2000) also reinforces this important point that public sector managers need to undergo management training in partnership working. He notes that traditionally, management training has been concentrated around managing in hierarchical situations and more lately around managing contracts. Now the emphasis should be on developing 'techniques for helping partnerships set clear objectives, understand cultural differences and review progress without blame' (Jupp, 2000, p 31). He further argues that: 'brokers also need some kind of professional infrastructure. They are currently scattered across a range of organizations. Often they have fallen into a brokerage role almost by accident' (Jupp, 2000, p 37). This chimes with the views of others who suggest that these people have 'anomalous or unconventional career skills' (Challis et al, 1988, p 213), often with 'no single path of educational preparation' (Radin, 1996, p 157). It seems to make little sense to promote a form of working across the public policy landscape without the support of relevant training, development and education, unaccompanied by appropriate levels of investment. Is it responsible to allow people to undertake social work without prior training and qualifications, or civil engineers to build bridges without professional accreditation? Surely the same argument must apply to those working as boundary spanners?

Designing training and development programmes

The design of any programme to develop and improve boundary spanning competencies needs to resolve at the outset the question of whether the emphasis should be focused on the creation of cadre of dedicated boundary spanners, or whether generic boundary spanning skills should be mainstreamed into the training, development or professional programmes of leaders, managers and practitioners who increasingly are required to be active within theatres of collaboration. The answer is probably both. Public institutions need specialist boundary spanners to identify, facilitate and support the areas of interdependence between organisations and people, but a sustainable collaborative paradigm will only develop if there is a sufficient critical mass of leaders, managers and practitioners comfortable and proficient in this form of working. Boundary spanning competencies need also to be mainstreamed into professional and management development programmes.

The differentiation alluded to in this study between boundary spanners who occupy specific job-related roles, and boundary spanning which is increasingly undertaken by a large number of managers and leaders in the course of their duties, has parallels in the distinction made by Day (2001) between leaders and leadership, and the consequent different emphasis demanded for the training and development for each. Day argues that leadership has traditionally been conceptualised as an individual-level skill undertaken exclusively by formally designated leaders. However, he maintains that leadership is more of a social process involving everyone in an organisation; it is an effect rather than a cause, and an emergent property of systems design. Taking this distinction forward to leaders and leadership development, Day proceeds to build a case for different types of training and development to enhance the effectiveness of each. In the case of leaders, he suggests that the emphasis here should be very much geared towards the development of individual human capital based on knowledge, skills and abilities associated with formal leadership roles. Here, attention is focused on intrapersonal competence through self-awareness, self-regulation and self-motivation. In contrast, leadership development shifts the focus towards the creation of social capital and: 'on building networked relationships among individuals that enhance cooperation and resource exchange in creating organizational value' (Day, 2001, p 585). The primary emphasis in leadership development should be geared towards the building and use of interpersonal competence which emphasises relational aspects such as trust and mutual respect, structural dimensions by means of network ties and cognitive dimensions as evidenced in attempts to achieve collective and shared meanings within an organisation.

The use of a similar distinction between boundary spanner and boundary spanning development offers a constructive basis from which to design a coherent training and development strategy for each. The advantages of a strategy that focuses on enhancing boundary spanning capacity throughout an organisation, with its emphasis on relational and interpersonal elements, is that the benefits can be reaped both internally to support cross-functional working and network management approaches, as well as externally in multiorganisational settings.

In the author's view, there is a strong case for a more explicit recognition of the need to develop education, training and development programmes designed to cultivate, develop and support boundary spanners. Managing within collaborative settings is highly complex, and close scrutiny of performance and outcomes over a number of years is far from convincing. One explanation for this must rest with the quality and capability of the actors involved in the process. Any programme that aims to design training and development opportunities needs to understand the relative merits of different learning solutions, particularly workplace or experiential practices as opposed to formal education. The notion of situated learning (Fox, 1997) challenges the supremacy of formal education routes and contexts by emphasising the more natural, informal and grounded learning processes of practitioners in the workplace. It rejects an overly 'educationalised' concept of the learning process: 'within a highly designed sequestered setting – the education institution, syllabus, classroom – classically divorced from the "messy" real world' (Fox et al, 2001, p 27). In contrast, situated learning emphasises the value of participation in the practice of concrete problem solving and management in the workplace, and the benefits of social networks and communities of practice. There is evidence that situated learning is favoured by some groups. For instance, in one study (2001) on the management and leadership in the professions, among professional practitioners there was a marked tendency to prefer informal means of learning more than formal methods. Of course, it may be that many practitioners do not have sufficient exposure to formal education methodologies, and may consider them to be abstract, theoretical and not relevant to real world situations. The author's view is that it is unlikely that there is any single or most effective approach to training and development, and that there is value in both formal and informal approaches to learning, and the most effective programmes are those that link theory with practice. Education, training and development strategies fall into a number of broad areas, as follows:

- professional
- academic
- experiential
- capacity building
- networking and communities of practice.

Professional

In the field of health and social care, but most probably in other policy areas as well, Hudson (2002, p 7) considers that the:

> Focus on interorganizational working has not been matched by equal attention to interprofessional relationships. To some extent, the assumption seems to be that once interagency partnership policies, processes and structures are established, then front line partnerships between a range of traditionally separate professions will fall into place.

The reality often suggests otherwise, and professionalism is identified as a significant stumbling block. Professional identity, status, discretion and accountability make forms of interprofessional and interagency working very challenging. Professionalism is associated with discrete bodies of knowledge, and with methods of socialisation and acculturation that are directed towards the promotion of particular core values, resulting in the unique framing of problems and solutions. Furthermore, it promotes accountabilities that are rooted in professional and ideological authority, as opposed to ones that reflect organisational and managerial imperatives. Cross-professional and collaborative working fundamentally challenge many professional tenets. It involves sharing knowledge and expertise, exposes value differences and requires the surrendering of professional territory and responsibility. One body of opinion argues that this results in a blurring of boundaries between professions and that this is a healthy outcome (Van de Ven, 1976; LGMB, 1997). Others, for example, Rushmer and Pallis (2002), take the opposite view, and argue that integrated working continues to require absolute clarity on boundaries in terms of roles, responsibilities and areas of legitimate action.

A training and development strategy that might encourage interprofessional working within collaborative settings is the inclusion of relevant boundary spanning competencies within the mainstream professional education, training and development programmes of the numerous professions that typically populate local and national government, health and other sectors involved in collaborative working. The advantage of this approach would be the preservation of the supremacy of professional accreditation and all the perceived attendant advantages of professional status and identity. The way in which boundary spanning knowledge could be included within a professional syllabus is through the identification of an 'irreducible core' of competence which would form part of the overall programme. Alternatively, it could be offered at post-qualification stage based on specialist practice development programmes, or as part of lifelong learning and continuous professional development requirements.

Of course, whether the inclusion of boundary spanning competencies is sufficient in itself to counter the forces of professionalism is open to debate. With this in mind, a possible improvement in this approach could involve the delivery of boundary spanning education and training on an interprofessional basis. This would be advantageous because it could begin to tackle, at their root, some of the issues and constraints involved in interprofessional working. It could also offer the skills necessary to assist in working in highly complex and contested public policy arenas. Initiatives to promote interprofessional training might more easily be accommodated in clearly defined complementary areas of public policy such as health and social care rather than in others where interprofessional collaboration is less clear-cut.

A competency framework could ensure an appropriate balance between the need to include sufficient competencies to cover the various boundary spanning roles, yet avoiding the accumulation of an over-elaborate list that would be difficult to operationalise and use in practice. Also, any framework should not aim to be totally prescriptive, but provide a workable scheme that would be capable of further elucidation and interpretation depending on its proposed use. It could be used for training and development purposes, but also for recruitment through the design of job descriptions (Table 8.1), assessment and job appraisal. It has the potential to be used in a team building context where the objective is to build teams of people who collectively rather than individually display these boundary spanning competencies.

Getha-Taylor (2008) has undertaken rigorous research on generating collaborative competencies resulting in 12 main competencies: initiative, information seeking, interpersonal understanding, organisational awareness,

Table 8.1: Job description for a boundary spanner

Qualifications
- Undergraduate degree
- Postgraduate degree (desirable)

Knowledge
- Appreciation of multiorganisational environments
- Understanding of the policy process
- Appreciation of different organisational contexts
- Some trans-disciplinary knowledge

Experience
- Experience of working in multiorganisational settings
- Cross-sector experience
- Experience of working in different types of organisation and policy area

Skills
- Networking
- Negotiation and conflict resolution
- Cultivation and maintenance of effective interpersonal relationships
- Able to build trusting relationships and cultures
- Effective communication skills
- Ability to work in teams and groups
- Critical analysis skills to cope with high complexity
- Innovative, creative and entrepreneurial
- Proven planning and coordination skills
- Comfortable working with cultural, professional and organisational diversity
- Ability to manage multiple accountabilities
- Ability to work in different modes of governance
- Well developed influencing skills

Personal attributes
Tolerant of ambiguity, risk taking, self-confident, respectful, personable, diplomatic/tactful, honest and committed, patient and persevering

relationship building, teamwork and cooperation, team leadership, analytical thinking, conceptual thinking, organisational commitment, self-confidence and flexibility. Further statistical analysis of the data that was used to generate these competencies revealed that interpersonal understanding, teamwork and cooperation, and team leadership were the most significant competencies for collaborative effectiveness. However, Getha–Taylor compared her findings with some other research in this area and concluded that: 'there exists a disconnect between human resource managers and superior collaborators with regard to the necessary skills for effective collaboration' (2008, p 114).

This underscores the need to take considerable care when using generic competency frameworks not least because, learned out of context, they may not enhance an individual's ability to perform effectively in a particular context. Therefore, it is important to tailor frameworks to specific organisational contexts and challenges, and to express the nuances, values and interpretations of individual competencies within different collaborative cultures and business objectives.

An interesting question relates to the appropriateness or otherwise of nurturing the development of a class of specialist boundary spanners as opposed to integrating boundary spanning competencies into the mainstream training and education portfolios of leaders, managers and practitioners. There are arguments for and against either option. The dedicated boundary spanner route has some attraction relating to the creation of highly competent individuals trained to operate in collaborative environments, majoring particularly on process issues and concentrating on facilitating connectivity between people and organisations. However, any attempt to professionalise such a group might at first sight appear to be counterproductive and in conflict with their intrinsic roles and purpose. Moreover, the public sector is already congested with existing professional bodies often competing for high status, and it is arguable whether a further addition would contribute any value in this area. The added danger of a professional group of boundary spanners is the perception by others that boundary spanning is not their role or responsibility, and that any such activity should be left to this specialist group. This is patently not the case. On the other hand, it is possible to sympathise with a group of actors who may feel genuinely undervalued by the absence of a professional body that can offer status, identity, regulation, advocacy and other forms of support that accompany this form of organisation. Professional bodies also help define career paths and forms of remuneration within areas of employment.

However, the integration route has much to commend it, as it is premised on influencing the behaviour of leaders, managers and practitioners in many different policy areas, and providing them with the tools and mindsets to work constructively and consensually on interrelated agendas. Building in boundary spanning capacities is preferable to building on boundary spanning capacities. It is more sustainable over a longer period of time, and can be translated into all stages of the policy process.

Academic

The issues involved in this option relate to whether collaborative working can be pursued as a separate and distinct subject or studied on some kind of trans-disciplinary basis, and at what level, undergraduate or postgraduate? One of the problems of studying this subject at a purely academic level is that there is no clear career entry or progression, as is the case with many professional disciplines. The safest route here is probably at a postgraduate level through the inclusion of studies of collaborative working within the programmes of Master's in Business Administration or Master's in Public Administration. Consideration of fast-track cohort programmes is also worthy of exploration.

Experiential

There is considerable value to be gained from the experience of working in a range of different organisations to understand better their cultures, ways of working, operating systems, accountabilities and motivations. Programmes designed to expose suitable candidates to such opportunities would be effective. In addition, if these opportunities were arranged within a particular interorganisational set, it would have the advantage of developing personal networks that could be beneficial in later collaborative working. The typical methods involved include secondments, mentoring, coaching and shadowing. Mentoring is based on some prior selection of candidates who are linked, either formally or informally, with an appropriate and competent practising boundary spanner. The advantage for the mentee is that he/she can learn about the role within a real organisational context, and can be encouraged to understand the complexities and challenges involved. There is, however, a paucity of studies that evaluate the success or otherwise of mentoring programmes and much depends on the skills of the mentor. Coaching is a possible variation on a similar theme to mentoring. It can be associated with negative performance, but in this context could be utilised in a similar fashion to executive coaching programmes, designed to improve performance and enhance career progression. Again, the choice of coach is important and the reality of such programmes is their variability in quality. An additional opportunity with coaching may be to offer it to a team or group rather than to a single individual. Shadowing is generally much weaker than both mentoring and coaching, as it is less proactive and formal, but the issues are similar.

In general, experience shows that programmes involving these methods need to be properly devised, planned and monitored to ensure that the learning experience is of an appropriately high quality and of benefit to both the individuals and organisations concerned. Problems of interrupted career progression, remuneration and terms and conditions of employment often prove difficult to overcome. However, they are not insurmountable, and effective and well-organised programmes linked to corporate organisational training and development plans can provide a sustainable learning method for raising local collaborative capacities and capabilities. In addition to the approaches discussed above consideration could be given to other models such as job rotation, job assignment, action learning sets and succession planning.

Capacity building

The context of active collaborative initiatives provides a significant opportunity for developing understanding and proficiency in boundary spanning. Evaluation studies of collaborations in many policy areas often point to the problems associated with insufficient capacity among the people involved in working in those particular arenas. An all too familiar story is that groups get carried away with the tasks facing them, neglect the process aspects and complain when their aspirations are not realised, or when intergroup conflicts reduce the effectiveness and potential of the overall collaboration. In the light of this, it is good practice for any new collaboration to attend to the issue of capacity and capabilities at the outset, and to revisit this issue on a regular basis throughout its lifetime. The use of partnership health checks is becoming more commonplace (Hardy et al, 2000). These aim to examine the effectiveness and fitness for purpose of particular collaborations through canvassing the strength of the opinions of stakeholders against an idealised model of collaboration. The health check covers issues of trust, communication, interpersonal relationships and working as a team, allowing action to be taken where problems are identified. Specific training and development needs can be addressed as a result of such exercises.

Ideally, both personal and collaborative capacity building needs to be embedded into the process from the inception of any new initiative. It should not be seen as an isolated event but treated as a continuous process of learning. It is also never too late to consider training and learning, and mature collaborations in need of some reflection, refocusing or revitalisation might equally benefit from this kind of action. It is a simple recognition that the course of numerous collaborations is often undermined by the lack of boundary spanning competencies in people and teams working together. High quality expertise and professional knowledge is assembled around the table, but the ability to devise mutually beneficial solutions to complex and interrelated issues is hampered by poorly developed boundary spanning competencies. Given the major effort that is often invested in collaborative working and the high profile nature of them, every effort should be made to ensure that they are effective. In this context, the value of action learning models and appreciative inquiry (Van der Haar and Hosking, 2004) can be considered. These approaches reject formal classroom learning in favour of a focus on real problem solving with an emphasis on reflective learning. They can also be used prospectively to consider how best to approach emerging challenges facing the learning group members. Membership that cuts across organisational boundaries, backgrounds and professions is likely to be the most exhilarating. In Wales, an example of this approach can be seen in the context of the Public Service Management Wales programme, in the form of the middle management development programme designed to build collaborative capacity among this cadre through knowledge of collaborative working methods and skills. The action learning model forms the basis of the programme that includes project work, coaching and mentoring, tutorials, visits to exemplar organisations, as well as formal programmes such as Leadership for Collaboration. Other examples include the Leading Powerful Partnerships programme organised by the National College of Police Leadership supported by the Home Office (Meaklim and Sims, 2011) and the Collaborative Leadership programme designed by the Skills for Justice network of voluntary organisations operating in the justice and community safety field.

The resourcing of capacity building programmes is not inexpensive, and in an austere financial climate there is an urgent need for more robust evidence of the value of investment in training, development and capacity building in relation to performance and outcomes. Evidence of the benefits of training and development programmes is needed at an individual, team, organisational and interorganisational level. For example, as a result of a particular individual taking part in a secondment opportunity, what impact did he or she subsequently have in the work situation? Or what was the effect of a training programme on collaborative skills undertaken by a local strategic partnership on its subsequent way of working and outcomes on the ground? On receipt of such evidence, government and individual organisations/sectors might consider including ring-fenced budgets within special collaborative initiatives to promote such practices. A further consideration for many public organisations is the extent to which boundary spanning activity could be actively rewarded, in the form of enhanced remuneration attached to performance management strategies or other non-pecuniary mechanisms. Job appraisal frameworks could certainly include this as an element, and the development of individual CVs could be enhanced through recognition of this area of expertise and knowledge.

Networking and communities of practice

In the absence of professional bodies to promote and regulate learning, forms of networking offer a very practical route for enhancing individual learning on collaborative capabilities. Networking can be both formal and informal, and is likely to be sustained over longer periods than methods such as shadowing, mentoring or coaching. A number of formal networks have emerged around specific policy-based boundary spanning fields, such as community safety, anti-poverty and sustainable development. It reflects a need by boundary spanners in these areas, often facing similar stresses, strains and challenges in the isolation of their home organisations, to seek the comfort of like-minded and motivated people, to share experiences and to offer mutual support. Such networks can provide a number of functions but shared learning and practice is particularly high on the agenda of most. Knowledge transfer can be tacit as well as explicit. Tacit knowledge is difficult to articulate through reports or studies and is best transmitted face to face in the form of stories and anecdotes about working life experiences. Network activities are often formalised into jointly arranged workshops, seminars, studies, newsletters, websites and training opportunities. Facilitation at network events is regarded as very useful, and those individuals who are the most proactive and invest heavily in network experiences realise the greatest benefits.

Networks confined to specific policy fields risk the development of 'groupthink' and ossification because of similarities between group members. Therefore, some diversity within networks is considered valuable as a source of challenge to existing conventions and assumptions, and networks that cross different boundary spanning fields are potentially more rewarding. This can be realised in a number of ways – first, on an individual basis, boundary spanners can be a member of different networks. Second, different networks can attempt to forge linkages with other networks through a shared realisation of mutual agendas resulting in some communication. Third, specialist boundary spanners from different policy areas can be encouraged to form networks.

Linked to networking is the potential of communities of practice. In relation to management and leadership, Perren and Burgoyne (2002a, 2000b) note that the sharing of knowledge and practice is often sporadic, isolated and rarely communicated between different communities of interest – individuals, employers and providers. They propose to rectify this deficiency through the development of a web-based database of management and leadership practices and development opportunities built around a shared framework of abilities. This would have the effect of bridging the communities with a central core of shared constructs and a set of peripheral, community-specific constructs.

A similar approach might well be applicable for boundary spanning, to help foster learning and shared practice between different providers of education and training, the different organisations employing boundary spanners at local and national level and individual actors themselves. A register of competencies could be established to link individuals to organisations that may be faced with specific needs, offer secondment opportunities or other development options; a chat room could provide support and information for often isolated boundary spanners; and details of training and development opportunities could be posted. User feedback from both individuals and organisations could usefully provide valuable information on the most effective pedagogic approaches to learning outcomes.

Developing boundary spanning leaders and managers

Osborne (2010, p 421) comments that:

> The reality of contemporary public service management is that it is an interorganizational and collaborative activity, and requires the governance of complex systems and interorganizational processes. Despite this, training has often remained rooted in organizational needs rather than embracing the requirement to develop skills in managing the complex processes of interorganizational, network and systems governance.

Likewise, Morse (2008), in examining the leadership development implications of boundary spanning leaders, reflects that the focus, particularly in the public sector, is biased towards intraorganisational settings which fail to take account of the demands of interorganisational arenas. His view is that leadership for collaboration is definitely different from traditional notions of leadership that are premised on power, status and hierarchy. He then pursues this line of argument to suggest that, using as a baseline the public organisational leadership competencies generated by Van Wart (2005), an additional or enhanced set of competencies are needed for collaborative leadership. These competencies consist of attributes, skills and behaviours, as listed in Table 8.2.

A number of competencies clearly span both intra and interorganisational leadership, and Morse (2008) asserts that six meta-skills (communication, social skills, influence skills, analytic skills, technical skills and continual learning) are applicable in both settings. However, the list in Table 8.2 contains ones that are either unique to collaborative settings or are enhanced versions of those applicable in intraorganisational situations. In terms of developing leaders, the implication here is that they must first be trained as public managers and only then would they be subject to a programme that aims to make them proficient in the competencies for collaborative leadership.

Table 8.2: Collaborative leadership competencies

Attributes	Skills	Behaviours
Collaborative mindset	Self-management	Stakeholder identification
Passion towards outcomes	Strategic thinking	Stakeholder assessment
Systems thinking	Facilitation skills	Strategic issue framing
Openness and risk taking		Convening working groups
Sense of mutuality and connectedness		Facilitating mutual learning processes
Humility		Inducing commitment
		Facilitating trusting relationships among partners

Source: After Morse (2008)

Posner (2009, p 241) takes up the training and development challenge of collaborative public managers by asserting that: 'public managers working in third-party governance arrangements increasingly confront a world where a premium is placed on other skills and capacities'. This follows a similar view propounded by a number of researchers including Goldsmith and Eggers (2004) and Agranoff and McGuire (2003). Posner (2009) summarises these as:

- activating disparate actors to come together using various tools and incentives to gain participation and consensus;
- negotiating and bargaining using leverage and/or withholding critical resources to achieve joint enterprise;
- understanding the incentives to mobilise actors;
- communicating shared goals, common purpose and measured outcomes;
- building social capital through trust;
- developing 'soft' leadership skills;
- establishing policy learning institutions to steer loosely connected networks.

However, in terms of graduate and postgraduate public administration programmes, both in the US and UK, there are preciously few academic institutions that offer an integrated programme on either collaborative management or collaborative leadership. One exception is the Suffolk University MPA (Master's of Public

Administration) and MHA (Master's of Health Administration) which include a mandatory model on collaborative leadership and sets a precedent that:

> … all our students need to understand this new way of doing business, can reflect on what it means in their own professional environment, and have the opportunity to develop and practice collaborative leadership skills. (Bramson, 2005, p 136)

Another is the University of Southern California that includes 'intersectoral leadership' as a core subject in its Master's in Policy Studies and 'non-profit management and leadership' as an elective. The MPA also has 'intersectoral management' as a specialised elective. The Weil Program on Collaborative Governance at Harvard University's Kenny School of Government also offers degree programmes that embrace cross-sector leadership. The Consortium on 'Collaborative Governance' between the Universities of Southern California, Washington and Arizona acknowledge the need for universities to work together on this agenda.

In a world where public, private and third sectors increasingly collaborate in different forms spawning new models of governance, there is a need for academic programmes to reflect the cross-sector nature of this phenomenon, and to equip students accordingly with the appropriate knowledge and skills. Although this may involve imparting bodies of explicit knowledge, the relatively high component of tacit knowledge involved needs to be reflected in the forms of learning and delivery mechanisms adopted – case studies, reflective practice, action learning and experiential learning.

The trend towards increasing specialisation in government has been accompanied by attempts to 'professionalise' that work, and to fit it into hierarchical forms of organisation. This has led to professional bodies seeking to clearly demarcate and jealously guard discrete areas of knowledge and expertise. Arguably, the cultivation of collaborative public managers is not best served through a professional route because of the nature, depth and spread of the knowledge and skills required. Local and national government agencies will need to be far more creative in terms of recruitment, progression, training, development and incentivisation of collaborative public managers than they have been in the past to reflect the importance of collaborative working. How can graduates be recruited into this area of work? How can the movement of people between sectors be encouraged, and barriers pulled down? How can remuneration and performance appraisal systems reflect the job of a collaborative public manager? Should there be equal status between traditional public managers and collaborative public managers? These and other related questions need to be addressed as a matter of urgency.

Review of main points

- Collaboration is a permanent and important feature of the public policy landscape. However, given its indifferent success, there is a pressing need to understand 'what works' in general and particularly in relation to the role and behaviour of boundary spanners.
- Appropriate capabilities and capacities need to be built into the design and delivery processes of collaboration. Attention needs to be given to promoting the necessary supportive cultures and institutional arrangements to facilitate the work of boundary spanners.
- The public policy community has to ensure that enabling mechanisms for learning and knowledge management are installed to enhance, embed and sustain the benefits of collaboration.
- Explicit and planned learning strategies need to be informed by an understanding of different levels, types and forms of learning.
- Tacit and explicit forms of knowledge management demand different approaches, and knowledge conversion and transfer strategies must be grounded in an appreciation of the different structures, processes and carriers underpinning them.
- The notion of absorptive capacity is critically important in terms of the receptivity, resources, attitudes, competences and experiences of agencies working in collaboration.
- Meaning, power and interpersonal relationships are highly influential phenomena at an individual level in relation to learning and knowledge management, and boundary spanners have an important role in mediating these processes.
- This book's exposition on boundary spanners has profound implications for their training, education and development; the question of whether the purpose is to develop a special cadre of boundary spanners, or to build boundary spanning competencies into leadership, management and professional development, is a key strategic choice.
- Specific strategies fall into a number of broad categories – professional, academic, experiential, capacity building and networking/communities of practice.

Questions for discussion

1. Think of an effective boundary spanner you are familiar with, and identify the main competencies that you consider make him/her effective in that role. Develop a training and education programme based on those competencies.
2. What steps would you take to establish an effective community of practice/network of boundary spanners in a particular area or policy field?
3. Design a Master's level programme in boundary spanning.
4. Design a capacity building programme to accompany a new collaboration.
5. How should boundary spanners be trained, developed and supported?

Suggested further reading

Getha-Taylor, H. (2008) 'Identifying collaborative competencies', *Review of Public Personnel Administration*, vol 28, no 2, pp 103-19.

Morse, R.S. (2008) 'Developing public leaders in an age of collaborative governance', in R.S. Morse and T.F. Buss (eds) *Innovations in public leadership development*, Armonk, NY: M.E. Sharpe.

NINE

Reflections and conclusion

Boundaries are exciting, intriguing and turbulent places to inhabit. They are 'like fault lines: they are the locus of volcanic activity. They allow movement, they release tension; they create new mountains; they shake existing structures' (Wenger, 1998, p 254). Boundaries are often the sites of conflict, miscommunication and misunderstanding, resulting in a lack of coordination and duplication – they are too often perceived as barriers and protected by organisational, sectoral and professional walls. Alternatively, they can be the locus of transformation, collaboration, imagination, energy, innovation and creativity through the juxtapositioning of multiple communities of practice and interests. Boundary encounters are healthy for people and organisations – they avoid atrophy, groupthink and inbreeding, and offer new opportunities for learning, knowledge acquisition and windows on the world.

A preoccupation with understanding boundaries and managing their implications is critical in a UK public policy landscape that is defined by a number of particular characteristics. First, the type of policy issues and problems that are presented fall into the category of being 'wicked' – complex, tangled, lacking optimal solutions and multiply framed in terms of structure and meaning. These problems are not only persistent – social and health inequality, unemployment, an ageing population – but demand collaborative approaches to their management because they cross boundaries. However, some care is needed to avoid overstating the prevalence of 'wicked issues' because not all public problems and issues fall into this category. The Type 1 and Type 2 problems referred to by Chrislip and Larson (1994), which have relatively clear definitions and solutions, are best dealt with through conventional management and governance approaches predominantly by single organisations. There has been a tendency in the UK, fuelled by the mantra of 'joined-up' working, to apply collaborative approaches in an indiscriminate fashion to any type of problem. An important message for policy makers about to embark on collaboration is to decide exactly what business is best conducted through collaboration, and what business is best left in the hands of individual organisations.

Second, the public policy landscape is characterised by an institutional and governance architecture that is fragmented and multilevel, with frequent changes in the relationship between the state, the private sector and civil society. Devolution, decentralisation and localism are variously influencing the shape of local governance, often dependent on central government persuasion and direction. The balance between the state and non-state institutions has changed, with a greater involvement of the private sector in the design and provision of public services sometimes managed through PPPs. This is likely to expand in the current political climate, with a planned diminution in the role of the state. Also, the third sector is poised to expand to fill some of the gaps vacated by government, stimulating new and innovative forms of social enterprise alongside traditional voluntary and community endeavours.

Third, the public, in various guises as citizens, clients and service users, are increasingly aware and informed about public services particularly at a time of 'cuts', and they are actively invited to participate in the design and delivery of public services through public and community involvement processes. Notions from the private sector such as 'quality', 'choice' and 'customer service' have entered public sector arenas, and have been reinterpreted in this different context. Users of public services represent the point at which effectiveness is experienced – whether it is seamless, efficient and integrated, or whether it is uncoordinated and unresponsive. Among a daunting list of challenges facing collaborative working, securing the effective involvement of citizens and service users continues to be a difficult proposition.

Lastly, public service providers and commissioners are faced with an unprecedented period of austerity, with deep cuts in public service budgets and significant restrictions in planned budget levels going forward. This reinforces the case for collaboration between organisations and sectors to reduce inefficiencies and areas of duplication, and to promote better coordination and synergy. The prospect of major reconfiguration and a re-engineering of public services is already being manifested in moves to develop shared services, community budgets, joint appointments, joint working arrangements, merged departments, joint procurement of services and commissioning of services from the private sector and new social enterprises. This reflects the potential of collaboration as a source of institutional entrepreneurship (Lawrence et al, 2002; Maguire et al, 2004), with its ability to transcend existing rules, technologies and practices through the creation of 'proto-institutions', leading in turn to the possibility of fully fledged new institutions. In their research, collaborations that exhibited deep and extensive interactions between partners, multidirectional flows of information and highly embedded relationships were positively associated with the development of these so-called 'proto-institutions'.

In these circumstances, it is imperative that appropriate roles, capabilities and competencies are cultivated in public servants to match these challenges of collaborative working. The logic is that if boundary spanning activities and processes have become a major component of the design and delivery of contemporary public services, the role and work of boundary spanners must now occupy centre stage. A rebalancing of relationships between sectors, the creation of new institutional arrangements and other structural reconfigurations need to be supported by the cultivation of appropriate competencies and capabilities in boundary spanning actors.

Rieple et al (2002, p 8) came to the conclusion that:

> There is almost no research on the role that boundary spanners have
> in hybrid organizational structures, and yet they are arguably likely
> to be some of the most important people in ensuring their success.

This book sets out to redress this gap in our knowledge, with its focus on the life
and times of boundary spanners in UK public policy. A number of key questions
provide the scaffolding for a detailed exploration of their role and behaviour.
Specifically, who are the boundary spanners? What roles do they undertake?
Which competencies are needed to undertake these roles effectively? And what
particular challenges do they face when undertaking these roles? The subsequent
examination has generated different types of boundary spanner that has allowed
contrasts and comparisons to be made, and also private sector perspectives explored
to factor in additional learning and insights. Table 9.1 summarises some of the
main features of this analysis.

Who are the boundary spanners?

At times, academic discourse has a tendency to be overly preoccupied by
definitions, but it is unavoidable in the present discussion. Who are the boundary
spanners, and does this notion have sufficient clarity to be a useful analytical and
practical construct? Different academics and researchers in different disciplines
have coined a variety of terms to describe people who undertake boundary
spanning roles, tasks and activities. These are not formal role titles but are designed
to capture the essence of their work and functions. The term 'boundary spanner'
serves a similar purpose and is analogous in part to other descriptions. However,
among a minefield of terminology, the author has attempted here to present
an interpretation of a boundary spanner with reference to two main types.
First, those actors who have a formal, dedicated position and role to operate in
collaborative settings – having a clear mandate to manage, support and operate
at the boundary. Second, those managers and leaders who are considerably larger
in number and whose roles straddle intra and interorganisational working. This
reflects the growing trend for many managers and leaders to divide their time
between managing within their organisations, and being involved with people
and organisations in collaborative endeavours.

The definition of the second type invites the criticism that this is too broad an
interpretation, includes a very large number of people and offers little scope for
exposing the differentiation and nuances that may exist between them. However,
there can be little doubt that this group of actors does engage in boundary
spanning activities to varying degrees, and as has been discussed in previous
chapters, the juggling between different modes of governance demands sensitive
judgements and particular responses in terms of approach and competence. The
very co-existence of these different modes creates dilemmas and ambiguities in
accountability, authority, legitimacy and responsibility. The author's general view
here, arrived at over a period of sustained fieldwork research in collaborative

Table 9.1: Summary of boundary spanners' profiles

	Roles	Competencies	Personal qualities	Tensions and ambiguities
Dedicated	**Reticulist** Informational intermediary Gatekeeper Entrepreneur of power	Networking, political sensitivity, diplomacy, bargaining, negotiation, persuasion	• Respect for others • Honesty • Trustworthiness • Approachability • Diplomatic • Positive • Enthusiastic • Confident • Calm	• Managing in and across multiple modes of governance • Blurred personal and professional relationships • Dilemmas of multiple accountabilities • Appreciation of multiple framing processes
	Interpreter/ communicator Culture breaker Frame articulator	Inter-personal, listening, empathising, communication, sensemaking, trust building, conflict management		
	Coordinator Liaison person Organiser	Planning, coordination, servicing, administration, information management, monitoring, communication		
	Entrepreneur Initiator Broker Catalyst	Brokering, innovation, whole systems thinking, flexibility, lateral thinking, opportunistic		

Manager	Facilitator Coordinator Broker Maestro	• Managing complexity and strategic appreciation • Communication • Networking • Negotiation/mediation and conflict resolution • Facilitation • Team building • Interpersonal skills • Network design and structuring	• Patience • Sensitivity • Creativity	• Sources of uncertainty – substantive, strategic and institutional • Network tensions – efficiency versus inclusiveness, internal versus external legitimacy, flexibility versus stability • Hierarchical and network forms of governance – autonomy/interdependence, participative/authoritarian, advocacy and enquiry
Leader	Convenor Integrator Manager of meaning	• Negotiation/mediation and conflict resolution • Interpersonal skills • Facilitation • Critical thinking • Group working	• Being respectful • Humble • Personable • Calm • Humorous • Charismatic	• Knowing when to lead and when to follow • Independence versus interdependence • Inclusivity versus effectiveness
Alliance manager	Champion Point man Ambassador Intermediary	• Interpersonal relationships • Building trust • Communication • Conflict management • Learning • Team working • Negotiation	• Self-confidence • Inspiring others • Respectful • Credible • Adaptability	• Balancing competition and cooperation • Managing accountabilities • Coping with complexity • Managing without power • Switching between different management approaches

environments, is that the notion of a boundary spanner does resonate well with policy makers and practitioners. The author has had many conversations with managers and practitioners who recognise themselves as boundary spanners rather than in terms of a formal role title. Also, it is a particularly useful construct in underlining the value of this type of actor in helping to shape the outcomes of collaboration, and to understand the resource implications of building this capacity within collaborations. However, as an analytic construct, the case may be less compelling. It is an inherently imprecise notion that attracts different interpretations and meanings. The accumulated body of research on boundary spanners is not extensive, and in the absence of a greater depth and breadth of understanding of boundary spanners in different contexts and challenges, with researchers sharing common understandings of the notion, achieving consensus will be difficult.

Roles and competencies

The role of the dedicated class of boundary spanner is made up of a number of elements – reticulist, interpreter/communicator, coordinator and entrepreneur – each associated with a particular mix of competencies. Although in certain tasks a predominant role can be detected, in reality many challenges require a careful combination of these role elements. The work of these boundary spanners are characterised by a number of particular features: managing and influencing without formal sources of power – facilitating and convening; dealing with complexity and interdependence because it is a job for 'clever' people (Kanter, 1997); working with diversity and different cultures arising from a variety of interests and agencies; managing conflict (O'Leary and Bingham, 2009) as much as collaboration, requiring diplomacy and negotiation; managing in different modes of governance; and building and sustaining interpersonal relationships constructed around trust and networking – although like 'shares', trust can go down as well as up! As a result of these capabilities, boundary spanners are in potentially influential positions to help frame, interpret and make sense of reality and shape the course of strategic action. Finally, these actors have a strong inclination towards innovation and risk, the 'prosecutors' in Miles and Snow's (1978) conceptualisation of the most highly performing strategic agents, with even a capacity for institutional entrepreneurship (Maguire et al, 2004).

Managers and leaders who undertake boundary spanning roles have many similarities with their dedicated counterparts. The reticulist element of the manager's role reflects the need to practise effective network design and management. Coordination, facilitation and brokering are familiar aspects of this role with communication, negotiation and conflict resolution skills being highly prized. Responsibility for building teams and groups is perhaps more of a preoccupation with managers and leaders, as is leadership. Leaders have to take prime responsibility for the process of collaboration – for convening relevant interests and building collaborative cultures intent on shared purposes. Integrators and managers of meaning stand out as apt metaphors for the work of leaders as boundary spanners. Critically, all types of boundary spanner face the problem of dealing with complexity that is generated from a number of different sources, requiring them to demonstrate a number of specific competencies. Above all else, they must be strategists who are conversant in whole systems and critical thinking, and convey an acute 'appreciation of interdependence' – that is, an in-depth knowledge of the individuals, agencies and organisations that make up a collaborative domain – their roles, responsibilities, cultures, histories and purposes – and the jigsaw of connections that tie, or potentially tie, them together to achieve some form of collective purpose and synergy. The sources of such knowledge can be acquired academically, but are more likely to be honed through cross-sector experience, networking and collaborative working. The analytical skills to appreciate areas of connectivity must be present to convert 'collaborative knowledge' into the potential for policy and practice.

Uncertainty is the everyday reality of modern public management, compounded within collaborative settings by the challenges of assembling multiple agencies together and sustaining their commitment, of coordinating individual actions within a collective umbrella, of managing different accountabilities and performance regimes and of securing effective resourcing, often from multiple sources. Levels of risk are likely to be higher in such situations, and boundary spanners need to be comfortable operating within such frameworks. Collaboration invites a preoccupation with boundaries – real and imagined – and challenges are invariably couched in terms of scaling, crossing or permeating them. However, many are becoming increasingly blurred, and that provides an opportunity for boundary spanners to frame problems and solutions within different paradigms based on effectiveness, efficiency or customer focus, and to help envisage a reordering of resource possibilities. This involves encouraging people to move from what Sarason and Lorentz (1998) refer to as an 'organisation chart mentality' to 'a boundary crossing mentality'. But, whereas blurring may allow different formulations of problems and issues to emerge, boundary clarity is especially important at a time of delivery and implementation.

Both the literature and empirical research makes reference to the sorts of people who are attracted to working as boundary spanners. This prompts questions as to whether they are of a particular type, whether they project a certain disposition or whether it has anything to do with personal traits or attributes. A largely similar set of personal qualities are advanced for the different types of boundary spanner, and there is anecdotal evidence to support the view that people occupying boundary spanning positions need to display certain attributes which may be rooted in their personal demeanour and behaviour. If you crave a working life that is consistent, regular, organised, low risk and uncomplicated, the life of a boundary spanner is not for you. On the other hand, if you relish tension, difference, challenge, flexibility, risk and learning, the reverse is the case. Wenger (1998, p 109) considers that:

> Certain individuals seem to thrive on being brokers: they love to create connections and engage in "import-export", and so would rather stay at the boundaries than move to the core of any one practice.

A question that arises regularly in the literature and policy practice is whether the competencies to work in boundary spanning roles set out above are materially different or similar to those needed to operate within single organisations. There are suggestions in particular that boundary spanners have to switch their behaviours and management styles between different modes of governance. Is this a realistic view of management practice, or do actors adopt default styles that they use irrespective of context? Unfortunately, the available evidence is largely inclusive and there is no real consensus on this question. Some argue that working in collaboration is clearly different from working within a single organisation and necessarily demands different approaches and skills. Others are not so convinced and point to the increasing use of collaborative approaches to management within organisations, and the general blurring of modes of governance. One view is that there are a common set of skills needed by public managers, and collaboration needs much more of some than others, for example, mediation, whereas others identify a specific skill set that is unique to collaborative settings. This may seem a somewhat academic discussion but it does have important practical implications when it comes to the design and content of education and training strategies. My view is that, while there is clearly communality between organisations that pursue network and collaborative approaches within their organisations and interorganisational collaboration, the context and nature of the challenges faced by the latter certainly demand particular competencies. For example, sharing power is not an option in collaboration, although it is within single organisations, and consensus seeking is not an option in collaboration in contrast to single organisations where central directives are feasible courses of action.

A life of paradox and ambiguity

The context for collaboration is complex and challenging – typically characterised by an absence of clarity around purposes and problems; different value orientations, frames and systems of belief; unclear, multiple, shifting or conflicting goals; lack of precision around personal and organisational roles and responsibilities; differences in interpretation over what constitutes 'success'; variations in culture and language; multiple accountabilities and performance management regimes; and conflicts between different modes of governance. These are a direct consequence of the assembly of a diverse set of people and organisations intent on some form of collaboration. However, as a consequence, managing in this context is complex, and the working life of any type of boundary spanner is replete with paradox, ambiguity and tension. The preceding chapters have identified and discussed a number of problematic areas which require careful judgements and balances to be made, particularly around managing in different modes of governance, multiple accountabilities, relationships and framing processes.

The interpersonal nature of the boundary spanning role is an especially sensitive one. Much of the work of the boundary spanner has been seen to be close and personal. Investing in a rich network of interpersonal relationships forged through trust, regular communication and common purpose are considered to be the hallmarks of an effective boundary spanner. The cultivation of relationships with other partners often spills over from the professional into more personal spheres, offering the prospect of deeper and more sustained understanding and collaboration. Setting aside the argument of whether this way of working is chosen as a matter of choice or necessity, clearly collaborative forms of governance and management do not lend themselves to more formal interactions based on traditional forms of organising and power relationships. However, despite the attraction of this form of working, it does have its problems, relating in part to the nature of interpersonal relationships. They can be dysfunctional and unstable, they can be tiring, they can be exclusive and discriminatory, and in transaction terms, they can be lengthy. The sustainability of collaboration is highly risky if it is constructed solely on the scaffolding of inherently fragile personal relationships.

Boundary spanners continually confront the challenges of how far to develop personal relationships – to listen respectfully and sympathetically or to genuinely empathise and support. Even the process of building trust can be a façade – manipulated or subverted to conceal or mask the reality of power. The dedicated type of boundary spanner can at the same time be highly connected, but also to some extent be in limbo from their home organisation because of their outward-looking focus – as mavericks and outsiders? They often have better connections to the top of their organisation despite their formal status, and are less connected with their peers at other levels. The challenge for boundary spanners is to ensure that they maintain and cultivate internal networks as much as external ones, otherwise the fruits of collaboration risk being marginalised and peripheral. In particular, where collaborative action is dependent on organisational change, unless sufficient investment has been placed on securing the commitment and understanding of mainstream managers and practitioners, delivery issues are likely to ensue.

There are arguments set out in the literature that boundary spanners of all types face the prospect of managing without power. Herranz (2008, p 2), for instance, makes the point that: 'public managers face the quandary of being expected to work more in networks where they have less authority, while at the same time increasingly being held more accountable for performance and improved outcomes'. The underlying proposition here is that, within their own organisations, managers and leaders acquire power by virtue of their formal position and status, and are largely able to control and direct decision-making processes particularly in relation to resources such as capital, land and manpower. As O'Toole (2009, p 145) argues: 'managers can expect to have some significant ability to give orders and direct resources over the central part of their domain'. Indeed, this capacity can be useful in collaborative settings, particularly in terms of delivery, because managers and leaders, by virtue of their embedded positions within the core of their organisations, are more able to commit resources and effect policy change. However, in general, in the world of collaboration where a number of autonomous organisations are assembled, the use of sovereign power frequently is not possible, and power needs to be shared and negotiated, and different ways of influencing embraced.

The true skill of a boundary spanner is to demonstrate an ability to mobilise other sources of power (Palmer and Hardy, 2000) to influence the outcomes of collaboration. These include influencing the process of decision making (Lukes, 1974) through the manipulation of participants and agendas; using the power of meaning to help frame and shape understandings and meanings; and drawing on other sources of power such as expertise and knowledge, credibility, control of information flows, attracting group support and using political connections and networks to exert influence. Tactics for mobilising power are varied and typically involve socialising, networking, coalition building, brokering, negotiating and envisioning. Power is often wielded unobtrusively, covertly and behind the scenes. This is just as effective as more direct methods, although it risks being associated with manipulation and lack of transparency by weaker parties.

Boundary spanners, particularly the many managers and leaders who actively engage in collaborative working, are often torn between the respective accountabilities of their home organisation and a collaborative. Securing clarification on the questions of 'to whom am I accountable' and 'for what' is not easily resolved. Different forms of accountability might align, but equally they could be blurred or even compete with one another. Accountability is inextricably linked to performance and outcomes, issues that are particularly complex in collaborations, and further exacerbated by differences in frameworks, regimes and regulatory mechanisms. In practice, boundary spanners are likely to have to engage in trade-offs between different sources of accountability depending on different circumstances. This involves a great deal of juggling to maintain personal credibility in the face of often opposing organisational and collective interests. The consequences of being involved in different forms of governance with their different rules, rationales and accountabilities, are that boundary spanners, particularly the dedicated variety, can also face a dilemma of organisational identity. There is some evidence from the alliance management literature that the demands of competing intra and interorganisational interests often appear as a disincentive to recruitment – alliance management being viewed as a career backwater away from the mainstream of company business. A contrasting view is that boundary spanners: 'have elite status in the organization and an ability to influence senior and operational managers outside of traditional authority relations' (Wright, 2009, p 320), and they are presented with 'a diversity of experience closed off to other members' (Aldrich, 1979, p 262) with a consequent enhancement in their employment prospects.

Finally, although collaboration is ideally premised on the values of equality, shared purpose and common goals:

> Unless people see it as their immediate self-interest voluntarily and
> safely to consider and explore bridge-building, whatever you mean
> by co-ordination and collaboration will not likely occur and survive.
> (Sarason and Lorentz, 1998, p 3)

The coming together of different stakeholders with often divergent aims makes life difficult. The imperatives of personal, professional and organisational self-interest are difficult to break down as many are highly demarcated and institutionalised by statutory duties and legislation. Although outright competition is not the norm in the public sector, the introduction of 'quasi-markets' and similar mechanisms invite competition between agencies, and in times of severe austerity with restricted resources, the default position of organisational self-interest may well prevail. This presents a huge challenge for boundary spanners to provide compelling reasons for collaboration, to provide a business case where benefits outweigh costs and to balance the protection of organisational interests and identities within an overall collaborative framework. Boundary spanners need to understand the multiple motivations that drive people and organisations together, both voluntary and mandated. Organisational self-interest is perhaps more acutely felt by managers and leaders as boundary spanners as opposed to their dedicated counterparts who can sometimes claim more independence. Dedicated boundary spanners have the opportunity of playing the 'honest broker' role to secure negotiated outcomes, whereas managers and leaders are more constrained by virtue of their organisational allegiances. However, the ability to align organisational self-interests with collaborative interests is a valuable commodity.

Perspectives from the private sector

An earlier chapter interrogated the private sector literature in search of perspectives and learning that might contribute to a better understanding of collaboration in the public sector. Certainly alliance management in general has a much clearer purpose than its public sector comparators, and there is some evidence to link its effectiveness with performance. In public sector collaborations, there is little evidence to connect interventions to collaborative performance, and, what constitutes 'success' is often hazy and contested. However, it is difficult to generalise as it is practised in diverse settings and driven by different purposes. Although competitive advantage underpins the overall purpose, businesses are motivated to cooperate for different reasons including learning, skill substitution and resource exchange. This colours the nature of the alliance management function including the management of risk and prevention of opportunistic behaviour, division of rewards and approach to managing cultural diversity through strategies of integration or differentiation.

In terms of competencies, the evidence presented suggests a degree of compatibility between boundary spanners operating in both contexts, focusing on personal relationships, building trust, communication, negotiation and managing complex power relationships. One key difference rests in the broader role that public sector boundary spanners adopt as opposed to their private sector counterparts who can be limited to simple relationship management. It might also be argued that the public sector, with its diverse purposes and actors, is a potentially more complex arena in which to manage than the private sector. The legislative and bureaucratic context which dominates the public sector, problems of transparency and democratic accountability, coupled with unclear and sometimes perverse incentive systems further complicate the picture. Importantly, as Ingraham and Getha–Taylor (2008) point out, financial recognition is not the only way to achieve enhanced collaborative performance primarily because it is not an individual endeavour, and people can be motivated by a different set of assumptions.

Manufacturing boundary spanners

The reality of modern public governance is that it is networked, collaborative and interorganisational, and this demands a particular set of behaviours and competencies by actors wishing to be effective in this field. Too often perhaps, collaboration is practised by ill-trained and poorly motivated actors, who exhibit a lack of sincerity to the objects of collaboration. As Rubin (2002, p 20) poetically points out:

> An inauthentic collaborative leader, like an unloving lover, may be able to put on a convincing performance for a brief time but will ultimately be brought down by the truth.

However, 'despite this, training has often remained rooted in organizational needs rather than embracing the requirement to develop skills in managing the complex processes of inter-organizational, network and systems governance' (Osborne, 2010, p 421). Recent innovations in both academic and professional programmes to redress this imbalance are encouraging but nevertheless remain at the margin. The mainstream focus is clearly in favour of professional and organisational self-interest and performance. This needs to change if the existing trends in public governance continue into the future. It is, of course, dependent on much more clarity on the exact nature of the skills and competencies required, and the precise impact of agency on collaborative outcomes in different collaborative settings.

Future research agenda

Writing over 30 years ago, Aldrich and Herker (1977, p 228) came to the conclusion that:

> More empirical studies are needed on how personnel in boundary spanning units or roles carry out their duties, and in particular how

such role performance varies under different environmental conditions and over time.

In many ways, this plea for more research has not been met and the challenge still remains to be filled. There is a need to rebalance the attention that has hitherto been given to macro-level and institutional perspectives, but more importantly to couch future research within the 'structure–agency–ideas' framework discussed earlier in this book. What contextual conditions enable effective agency and what factors constrain it? How do actors interpret their context to act strategically? What lenses do they use to undertake this task? Are boundary spanners gifted in some way, or powerfully placed to frame and articulate strategic action? Are the processes involved dynamic, and in what ways do actors learn? In the light of the different purposes and meanings ascribed by diverse actors and interests to the notion of collaboration, in what ways do/can boundary spanners act as cognitive filters, and how are they influenced in this process by structural factors?

The framework provided by the notion of 'institutional entrepreneurship' advanced by Garud et al (2007) may be useful in relation to these questions. It provides a theoretical mechanism for balancing the role of agency within institutional analysis, while acknowledging the paradox of embedded agency.

Future research agendas need to focus on a number of key areas:

- They must examine the different contexts within which boundary spanners operate, particularly public and private, exploring the extent to which 'context' influences the role and behaviour of boundary spanners. Also, given the increased importance of the third sector and the potential expansion of social enterprises, research should be extended to include situations where boundary spanners from this sector are involved. Context is reflected in value systems and beliefs, organisational and professional cultures, relationships to service users and citizens, management practices and ways of working. It both enables and constrains the operating space for key actors.
- They need to provide more empirical evidence on the role of different types of boundary spanner and their accompanying competencies – the dedicated boundary spanners as opposed to the managers and leaders who increasingly incorporate boundary spanning into their mainstream job roles. Can a differentiation be made to boundary spanners operating in strategic as opposed to operational arenas? Who are the 'street-level' boundary spanners, and what roles do they undertake?
- Boundary spanners provide a contribution in a wide range of different policy areas and issues – health, economic regeneration, sustainable development, community safety – but are their roles and behaviours shaped or influenced in any material way by them?
- Collaboration is manifested in all shapes, sizes and forms – alliances, strategic partnerships, networks, integration – involving different permutations of

stakeholders from different organisations and sectors. Do the roles and behaviours of boundary spanners differ between these?

- To what extent do levels of governance matter? Collaboration occurs at a local and community level; it happens across local authority areas, at sub-regional, regional and national levels. Again, what implications, if any, do these have for boundary spanning behaviours?

- The policy process typically proceeds through a number of different stages – from planning and policy formulation, through to implementation and delivery, and finally to evaluation. Various models of partnership envisage a progression through different stages (Gray, 1989; Wilson and Charleton, 1997; Lowndes and Skelcher, 1998). Does the role and interventions of boundary spanners differ at these different stages?

- Although a structure–agency framework has been used as the conceptual underpinning of the examination of boundary spanners in this book, do any other theoretical constructions offer potential insights?

Remarkably, there is a general lack of research evidence on the effectiveness of boundary spanning roles, strategies and interventions, particularly in the public sector. This is partly a reflection of the problems associated with the measurement and evaluation of their effectiveness, compounded by the difficulties of unpicking and separating single contributions from those delivered collectively through teams and organisations.

Finally, the research agenda in this area needs to be more innovative methodologically to generate more in-depth and nuanced agency-centred accounts and explanations of boundary spanners in practice. The two-dimensional focus on actor types and skills need to be extended through qualitative research methods – ethnographic, case study and action research – to collectively build up a picture of their operation and behaviour in a variety of different settings. They need to reflect what Emirbayer and Mische (1998, p 1012) refer to as 'relational pragmatics', or the fact that actors live simultaneously in the past, present and future, adjusting their patterns of engagement and action accordingly. Such a perspective 'lays the basis for a richer and more dynamic understanding of the capacity that actors have to mediating the structuring contexts within such action enfolds' (Emirbayer and Mische, 1998, p 1013). The accumulated body of evidence generated by such research will be invaluable to academics, but also to the policy community, helping to inform the future training and development of this special cadre of collaborative actors – the boundary spanners.

This book has examined the role of 'agency' in collaboration through the work of a class of actors known as 'boundary spanners' – actors who operate in multiorganisational and multisectoral environments. This form of governance is characterised by a particular set of operating conditions, rationales, set of rules and systems that stand in contrast to other forms of organising. Although collaboration now occupies a central position in public policy, the role and behaviour of individual actors within it remains a significant gap in research and practice. The author's view is that this is especially perverse considering the importance that is often placed in them to achieve effective outcomes in the highly complex and turbulent environments of collaboration. It is sincerely hoped that this book has in some small measure contributed to a greater understanding of the life of a boundary spanner in public policy, and will act as a stimulus to others to undertake further research and enquiry in this important area.

References

6, P. (1997) *Holistic government*, London: Demos.

6, P. (2004) 'Joined-up government in the Western world in comparative perspective: a preliminary perspective literature review and exploration', *Journal of Public Administration Research and Theory*, vol 14, no 1, pp 103-38.

6, P., Leat, D., Seltzer, K. and Stoker, G. (1999) *Governing in the round: Strategies for holistic government*, London: Demos.

Adams, J.S. (1976) 'The structure and dynamics of behaviour in organizational boundary roles', in M.D. Dunnette (ed) *Handbook of industrial and organizational psychology*, Chicago: Rand and McNally.

Adobor, H. (2006) 'The role of personal relationships in inter-firm alliances: benefits, dysfunctions, and some suggestions', *Business Horizons*, vol 49, pp 473-86.

Agranoff, R. (2004) 'Leveraging networks: a guide for public managers working across organizations', in J.M. Kamensky and T.J. Burlin (eds) *Collaboration: Using networks and partnerships*, New York: Rowan & Littlefield. P 61-102

Agranoff, R. (2007) *Managing within networks: Adding value to public organizations*, Washington, DC: Georgetown University Press.

Agranoff, R. and McGuire, M. (2001) 'Big questions in public network management research', *Journal of Public Administration Research and Theory*, vol 3, pp 295-326.

Agranoff, R. and McGuire, M. (2003) *Collaborative public management: New strategies for local government*, Washington, DC: Georgetown University Press.

Aiken, M. and Hage, J. (1968) 'Organizational interdependence and intra-organizational structure', *American Sociological Review*, vol 33, pp 912-30.

Aldrich, H.A. (1979) *Organizations and environments*, Englewood Cliffs, NJ: Prentice Hall.

Aldrich, H.A. and Herker, D. (1977) 'Boundary spanning roles and organization structure', *Academy of Management Review*, vol 2, no 2, pp 217-30.

Alexander, J.A., Comfort, M.E., Weiner, B.J. and Bogue, R. (2001) 'Leadership in collaborative community health partnerships', *Nonprofit Management and Leadership*, vol 12, no 2, pp 159-75.

Allen, K.E., Bordas, J., Hickman, G.R., Matusak, L.R., Sorenson, G.J. and Whitmire, K.J. (1998) 'Leadership in the 21st century', in G.R. Hickman (ed) *Leading organizations: Perspectives for a new era*, London: Sage Publications. p. 572-580

Alter, C. and Hage, J. (1993) *Organizations and environments*, Englewood Cliffs, NJ: Prentice Hall.

Alvesson, M. and Billing, Y.B. (1997) *Understanding gender and organizations*, London: Sage Publications.

Archer, M.S. (1988) *Culture and agency: The place of culture in social theory*, Cambridge: Cambridge University Press.

Armistead, C., Pettigrew, P. and Aves, S. (2007) 'Exploring leadership in multi-sectoral partnerships', *Leadership*, no 3, pp 211-30.

Bacharach, S.B., Bamberger, P. and McKinney, V. (2000) 'Boundary management tactics and logics in action: the case of peer-support providers', *Administrative Science Quarterly*, vol 45, no 4, pp 704-36.

Bachmann, R. (2001) 'Trust, power and control in trans-organizational relations', *Organization Studies,* vol 22, no 2, pp 337-65.

Bamford, J.D., Gomes-Casseres, B. and Robinson, M.S. (2003) *Mastering alliance strategy*, San Francisco, CA: Jossey-Bass.

Bardach, E. (1998) *Getting agencies to work together*, Washington, DC: Brookings Institution Press.

Bardach, E. and Lesser, C. (1996) 'Accountability in human services collaboratives – for what? And to whom?', *Journal of Public Administration Research and Theory*, vol 6, no 2, pp 197-224.

Barringer, B.R. and Harrison, J.S. (2000) 'Walking a tightrope: creating value through interorganizational relationships', *Journal of Management*, vol 26, no 3, pp 367-403.

Belbin, M. (2001) *Managing without power*, Oxford: Heinemann.

Benford, R.D. and Snow, D.A. (2000) 'Framing processes and social movements: an overview and assessment', *Annual Review of Sociology*, vol 26, pp 611-39.

Bingham, L.B., Sandfort, J. and O'Leary, R. (2008) 'Learning to do and doing to learn: teaching managers to collaborate in networks', in L.B. Bingham and R. O'Leary (eds) *Big ideas in collaborative public management*, London: M.E. Sharpe. P 270-285

Benson, J.K. (1975) 'The interorganizational network as a political economy', *Administrative Science Quarterly*, vol 20, pp 229-48.

Beresford, P. and Trevillion, S. (1995) *Developing skills for community care*, Aldershot: Arena.

Boal, K.B. and Hooijberg, R. (2001) 'Strategic leadership research: moving on', *Leadership Quarterly*, vol 11, no 4, pp 515-49.

Bogason, P. (2000) *Public policy and local governance: Institutions in postmodern society*, Cheltenham: Edward Elgar.

Boon, S. (1994) 'Dispelling doubt and uncertainty: trust in romantic relationships', in S. Duck (ed) *Dynamics of relationships*, London: Sage Publications.

Bramson, R.A. (2005) 'Preparing MPA graduates to serve as intermediaries in community building and public engagement', in R.S. Morse and T.F. Buss (eds) *Innovations in public leadership development*, London: M.E. Sharpe. P 129-145

Brown, L.D. (1983) *Managing conflict at organizational interfaces*, Reading, MASS: Addison-Wesley (no page number available).

Brown, J.S. and Duguid, P. (2000) *The social life of information*, Boston, MA: Harvard Business Press.

Brown, M.E. and Gioia, D.A. (2002) 'Making things click: distributive leadership in an online division of an offline organization', *Leadership Quarterly*, vol 13, pp 397-419.

Brunas-Wagstaff, J. (1998) *Personality: A cognitive approach*, London: Routledge.

Bryson, J.M. and Crosby, B.C. (2005) *Leadership for the common good: Tackling public problems in a shared-power world*, San Francisco, CA: Jossey-Bass.

Burt, R.S. (1982) *Toward a structural theory of action*, New York: Academic Press.

Cabinet Office (2000) *Wiring it up*, London: Cabinet Office.

Capra, F. (1997) *The web of life*, London: Flamingo.

Carlile, P.R. (2004) 'Transferring, translating, and transforming: an integrative framework for managing knowledge across boundaries', *Organization Science*, vol 15, no 5, pp 555-68.

Cash, D.W., Adger, W.N., Berkes, F., Garden, P., Lebel, L., Olsson, P., Pritchard, L. and Young, O. (2006) 'Scale and cross-scale dynamics: governance and information in a multi-level world', *Ecology and Society*, vol 11, no 2, article 8.

Castells, M. (2000) *The rise of the network society*, Oxford: Blackwell.

Challis, L., Fuller, S., Henwood, M., Klein, R., Plowden, W., Webb, A., Whittingham, P. and Wistow, G. (1988) *Joint approaches to social policy*, Cambridge: Cambridge University Press.

Child, J. and Heavens, S.J. (2003) 'The social construction of organizations and its implications for organizational learning', in M. Dierkes, A. Berthoin Antal, J. Child and I. Nonaka (eds) *Handbook of organizational learning and knowledge*, Oxford: Oxford University Press.

Child, J., Faulkner, D. and Tallman, S. (2005) *Cooperative strategy: Managing alliances, networks, and joint ventures*, Oxford: Oxford University Press.

Chrislip, D.D. and Larson, C.E. (1994) *Collaborative leadership*, San Francisco, CA: Jossey-Bass.

Cobb, R.W. and Elder, C.D. (1981) 'Communication and public policy', in D.D. Nimmo and K.R. Sanders (eds) *Handbook of political communication*, London: Sage Publications.

Cockburn, C. (1991) *In the way of women*, London: Macmillan.

Connelly, D.R. (2007) 'Leadership in the collaborative interorganizational domain', *International Journal of Public Administration*, vol 30, pp 1231-62.

Connelly, D.R., Zhang, J. and Faerman, S.R. (2008) 'The paradoxical nature of collaboration', in L.B. Bingham and R. O'Leary (eds) *Big ideas in collaborative public management*, London: M.E. Sharpe. P 17-35

Contractor, F.J. and Lorage, P. (1988) 'Why should firms cooperate? The strategy and economic basis for cooperative ventures', in F.J. Contractor and P. Lorage (eds) *Cooperative strategies in international business*, New York: Lexington.

Cooper, T.L., Bryer, T.A. and Meek, J.W. (2006) 'Citizen-centred collaborative public management', *Public Administration Review*, Special Issue, pp 76-88.

Coote, A., Allen, J. and Whitehead, D. (2004) *Finding out what works: Understanding complex, community-based initiatives*, London: The King's Fund.

Cropper, S. (1996) 'Collaborative working and the issue of sustainability', in C. Huxham (ed) *Creating collaborative advantage*, London: Sage Publications. p 80-100

Cropper, S., Ebers, M., Huxham, C. and Smith Ring, P. (2009) *The Oxford handbook of inter-organizational relations*, Oxford: Oxford University Press.

Crosby, B.C. and Bryson, J.M. (2005a) *Leadership for the common good: Tackling public problems in a shared-power world*, San Francisco, CA: Jossey-Bass.

Crosby, B.C. and Bryson, J.M. (2005b) 'A leadership framework for cross-sector collaboration', *Public Management Review*, vol 7, issue 2, pp 177-201.

Crosby, B.C. and Bryson, J.M. (2010) 'Integrative leadership and the creation and maintenance of cross-sector collaborations', *The Leadership Quarterly*, vol 21, issue 2, pp 211-30.

Cummings, L.L. and Bromily, P. (1996) 'The Organizational Trust Inventory (OTI)', in R.M. Kramer and T.R. Tyler (eds) *Trust in organizations*, London: Sage Publications.

Das, T.K. and Teng, B.-S. (2001) 'Trust, control, and risk in strategic alliances: an integrated framework', *Organization Studies*, vol 22, no 2, pp 251-83.

Day, D.V. (2001) 'Leadership development: A review in context', *Leadership Quarterly*, vol 11, no 4, pp 581-613.

Degeling, P. (1995) 'The significance of "sectors" in calls for urban public health intersectoralism: an Australian perspective', *Policy & Politics*, vol 23, no 4, pp 289-301.

DeLeon, L. (1996) 'Ethics and entrepreneurship', *Policy Studies Journal*, vol 24, no 3, pp 495-510.

de Long, D.W. and Fahey, L. (2000) 'Diagnosing cultural barriers to knowledge management', *Academy of Management Executive*, vol 14, no 4, pp 113-27.

Denis, J.-L., Lamothe, L. and Langley, A. (2001) 'The dynamics of collective leadership and strategic change in pluralistic organizations', *Academy of Management*, vol 44, no 4, pp 809-37.

Donahue, J. (2004) *On collaborative governance*, Working Paper No 2, Cambridge, MA: John F. Kennedy School of Government.

Dowling, B., Powell, M. and Glendinning, C. (2004) 'Conceptualizing successful partnerships', *Health and Social Care in the Community*, vol 12, no 4, pp 309-17.

Doz, Y.L. and Hamel, G. (1998) *Alliance advantage: The art of creating value through partnering*, Boston, MA: Harvard University Press.

DTLR (Department for Transport, Local Government and the Regions) (2002) *Collaboration and co-ordination in area-based initiatives*, London: DTLR.

Dyer, J.H., Kale, P. and Singh, H. (2001) 'How to make strategic alliances work', *Sloan Management Review*, vol 42, no 4, pp 37-43.

Ebers, M. (1997) 'Explaining inter-organizational network formation', in M. Ebers (ed) *The formation of inter-organizational networks*, Oxford: Oxford University Press. P 3-40

Emerson, K. (2009) 'Synthesizing practice and performance in the field of environmental conflict resolution', in R. O'Leary and L.B. Bingham (eds) *The collaborative public manager*, Washington, DC: Georgetown University Press. P 215-231

Emirbayer, M. and Mische, A. (1998) 'What is agency?', *American Journal of Sociology*, vol 103, pp 962-1023.

Engel, C. (1994) 'A functional anatomy of teamwork', in A. Leathard (ed) *Going interprofessional*, London: Routledge.

Ernst, C. and Yip, J. (2009) 'Boundary-spanning leadership', in T.L. Pittinsky (ed) *Crossing the divide: Intergroup leadership in a world of difference*, Boston, MA: Harvard Business Press. P 87-99

Etzioni, A. (1967) 'Mixed scanning: a "third" approach to decision making', *Public Administration Review*, vol 27, no 5, pp 385-92.

Eyestone, R. (1978) *From social issues to public policy*, New York: John Wiley & Sons.

Eysenck, H.J. (1994) 'Trait theories of personality', in S.E. Hampson and A.M. Colman (eds) *Individual differences and personality*, London: Longman. P . 40-57

Evan, W.E. (1971) 'The organizational-set: toward a theory of interorganizational relations", in J.D. Thompson (ed) *Approaches to organizational design*, Pittsburgh: University of Pittsburgh Press (no page number available).

Exworthy, M. (2011) 'Policy entrepreneurship in the development of public sector strategy: the Case of the London Health Service Review', *Public Administration*, vol 89, no 2, pp 325-44.

Fairtlough, G. (1994) *Creative compartments*, London: Adamantine Press.

Ferlie, E. and Pettigrew, A. (1996) 'Managing through networks: some issues and implications for the NHS', *British Journal of Management*, vol 7, Special Issue, pp S81-S99.

Feyerherm, A.E. (1994) 'Leadership in collaboration: a longitudinal study of two interorganizational rule-making groups', *Leadership Quarterly*, vol 5, no 3/4, pp 253-70.

Fischbacher, M. and Beaumont, P.B. (2003) 'PFI, public–private partnerships and the neglected importance of process: stakeholders and the employment dimension', *Public Money and Management*, July, pp 171-6.

Fitzpatrick, D. (1999) 'Drowning in a sea of initiatives', *New Society*, 26 April, pp xii-xiv.

Fletcher, J.K. and Kaufer, K. (2003) 'Shared leadership: paradox and possibility', in C.L. Pearce and J.A. Conger (eds) *Shared leadership: Reframing the hows and whys of leadership*, London: Sage Publications. p 21-47

Fox, S. (1997) 'Situated learning theory versus traditional cognitive learning theory: why management education should not ignore management learning', *Systems Practice*, vol 10, no 6, pp 727-47.

Fox, S., Dewhurst, F., Eyres, J. and Vickers, D. (2001) *The nature and quality of management and leadership in the professions: A qualitative study*, London: The Management and Leadership Council.

Freeman, R. (2006) 'Learning in public policy', in M. Moran, M. Rein and R.E. Goodin (eds) *The Oxford handbook of public policy*, Oxford: Oxford University Press. P 367-388

Friedman, T.L. (2005) *The world is flat: A brief history of the twenty-first century*, New York: Farrar, Straus and Giroux.

Friend, J.K., Power, J.M. and Yewlett, C.J.L. (1974) *Public planning: The inter-corporate dimension*, London: Tavistock.

Gajda, R. (2004) 'Utilizing collaboration theory to evaluate strategic alliances', *American Journal of Evaluation*, vol 25, no 1, pp 65-77.

Garud, R., Hardy, C. and Maguire, S. (2007) 'Institutional entrepreneurship as embedded agency: an introduction to the Special Issue', *Organization Studies*, vol 28, no 7, pp 957-69.

Geddes, M. (1998) *Local partnership: A successful strategy for local cohesion?*, Dublin: European Foundation for the Improvement of Living and Working Conditions.

Getha-Taylor, H. (2008) 'Identifying collaborative competencies', *Review of Public Personnel Administration*, vol 28, no 2, pp 103-19.

Giddens, A. (1984) *The constitution of society*, Cambridge: Polity Press.

Giddens, A. (1991) *Modernity and self-identity*, Oxford: Polity Press.

Gilchrist, A. (2000) 'The well-connected community: networking to the "edge of chaos"', *Community Development Journal*, vol 35, no 3, pp 264-75.

Glasby, J. and Lester, H. (2004) 'Cases for change in mental health: partnership working in mental health services', *Journal of Interprofessional Care*, vol 18, no 1, pp 7-16.

Goldsmith, S. and Eggers, W.D. (2004) *Governing by network: The new shape of the public sector*, Washington, DC: Brookings Institution.

Grandori, A. (1997) 'An organizational assessment of interfirm co-ordination models', *Organization Studies*, vol 18, no 6, pp 897-925.

Gray, B. (1989) *Collaborating*, San Francisco, CA: Jossey-Bass.

Gray, B. (2003) 'Framing of environmental disputes', in R.J. Lewicki, B. Gray and M. Elliott (eds) *Making sense of intractable environmental conflicts*, Washington, DC: Island Press. P 11-34

Greve, C. and Hodge, G. (2010) 'Public–private partnerships and public governance challenges', in S.P. Osbourne (ed) *The new public governance? Emerging perspectives on the theory and practice of public governance*, London: Routledge. P 149-162

Grint, K. (2005a) 'Problems, problems, problems: the social construction of "leadership"', *Human Relations*, vol 58, pp 1467-94.

Grint, K. (2005b) *Leadership: Limits and possibilities*, Basingstoke: Palgrave Macmillan.

Gronn, P. (2002) 'Distributed leadership as a unit of analysis', *Leadership Quarterly*, vol 13, pp 423-51.

Hambleton, R. Stewart, M. Sweeting, D. Huxham, C. and Vangen, S.(2001) *Leadership in urban governance: The mobilisation of collaborative advantage*, Bristol: UWE.

Hampson, S.E. (1994) 'The construction of personality', in S.E. Hampson and A.M. Colman (eds) *Individual differences and personality*, London: Longman.

Hansen, M.T. (2009) 'When internal collaboration is bad for your company', *Harvard Business Review,* April, pp 82-8.

Hardy, B., Hudson, B. and Waddington, E. (2000) *What makes a good partnership? A partnership assessment tool*, Leeds: Nuffield Institute for Health.

Hardy, C., Phillips, N. and Lawrence, T. (1998) 'Distinguishing trust and power in interorganizational relations: forms and facades of trust', in C. Lane and R. Bachmann (eds) *Trust in and between organizations*, Oxford: Oxford University Press.

Hay, C. (1995) 'Structure and agency', in G. Stoker and D. Marsh (eds) *Theory and methods in political science*, London: Macmillan. P 189-206

Hay, C. (2002) *Political analysis: A critical introduction*, Basingstoke: Palgrave.

Heclo, H. (1974) *Modern social politics in Britain and Sweden: From relief to income maintenance*, New Haven, CT: Yale University Press.

Herranz, J. (2008) 'The multisectoral trilemma of network management', *Journal of Public Administration, Research and Theory*, vol 18, no 1, pp 1-31.

Hornby, S. (1993) *Collaborative care: Interprofessional, interagency and interpersonal*, Oxford: Blackwell.

Hosking, D.-M. and Morley, I.E. (1991) *A social psychology of organizing*, London: Harvester Wheatsheaf.

Hudson, B. (2002) 'Interprofessionality in health and social care: the Achilles' heel of partnership?', *Journal of Interprofessional Care*, vol 16, no 1, pp 7-17.

Hudson, B. (2004) 'Trust: towards conceptual clarification', *Australian Journal of Political Science*, vol 39, no 1, pp 75-87.

Hutt, M.D., Stafford, E.R., Walker, B.A. and Reingen, P.H. (2000) 'Defining the social network of a strategic alliance', *Sloan Management Review*, winter, pp 51-62.

Huxham, C. and Vangen, S. (2005) *Managing to collaborate: The theory and practice of collaborative advantage*, London: Sage Publications.

Ingraham, P.W. and Getha-Taylor, H. (2008) 'Incentivizing collaborative performance', in L.B. Bingham and R. O'Leary (eds) *Big ideas in collaborative public management*, New York: M.E. Sharpe. P 79-96

Inkpen, A. (2000) 'Learning through joint ventures: a framework of knowledge acquisition', *Journal of Management Studies*, vol 37, no 7, pp 1019-43.

Innes, J.E. and Booher, D.E. (1996) 'Consensus building and complex adaptive systems: a framework for evaluating collaborative planning', *Journal of the American Planning Association*, vol 65, no 4, pp 412-24.

Innes, J.E. and Booher, D.E. (2003) 'Collaborative policymaking: governance through dialogue', in M.A. Hajer and H. Wagenaar (eds) *Deliberative policy analysis: Understanding governance in the network society*, Cambridge: Cambridge University Press. P 33-59

Jansen, J.J.P., Vera, D. and Crossan, M. (2009) 'Strategic leadership for exploration and exploitation: the moderating role of environmental dynamism', *Leadership Quarterly*, vol 20, pp 5-18.

Javidan, M. and Waldman, D.A. (2003) 'Exploring charismatic leadership in the public sector: measurement and consequences', *Public Administration Review*, vol 63, no 2, pp 229-42.

Jessop, B. (1996) 'Interpretive sociology and the dialectic of structure and agency', *Theory, Culture and Society*, vol 13, no 1, pp 119-28.

Jessop, B. (1997) 'The governance of complexity and the complexity of governance: preliminary remarks on some problems and limits of economic guidance', in A. Amin and J. Hausner (eds) *Beyond market and hierarchy*, Cheltenham: Edward Elgar. P95-127

Jones, C., Hesterly, W.S. and Borgatti, S.P. (1997) 'A general theory of network governance: exchange conditions and social mechanisms', *Academy of Management Review*, vol 22, no 4, pp 911-45.

Jones, R. and Noble, G. (2008) 'Managing the implementation of public–private partnerships', *Public Money and Management*, April, pp 109-14.

Jupp, B. (2000) *Working together*, London: Demos.

Kale, P., Singh, H. and Perlmutter, H. (2000) 'Learning and protection of proprietary assets in strategic alliances: building relational capital', *Strategic Management Journal*, vol 21, no 3, pp 217-37.

Kanter, R.M. (1997) 'World-class leaders', in F. Hesselbein, M. Goldsmith and R. Beckhard (eds) *The leader of the future*, San Francisco, CA: Jossey-Bass.

Kanter, R.M. (2009) 'Creating common ground', in T.L. Pittinsky (ed) *Crossing the divide: Intergroup leadership in a world of difference*, Boston, MA: Harvard Business Press. P 73-85

Katz, D. and Kahn, R.L. (1966) *The social psychology of organizations*, New York: John Wiley.

Katz, R. and Tushman, M.L. (1983) 'A longitudinal study of the effects of boundary spanning supervision on turnover and promotion in research and development', *Academy of Management Journal*, vol 26, no 3, pp 437-56.

Kickert, W.J.M. (1997) 'Public governance in the Netherlands: an alterative to Anglo-American "managerialism"', *Public Administration*, vol 75, no 4, pp 731-52.

Kickert, W.J.M., Klijn, E.-H. and Koppenjan, J.F.M. (1997) *Managing complex networks*, London: Sage Publications.

Kingdon, J.W. (1984) *Agendas, alternatives, and public policies*, Boston: Little, Brown and Company

Klijn, E.-H. and Teisman, G.R. (2003) 'Institutional and strategic barriers to public–private partnership: an analysis of Dutch cases', *Public Money and Management*, July, pp 137-46.

Kogut, B. (1988) 'Joint ventures: theoretical and empirical perspectives', *Strategic Management Journal*, vol 9, pp 319-32.

Koliba, C., Meek, J.W. and Zia, A. (2011) *Governance networks in public administration and public policy*, London: CRC Press.

Kooiman, J. (2000) 'Societal governance: levels, modes, and orders of socio-political interaction', in J. Pierre (ed) *Debating governance*, Oxford: Oxford University Press. P 138-163

Koppenjan, J. and Klijn, E.-H. (2004) *Managing uncertainties in networks*, London: Sage Publications.

Lane, C. (1998) 'Introduction: theories and issues in the study of trust', in C. Lane and R. Bachmann (eds) *Trust in and between organizations*, Oxford: Oxford University Press.

Lane, C. (2003) 'Organizational learning in supplier networks', in M. Dierkes, A. Berthoin Antal, J. Child and I. Nonaka (eds) *Handbook of organizational learning and knowledge*, Oxford: Oxford University Press.

Lasker, R.D., Weiss, E.S. and Miller, R. (2001) 'Partnership synergy: a practical framework for studying and strengthening the collaborative advantage', *Milbank Quarterly*, vol 79, no 2, pp 179-205.

Lawrence, T.B., Hardy, C. and Phillips, N. (2002) 'The institutional effects of interorganizational collaboration: the emergence of proto-institutions', *Academy of Management Journal*, vol 55, no 1, pp 281-90.

Lawrence, T.B., Phillips, N. and Hardy, C. (1999) 'Watching whale watching: exploring discursive foundations of collaborative relationships', *The Journal of Applied Behavioral Science*, vol 35, no 4, pp 479-502.

Leadbeater, C. and Goss, S. (1998) *Civic entrepreneurship*, London: Demos.

Leifer, R. and Delbecq, A. (1976) 'Organizational/environmental interchange: a model of boundary spanning activity', *Academy of Management Review*, January, pp 40-50.

Levine, S. and White, P. (1961) 'Exchange as a conceptual framework for the study of interorganizational relationships', *Administrative Science Quarterly*, vol 5, pp 583-601.

Lewicki, R.J. and Bunker, B.B. (1996) 'Developing and maintaining trust in work relationships', in R.M. Kramer and T.R. Tyler (eds) *Trust in organizations*, London: Sage Publications. p. 114-137

LGMB (Local Government Management Board) (1997) *Networks and networking*, London: LGMB.

Linden, R.M. (2002) *Working across boundaries: Making collaboration work in government and nonprofit organizations*, San Francisco, CA: Jossey-Bass.

Ling, T. (2000) 'Unpacking partnership: the case of health care', in J. Clarke, S. Gewirtz and E. McLaughlin (eds) *New managerialism, new welfare?* London: Sage Publications. p 82-101

Ling, T. (2002) 'Delivering joined-up government in the UK: dimensions, issues and problems', *Public Administration*, vol 80, no 4, pp 615-42.

Lipsky, M. (1980) *Street-level bureaucracy: Dilemmas of the individual in public services*, New York: Russell Sage Foundation.

Lipman-Blumen, J. (1996) *The connective edge: Leading in an interdependent world*, San Francisco, CA: Jossey-Bass.

Lowndes, V. and Skelcher, C. (1998) 'The dynamics of multi-organizational partnerships: an analysis of changing modes of governance', *Public Administration*, vol 76, pp 313-33.

Lubell, M. (2005) 'Do watershed partnerships enhance beliefs conducive to collective action?', in P.A. Sabatier, W. Focht, M. Lubell, Z. Trachtenberg, A. Vedlitz and M. Matlock (eds) *Swimming upstream: Collaborative approaches to watershed management*, Cambridge, MA: The MIT Press. P 201-232

Luke, J.S. (1998) *Catalytic leadership: Strategies for an interconnected world*, San Francisco, CA: Jossey-Bass.

Lukes, S. (1974) *Power: A radical view*, Basingstoke: Macmillan.

Lynn, L.E. (2010) 'What endures? Public governance and the cycle of reform', in S.P. Osborne (ed) *The new public governance? Emerging perspectives on the theory and practice of public governance*, London: Routledge. P 105-123

McAnulla, S. (2002) 'Structure and agency', in D. Marsh and G. Stoker (eds) *Theory and methods in political science*, Basingstoke: Palgrave Macmillan. P 271-291

McLaughlin, H. (2004) 'Partnerships: panacea or pretence?', *Journal of Interprofessional Care*, vol 18, no 2, pp 103-13.

McGuire, M. (2006) 'Collaborative public management: assessing what we know and how we know it, *Public Administration Review*, vol 66, no 6 (Supplement) pp 33-4.

McQuaid, R.W. (2010) 'Theory of organizational partnerships: partnership advantages, disadvantages and success factors', in S. Osbourne (ed) *The new public governance? Emerging perspectives on the theory and practice of public governance*, London: Routledge. P 127-148

Machado, N. and Burns, T.R. (1998) 'Complex social organization: multiple organizing modes, structural incongruence, and mechanism of integration', *Public Administration*, vol 76, pp 355-86.

Mackintosh, M. (1993) 'Partnership: issues of policy and negotiation', *Local Economy*, vol 7, no 3, pp 210-24.

Maguire, S., Hardy, C. and Lawrence, T.B. (2004) 'Institutional entrepreneurship in emerging fields: HIV/AIDS treatment advocacy in Canada', *Academy of Management Journal*, vol 47, no 5, pp 657-79.

Mandell, M.P. (1990) 'Network management: strategic behaviour in the public sector', in R.W. Gage and M.P. Mandell (eds) *Strategies for managing intergovernmental policies and networks*, New York: Praeger.

Mandell, M.P. (1999) 'The impact of collaborative efforts: changing the face of public policy through networks and network structures', *Policy Studies Review*, vol 16, no 1, pp 5-17.

Marchington, M. and Vincent, S. (2004) 'Analysing the influence of institutional, organizational and interpersonal forces in shaping inter-organizational relations', *Journal of Management Studies*, vol 41, no 6, pp 1029-56.

Marion, R. and Uhl-Bien, M. (2001) 'Leadership in complex organizations', *Leadership Quarterly*, vol 12, pp 389-418.

Martin, G.P., Currie, G. and Finn, R. (2009) 'Leadership, service reform, and public-service networks: the case of cancer-genetics pilots in the English NHS', *Journal of Public Administration, Research and Theory*, vol 19, pp 769-94.

Mattessich, P.W. and Monsey, B.R. (1994) *Collaboration: What makes it work*, St Paul, MN: Amherst H. Wilder Foundation.

Meaklim, T. and Sims, J. (2011) 'Leading powerful partnerships – a new model of public sector leadership development', *The International Journal of Leadership in Public Services*, vol 7, issue 1, pp 21-31.

Meier, K.J. and O'Toole, L.J. (2001) '"Managerial strategies and behaviour in networks": a model with evidence from US public education', *Journal of Public Administration Research and Theory*, vol 3, pp 271-93.

Meyerson, D.E. and Scully, M.A. (1995) 'Tempered radicalism and the politics of ambivalence and change', *Organization Science*, vol 6, no 5, pp 585-600.

Miles, R.E. and Snow, C.C. (1978) *Organization strategy, structure and process*, New York: McGraw Hill.

Mintrom, M. (2000) *Policy entrepreneurs and school choice*, Washington, DC: Georgetown University Press.

Mishra, A.K. (1996) 'Organizational responses to crisis', in R.M. Kramer and T.R. Tyler (eds) *Trust in organizations*, London: Sage Publications.

Mitchell, S.M. and Shortell, S.M. (2000) 'The governance and management of effective community health partnerships: a typology for research, policy, and practice', *The Milbank Quarterly*, vol 78, no 2, pp 241-89.

Mohr, J. and Speckman, R. (1994) 'Characteristics of partnership success: partnership attributes, communication behavior, and conflict resolution techniques', *Strategic Management Journal*, vol 15, no 2, pp 135-52.

Moore, M. (1995) *Creating public value: Strategic management in government*, Cambridge, MA: Harvard University Press.

Morgan, K. and Mungham, J. (2000) *Redesigning democracy: The making of the Welsh Assembly*, Bridgend: Poetry Wales Press.

Morse, R.S. (2008) 'Developing public leaders in an age of collaborative governance', in R.S. Morse and T.F. Buss (eds) *Innovations in public leadership development*, Armonk, NY: M.E. Sharpe. P 79-100

Morse, R.S. (2010) 'Integrative public leadership: catalyzing collaboration to create public value', *The Leadership Quarterly*, vol 21, issue 2, pp 231-45.

Newell, S. and Swan, J. (2000) 'Trust and inter-organizational networking', *Human Relations*, vol 53, no 10, pp 1287-328.

Newman, J. (1998) 'The dynamics of trust', in A. Coulson (ed) *Trust and contracts*, Bristol: The Policy Press.

Newman, J. (2000) 'Beyond the new public management? Modernizing public services', in J. Clarke, S. Gewirtz and E. McLaughlin (eds) *New managerialism, new welfare?*, London: Sage Publications. p 45-61

NLIAH (National Leadership & Innovation Agency for Healthcare) (2009) *Getting collaboration to work: Lessons from the NHS and partners*, Cardiff: NLIAH.

Nocon, A. (1989) 'Forms of ignorance and their role in the joint planning process', *Social Policy & Administration*, vol 23, no 1, pp 31-47.

Noble, G. and Jones, R. (2006) 'The role of boundary-spanning managers in the establishment of public–private partnerships', *Public Administration*, vol 84, no 4, pp 891-917.

Nonaka, I. (1994) 'A dynamic theory of organizational knowledge creation', *Organization Science*, vol 5, no 1, pp 15-37.

Nooteboom, B. (2008) 'Learning and innovation in inter-organizational relationships', in S. Cropper, M. Ebers, C. Huxham and P. Smith Ring (eds) *The Oxford handbook of inter-organizational relations*, Oxford: Oxford University Press. P 607-634

Oborn, E., Barrett, M. and Exworthy, M. (2011) 'Policy entrepreneurship in the development of public sector strategy: the case of London health reform', *Public Administration*, vol 89, no 2, pp 325-44.

O'Leary, R. and Bingham, L.B. (2009) *The collaborative public manager*, Washington, DC: Georgetown University Press.

Oliver, C. (1990) 'Determinants of interorganisational relationships: integration and future directions', *Academy of Management Review*, vol 15, no 2, pp 241-65.

Oliver, C. and Ebers, M. (1998) 'Networking network studies: an analysis of conceptual configurations in the study of inter-organizational relationships', *Organization Studies*, vol 19, no 4, pp 549-83.

Osborne, S.P. (2010) 'Conclusions', in S.P. Osborne (ed) *The new public governance? Emerging perspectives on the theory and practice of public governance*, London: Routledge. p 413-428

Osbourne, D. and Gaebler, T. (1992) *Reinventing government*, Reading, MA: Addison-Wesley.

Ospina, S. and Foldy, E. (2010) 'Building bridges from the margins: the work of leadership in social change organizations', *The Leadership Quarterly*, vol 21, issue 2, pp 292-307.

O'Toole, L.J. (2009) 'Interorganizational relations in implementation', in B.G. Peters and J. Pierre (eds) *The handbook of public administration*, London: Sage Publications. p 142-152

Page, S. (2010) 'Integrative leadership for collaborative governance: civic engagement in Seattle', *The Leadership Quarterly*, vol 21, issue 2, pp 246-64.

Palmer, I. and Hardy, C. (2000) *Thinking about management*, London: Sage Publications.

Parise, S. and Prusak, L. (2006) 'Partnerships for knowledge creation', in L. Prusak and E. Matson (eds) *Knowledge management and organizational learning: A reader*, Oxford: Oxford University Press. P 125-135

Parry, K.W. and Bryman, A. (2006) 'Leadership in organizations', in S.R. Clegg, C. Hardy, T.B. Lawrence and W. Nord (eds) *The SAGE handbook of organization studies*, London: Sage Publications.

Pasquero, J. (1991) 'Supraorganizational collaboration: the Canadian environmental experiment', *Journal of Applied Behavioral Science*, vol 27, no 1, pp 38-64.

Payne, M. (2000) *Teamwork in multiprofessional care*, Basingstoke: Macmillan.

Pearce, C.L. and Conger, J.A. (2003) *Shared leadership: Reframing the hows and whys of leadership*, London: Sage.

Peck, E. and Dickinson, H. (2008) *Managing and leading in inter-agency settings*, Bristol: The Policy Press.

Perren, L. and Burgoyne, J. (2002a) *Management and leadership abilities: An analysis of texts, testimony and practice*, London: Council for Excellence in Management and Leadership.

Perren, L. and Burgoyne, J. (2002b) *The Management and Leadership Nexus: Dynamic sharing of practice and principle* London: Council for Excellence in Management and Leadership.

Perrone, V., Zaheer, A. and McEvily, B. (2003) 'Free to be trusted? Organizational constraints in boundary spanners', *Organization Science*, vol 14, no 4, pp 422-39.

Petchey, R., Williams, J. and Carter, Y.H. (2007) 'From street-level bureaucrats to street-level policy entrepreneurs? Central policy and local action in lottery-funded community cancer care', *Social Policy & Administration*, vol 42, no 1, pp 59-76.

Peters, B.G. (1998) 'Managing horizontal government: the politics of co-ordination', *Public Administration*, vol 76, pp 295-311.

Peters, B.G. and Pierre, J. (1998) 'Governance without government? Rethinking public administration', *Journal of Public Administration Research and Theory*, vol 8, no 2, pp 223-44.

Peters, B.G. and Pierre, J. (2001) 'Developments in intergovernmental relations: towards multi-level governance', *Policy & Politics*, vol 29, no 2, pp 131-5.

Pittinsky, T.L. (2009) 'Introduction', in T.L. Pittinsky (ed) *Crossing the divide: Intergroup leadership in a world of difference*, Boston, MA: Harvard Business Press. p xi-xxvii

Pollitt, C. (2002) 'The new public management in international perspective: an analysis of impacts and effects', in K. McLaughlin, S.P. Osborne and E. Ferlie (eds) *New public management: Current trends and future prospects*, London: Routledge. P 274-292

Pollitt, C. (2003) 'Joined-up government: a survey', *Political Studies Review*, vol 1, pp 340-9.

Pollock, A., Price, D. and Player, S. (2007) 'An examination of the UK Treasury's evidence base for cost and time overrun data in UK value-for-money policy and appraisal', *Public Money and Management*, April, pp 127-33.

Porter, M.E. and Fuller, M.B. (1986) 'Coalitions and global strategy', in M.E. Porter (ed) *Competition in global industries*, Boston, MA: Harvard Business School Press.

Posner, P.L. (2009) 'A public administration education for the third-party governance era: reclaiming leadership of the field', in R. O'Leary and L.B. Bingham (eds) *The collaborative manager: New ideas for the twenty-first century*, Washington, DC: Georgetown University Press. P 233-253

Powell, M., Glendinning, C. and Dowling, B. (2004) 'Conceptualising successful partnerships', *Health and Social Care in the Community*, vol 12, no 4, pp 309-17.

Poxton, R. (1999) *Working across the boundaries*, London: The King's Fund.

Provan, K.G. and Kenis, P. (2008) 'Modes of network governance: structure, management, and effectiveness', *Journal of Public Administration, Research and Theory*, vol 18, no 2, pp 229-52.

Radin, B.A. (1996) 'Managing across boundaries'', in D.F. Kettl and H.B. Milward (eds) *The state of public management*, Baltimore, MD: John Hopkins University Press. P 145-167

Rainey, H.G. (2003) *Understanding and managing public organizations*, San Francisco, CA: Jossey-Bass.

Ray, T., Clegg, S. and Gordon, R. (2004) 'A new look at dispersed leadership: power, knowledge and context', in J. Storey (ed) *Leadership in organizations: Current issues and key trends*, London: Routledge. P 319-336

Rein, M. (2006) 'Reframing problematic policies', in M. Moran, M. Rein and R.E. Goodin (eds) *The Oxford handbook of public policy*, Oxford: Oxford University Press. P 389- 405

Rethemeyer, R.K. (2005) 'Conceptualizing and measuring collaborative networks', *Public Administration Review*, vol 65, no 1, pp 117-21.

Rhodes, R.A.W. (1996) 'The new governance: governing without government', *Political Studies*, vol 33, pp 652-67.

Rhodes, R.A.W. (1999) 'Foreword: governance and networks', in G. Stoker (ed) *The new management of British local governance*, London: Macmillan. P xii -xxvi

Rhodes, R.A.W. (2000) 'Governance and public administration', in J. Pierre (ed) *Debating governance*, Oxford: Oxford University Press. P 54-89

Rieple, A., Gander, J. and Haberberg, A. (2002) 'Factors contributing to the effectiveness of hybrid organizational forms: the case of new product development', Paper to the British Association of Management Conference, London.

Ring, P.S. and van de Ven, A.H. (1994) 'Development processes of co-operative interorganizational relationships', *Academy of Management Review*, vol 19, no 1, pp 90-118.

Rittel, H. and Webber, M. (1973) 'Dilemmas in a general theory of planning', *Policy Sciences*, vol 4, pp 155-69.

Roberts, N.C. and King, P.J. (1996) *Transforming public policy: Dynamics of policy entrepreneurship and innovation*, San Francisco, CA: Jossey-Bass.

Rubin, H. (2002) *Collaborative leadership: Developing effective partnerships in communities and schools*, Thousand Oaks, CA: Corwin Press.

Rugkasa, J., Shortt, N.K. and Boydell, L. (2007) ''The right tool for the task: 'boundary spanners' in a partnership approach to tackle fuel poverty in rural Northern Ireland'', *Health and Social Care in the Community*, vol 15, no 3, pp 221-30.

Rushmer, R. and Pallis, G. (2002) 'Inter-professional working: the wisdom of integrated working and the disaster of blurred boundaries', *Public Money and Management*, Oct-Dec, pp 59-66.

Sabatier, P.A. and Jenkins-Smith, H.C. (1999) 'The advocacy coalition framework: an assessment', in P.A. Sabatier (ed) *Theories of the policy process*, Boulder, CO: Westview Press. P 117-166

Saint-Onge, H. and Armstrong, C. (2004) *The conductive organization: Building beyond sustainability*, Oxford: Elsevier Butterworth-Heinemann.

Sarason, S.B. and Lorentz, E.M. (1998) *Crossing boundaries: Collaboration, coordination and the redefinition of resources*, San Francisco, CA: Jossey-Bass.

Schein, E.H. (1997) *Organizational culture and leadership*, San Francisco, CA: Jossey-Bass.

Schon, D.A. (1973) *Beyond the stable state: Public and private learning in a changing society*, Harmondsworth: Penguin.

Schon, D.A. (ed) (1987) *Educating the reflective practitioner*, San Francisco, CA: Jossey-Bass.

Schon, D.A. and Rein, M. (eds) (1994) *Frame reflection: Toward the resolution of intractable policy controversies*, New York: Basic Books.

Scott, J. (1991) *Social network analysis*, London: Sage Publications.

Scott, W.R. (1998) *Organizations: Rational, natural, and open systems*, Upper Saddle River, NJ: Prentice Hall.

Scott, W.R. (2001) *Institutions and organizations*, London: Sage Publications.

Sewell, W.H. (1992) 'A theory of structure: duality, agency and transformation', *American Journal of Sociology*, vol 98, no 1, pp 1-29.

Skelcher, C. (1998) *The appointed state: Quasi-governmental organizations and democracy*, Buckingham: Open University Press.

Skelcher, C., McNabe, A., Lowndes, V. and Nanton, P. (1996) *Community networks in urban regeneration*, Bristol: The Policy Press.

Silvia, C. and McGuire, M. (2010) 'Leading public sector networks: an empirical examination of integrative leadership behaviors', *The Leadership Quarterly*, vol 21, issue 2, pp 264-77.

Slater, L. (2005) 'Leadership for collaboration: an affective process', *International Journal in Education*, vol 8, no 4, pp 321-33.

Snow, C.C. and Thomas, J.B. (1993) 'Building networks: broker roles and behaviours', in P. Lorange, B. Chakravarthy, J. Roos and A.H. van de Ven (eds) *Implementing strategic processes: Change, learning and co-operation*, Oxford: Blackwell. P 217-238

Spillane, J.P. (2006) *Distributed leadership*, San Francisco, CA: Jossey-Bass.

Stogdill, R.M. (1950) 'Leadership, membership and organization', *Psychological Bulletin*, vol 47, pp 1-14.

Stohl, C. (1995) *Organizational communication*, London: Sage Publications.

Stoker, G. (1998) 'Governance as theory: five propositions', *International Social Science Journal*, vol 155, pp 7-28.

Stoker, G. (2000) 'Introduction', in G. Stoker (ed) *The new politics of British local governance*, Basingstoke: Macmillan. P 1-9

Stoker, G. (2004) *Transforming local governance: From Thatcherism to New Labour*, Basingstoke: Palgrave Macmillan.

Stone, D.A. (1989) 'Causal stories and the formation of policy agenda', *Political Science Quarterly*, vol 104, no 2, pp 281-300.

Stone, D.A. (1997) *Policy paradox: The art of political decision making*, New York: Norton & Co.

Sullivan, H. (2010) 'Collaboration matters', Inaugural Lecture, University of Birmingham.

Sullivan, H. and Skelcher, C. (2002) *Working across boundaries: Collaboration in public services*, Basingstoke: Palgrave Macmillan.

Sullivan, H. and Williams, P.M. (2009) 'The limits of co-ordination: community strategies as multi-purpose vehicles in Wales', *Local Government Studies*, vol 35, no 2, pp 161–80.

Sydow, J. (1998) 'Understanding the constitution of interorganizational trust', in C. Lane and R. Bachmann (eds) *Trust in and between organizations*, Oxford: Oxford University Press. P. 31–63

Taylor, M. (2000) *Top down meets bottom up: Neighbourhood management*, York: Joseph Rowntree Foundation.

Thompson, J.D. (1967) *Organizations in action*, New York: McGraw-Hill.

Thomson, A.M., Perry, J.L. and Miller, T.K. (2009) 'Conceptualizing and measuring collaboration', *Journal of Public Administration, Research and Theory*, vol 19, no 1, pp 23–56.

Thorpe, R., Gold, J., Anderson, L., Burgoyne, J., Wilkinson, D. and Malby, B. (2008) *Towards 'leaderful' communities in the North of England: Stories from the Northern Leadership Academy*, Cork: Oak Street Press.

Trevillion, S. (1991) *Caring in the community*, London: Longman.

Triandafyllidou, A. and Fotiou, A. (1998) 'Sustainability and modernity in the European Union: a frame approach to policy-making', *Sociological Research Online*, vol 3, no 1 (www.socresonline.org.uk/socresonline/3/1/2.html).

Trist, E. (1983) 'Referent organizations and the development of inter-organizational domains', *Human Relations*, vol 36, no 3, pp 269–84.

Tsasis, P. (2009) 'The social processes of interorganizational collaboration and conflict in nonprofit organizations', *Nonprofit Management and Leadership*, vol 20, no 1, pp 5–21.

Tushman, M.L. (1977) 'Special boundary roles in the innovation process', *Administrative Science Quarterly*, vol 22, pp 587–605.

Tushman, M.L. and Scanlan, T.J. (1981a) 'Characteristics and external orientation of boundary spanning individuals', *Academy of Management Journal*, vol 24, no 1, pp 83–98.

Tushman, M.L. and Scanlan, T.J. (1981b) 'Boundary spanning individuals: their role in information transfer and their antecedents', *Academy of Management Journal*, vol 24, no 2, pp 289–305.

Van der Haar, D. and Hosking, D.M. (2004) 'Evaluating appreciative enquiry: a relational constructionist perspective', *Human Relations*, vol 57, no 8, pp 1017–36.

Van de Ven, A.H. (1976) 'On the nature, formation, and maintenance of relations amongst organizations', *Academy of Management Review*, October, pp 24–36.

Van de Ven, A.H. (2007) *Engaged scholarship: A guide for organizational and social research*, Oxford: Oxford University Press.

Van Wart, M. (2003) 'Public-sector leadership theory: an assessment', *Public Administration Review*, vol 63, no 2, pp 214–28.

van Wart, M. (2005) *Dynamics of leadership in public service: Theory and practice*, Armonk, NY: M.E. Sharpe.

Vangen, S. and Huxham, C. (1998) 'The role of trust in the achievement of collaborative advantage', paper presented at the EGOS Colloquium, Maastrict.

Vickers, J. (1965) *The art of judgment: A study of policy making*, London: Chapman and Hall.

Webb, A. (1991) 'Co-ordination: a problem in public sector management', *Policy & Politics*, vol 19, no 4, pp 229-41.

Weick, K.A. (1995) *Sensemaking in organizations*, London: Sage Publications.

Weiss, C.H. (1998) 'Have we learned anything new about the use of evaluation?', *American Journal of Evaluation*, vol 19, no 1, pp 21-33.

Wenger, E. (1998) *Communities of practice: Learning, meaning, and identity*, Cambridge: Cambridge University Press.

Wildavsky, A.B. (1979) *The art and craft of policy analysis*, London: Macmillan.

Williams, P. (2002) 'The competent boundary spanner', *Public Administration*, vol 80, no 1, pp 103-24.

Williams, P. (2005) 'Collaborative capability and the management of interdependencies: the contribution of boundary spanner', Unpublished PhD thesis, University of Bristol.

Williams, P. and Sullivan, H. (2009) 'Faces of integration', *International Journal of Integrated Care*, vol 9, no 22, pp 1-13.

Wilson, A. and Charleton, K. (1997) *Making partnerships work*, York: York Publishing Services.

Wood, D.J. and Gray, B. (1991) 'Toward a comprehensive theory of collaboration', *Journal of Behavioral Science*, vol 27, no 2, pp 139-62.

Wright, C. (2009) 'Inside out? Organizational membership, ambiguity and the ambivalent identity of the internal consultant', *British Journal of Management*, vol 20, no 3, pp 309-22.

Yoshino, M.Y. and Rangan, U.S. (1995) *Strategic alliances: An entrepreneurial approach to globalization*, Boston, MA: Harvard Business School Press.

Zaheer, A., McEvily, B. and Perrone, V. (1998) 'Does trust matter? Exploring the effects of interorganizational and interpersonal trust on performance', *Organization Science*, vol 9, no 2, pp 141-59.

Index

6, P. 12, 13, 17

A

academic programmes 129, 134–5
accountabilities 17, 73–6, 87, 89, 107, 126, 148
action learning models 131
Adobor, H. 86
Advocacy Coalition Framework (ACF) approach 29
agency 23, 24, 25, 57, 85
    ideational influences 25–8, 30
    structure-agency debate 24–30, 87
Agranoff, R. 13–14, 73–4, 96, 99
Aiken, M. 84
Aldrich, H.A. 83, 148, 150–1
Alexander, J.A. 113, 115
Allen, K.E. 108
alliance management 85, 87–8, 90, 91, 148, 149
alliance managers 23, 85–8, 91, 143
    see also managers; public managers
alliances 18, 84–5, 86, 90
Alter, C. 40
ambiguities 64, 70–1, 87, 142–3, 146–9
appreciative systems 30
Armstrong, C. 108
Atkins, J. 53

B

Bacharach, S.B. 72
Bachmann, R. 48
Bamford, J.D. 23, 85, 87
Bardach, E. 14, 45, 74, 102
Beaumont, P.B. 89
behaviour differences, explanations for 69–70
belief-based trust 47–8
Benford, R.D. 29, 77
Beresford, P. 67
Bingham, L.B. 99

Boal, K.B. 104
Bogason, P. 24
Booher, D.E. 41
Boon, S. 47, 48, 52
boundaries 31, 32, 139
boundary spanners 1, 3–4, 32–3, 37, 58–60, 141–4
    see also boundary spanning
    alliance managers 23, 85–8, 91, 143
    competencies 37, 58, 72, 142–3, 144–6, 149–50
        alliance managers 87, 88, 143
        and gender 68–9
        leaders 108, 114, 125, 133–4, 143
        managers 143
        network managers 100
        public managers 99
        training and development 124, 127–8, 131, 134
    dedicated 32–3, 129, 142, 144, 149
        coordinator role 52–3, 58, 90, 142
        entrepreneur role 53–7, 58, 59, 67, 142
        interpreter/communicator role 42–52, 58, 59, 142
        reticulist role 38–42, 58, 72, 79, 90, 142
    and gender 68–9
    job description for 128
    leaders 100–13, 144–5
    managers 89, 96–100, 144–5
    personal qualities 37, 67–8, 128, 142–3, 145
        alliance managers 87, 88, 143
        leaders 102, 112, 115, 143
        managers 143
boundary spanning 30–2
    see also boundary spanners
    ambiguities 64, 70–1, 87, 142–3, 146–9
    private sector 83–4
    tensions 91, 142–3
        accountabilities 73–6
        framing processes 77–9
        governance, multiple modes 70–1

of leaders 115, 143
of managers 98, 100
private sector 87, 88
relationships, blurring of 71–3
training and development 123–4, 133–5
academic 129, 134–5
capacity building 130–2
communities of practice 133
experiential 129–30
networking 132
professional 126–32
programme design 124–6
Bramson, R.A. 135
brokering 45, 54–5
brokers 41–2, 108, 124
Bromily, P. 47–8
Brunas-Wagstaff, J. 69, 70
Bryman, A. 101
Bryson, J.M. 24, 54, 109–10
Bunker, B.B. 47
Burgoyne, J. 133
Burns, T.R. 70, 71

C

calculative trust 47, 50
capacity building 120, 130–2
Capra, F. 64
Cardiff, partnership structure 10, 11
Carlile, P.R. 121
Cash, D.W. 31
Castells, M. 59
catalytic leadership 111–12
cautionary distance 89
Challis, L. 40, 53, 124
characteristic-based trust 48
characteristics *see* personal qualities
charismatic leadership 104, 105
Charlton, K. 40, 45
Child, J. 85, 87, 107
children's disability services 112
Chrislip, D.D. 110
citizen-centred collaborative public
    management 14
civic entrepreneurs 53–4, 59
civil service 44
cliques 73
coaching 130
coalitions 29
Cobb, R.W. 54
cognitive psychology 69–70
collaboration 1
  definitions 14–15
  theories of 17–20

collaborative advantage 113
collaborative experience 64, 65
collaborative governance 14
collaborative knowledge 63, 64–6
collaborative leadership 103, 104, 107, 112,
    113, 133–4
Collaborative Leadership programme 131
collaborative leadership theory 101, 108–9
collaborative management 123–4
collaborative public management 13–14, 33
collaborative public managers 33, 95,
    96–100, 134, 135, 147
  see also alliance managers; managers
collaborative working
  costs and benefits of 16–17
  drivers of 16
  history of 9–10, 12
  motivation for 15–16
collaborative/reciprocal leadership 108–9
collateral leadership 113
collective leadership 109
communication 43–4, 71, 77, 86, 90
  see also interpreter/communicator role
communities of practice 30, 126, 133
community health partnerships 15, 20, 113
community regeneration initiatives 66
community strategy coordinators 79
community workers 71
competencies 37, 58, 72, 142–3, 144–6,
    149–50
  alliance managers 87, 88, 143
  and gender 68–9
  leaders 108, 114, 125, 133–4, 143
  managers 143
  network managers 100
  public managers 99
  training and development 124, 127–8,
    131, 134
competitive advantage 16, 84, 85
complex leadership 109
conceptual learning 121
conductive organisations 108
conflict 28, 70
conflict resolution 45, 86, 90, 114
connective leadership 108
Connelly, D.R. 115
consensus 41, 44–5
consensus building 41, 45
Conservative governments 9, 10, 12
contextual leadership 113
contingency leadership theory 101, 103
Cooper, T.L. 14
cooperation 19
cooperative strategies 16, 77, 84–5

see also alliances; joint ventures; partnerships
coordination 13, 19, 97
coordinator role 52–3, 58, 90, 142
Coote, A. 119
cosmopolitan leaders 112
creativity 55, 56
Crime Reduction Partnership 76
Crosby, B.C. 24, 54, 109–10
cultural breakers 44
cultural brokers 44
cultural distance 89
cultural diversity 85
cultural norms 44
culture 85, 90
Cummings, L.L. 47–8

D

Day, D.V. 125
decision making 44–5
dedicated boundary spanners 32–3, 129, 142, 144, 149
  see also boundary spanners
  coordinator role 52–3, 58, 90, 142
  entrepreneur role 53–7, 58, 59, 67, 142
  interpreter/communicator role 42–52, 58, 59, 142
  reticulist role 38–42, 58, 72, 79, 90, 142
deep trust 51
Degeling, P. 40, 53
Delbecq, A. 32
DeLeon, L. 55, 67
democratic legitimacy 17, 73
Denis, J.-L. 109
development and training 123–4, 133–5
  academic 129, 134–5
  capacity building 130–2
  communities of practice 133
  experiential 129–30
  networking 132
  professional 126–32
  programme design 124–6
devolution 10
diplomacy 66, 67
discretion 46
dispersed/distributed leadership theory 101, 105–7
distrust 51–2
Donahue, J. 14
Dowling, B. 10
Doz, Y.L. 85

E

Ebers, M. 18, 39
education, collaborative leadership in 109
Eggers, W.D. 59, 99, 100
egotism 67
Elder, C.D. 54
Emirbayer, M. 25, 29, 30, 152
empathy 44, 68
Engel, C. 44, 67
enthusiasm 67
entrepreneur role 40, 53–7, 58, 59, 142
  civic 53–4, 59
  policy 54–5, 56–7, 67
  public 55, 59, 67
environmental policy 27–8
equality 27, 30
Ernst, C. 113
evidence-based policy making 119
exchange relationships 18, 46
experience of collaborative working 64, 65
expertise 63, 66
explicit knowledge 121, 122, 135
exploitative learning 121
exploratory learning 121
Eyestone, R. 54
Eysenck, H.J. 69

F

facilitative leadership 102, 112
Fairtlough, G. 66
Ferlie, E. 70
Feyerherm, A.E. 110
Fischbacher, M. 89
Fletcher, J.K. 106
Foldy, E. 111
forms of ignorance 44
Fox, S. 125–6
frame articulators 29, 77
framing 28–30, 77–9
  reframing 113
Freeman, R. 26
Friedman, T.L. 12–13
Friend, J.K. 38–9
friendship 86
Fuller, M.B. 85
future research 150–3

G

gatekeepers 39
Geddes, M. 124
gender of boundary spanners 68–9
Getha-Taylor, H. 127, 150

Giddens, A. 24
Gilchrist, A. 71
globalisation 13
Goldsmith, S. 59, 99, 100
Goss, S. 53
governance 12, 13, 19, 70–1
Gray, B. 14, 19, 20
Gronn, P. 106

H

Hage, J. 40, 84
Hambleton, R. 103
Hamel, G. 85
Hampson, S.E. 69
Hardy, C. 48–9
Hay, C. 24, 25–6, 29
health and social care sector 51, 53, 110,
    114–15, 126
  locality model 77–8
health sector 27
health service in London, study 57
Heavens, S.J. 107
Herker, D. 83, 150–1
Herranz, J. 97, 147
heterarchic networks 98
honesty 48, 50, 66, 67, 142
Hooijberg, R. 104
Hornby, S. 44, 53, 72
Hosking, D.-M. 39, 106
Hudson, B. 126
Hutt, M.D. 2, 86
Huxham, C. 20, 49, 113

I

ideational factors 25–8, 30
ignorance, forms of 44
informational intermediaries 39
Ingraham, P.W. 150
Innes, J.E. 41
innovation 55, 56
institutional entrepreneurship 140, 151
institutional uncertainties 98
institutional-based trust 48
integrated children's disability services 112
integrated health and social care service 110
integration 13, 19, 30, 85
integrative leadership 111, 114, 115
intercultural boundary spanners 85
interdependency 98, 121
intergroup leadership 111, 112–13
internal boundary spanners 87–8
internal networks 147

international trends 12–14
interorganisational leadership 109–13,
    133–4
interorganisational movement 65–6
interorganisational relationships 14, 18, 24,
    86–7
interorganisational trust 87
interpersonal relationships 38–9, 43–5, 50,
    90
  potential problems with 79, 147
  private sector 86–7, 88
  and professional relationships, blurring
    71–3
interpersonal skills 90, 112
interpersonal trust 47, 49, 87
interpreter/communicator role 42–52, 58,
    59, 142
  see also communication
  personal relationships 43–5
  power and status 45–6
  trust 46–52
intersectoral movement 65–6
intraorganisational leadership 133–4

J

Jansen, J.J.P. 121
Javidan, M. 105
Jenkins-Smith, H.C. 29
Jessop, B. 24
job description for boundary spanners 128
joined-up government 10, 11, 26, 30
joint ventures 16, 18, 84, 85
Jones, R. 2, 89–90
Jupp, B. 124

K

Kahn, R.L. 83
Kale, P. 86
Kanter, R.M. 112–13
Katz, D. 83
Kaufer, K. 106
Kenis, P. 96–7
Kickert, W.J.M. 96
King, P.J. 55
Kingdon, J.W. 56, 67
knowledge conversion 121, 122
knowledge for collaboration 63, 64–6
knowledge management 88, 90, 91, 120–3
knowledge transfer 132
Kogut, B. 84
Koliba, C. 13
Kooiman, J. 10, 12

L

Lane, C. 47, 121
language 43, 44
    see also communication
Larson, C.E. 110
Lasker, R.D. 15, 20
Lawrence, T.B. 15
Leadbeater, C. 53
leaders 33, 95–6, 143, 144–5, 148
    see also leadership; leadership theories
    competencies 108, 114, 125, 133–4, 143
    development and training 125, 133–5
    paradoxes and dilemmas 115
    personal qualities 102, 112, 115, 143
    in the United States 13
leadership 100–1, 113–15
    see also leadership theories
    development 125
    interorganisational 109–13
    skills 111–12, 114
    traditional 115
leadership constellation 109
leadership theories 101
    collaborative 101, 108–9
    contingency 101, 103
    dispersed/distributed 101, 105–7
    new leadership 101, 104–5
    shared 105–7
    style 101, 102–3
    trait 101, 102
Leading Powerful Partnerships programme 131
learning 29–30, 86, 91, 120–3, 125–6, 132
Leifer, R. 32
Lesser, C. 74
Lewicki, R.J. 47
Linden, R.M. 112
Ling, T. 16, 100
Lipman-Blumen, J. 108
listening 43–4, 68
    see also communication
Local Government Management Board 71, 73
local partnerships 124
locality model 77–8
Lorentz, E.M. 66, 145, 149
Lowndes, V. 103
Luke, J.S. 1, 111
Lukes, S. 29

M

McAnulla, S. 24
McLaughlin, H. 14
McGuire, M. 13–14, 73–4, 115
Machado, N. 70, 71
macro-level theories 17–19
management development and training 123–4
managers 33, 89, 133–5, 143, 144, 147–8
    see also alliance managers; network managers; public managers
managing meaning 104–5, 111, 114
Mandell, M.P. 108, 123–4
Marchington, M. 24
Marion, R. 109
Martin, G.P. 24
Mattessich, P.W. 19–20
meaning, managing 104–5, 111, 114
mediation 114
Meier, K.J. 40
mentoring 130
Meyerson, D.E. 75
Mintrom, M. 56
Mische, A. 25, 29, 30, 152
Mishra, A.K. 48
Mitchell, S.M. 20
Mohr, J. 87
Monsey, B.R. 19–20
Morley, I.E. 39, 106
Morse, R.S. 45, 53, 102, 133–4
motivations 15–16, 63, 84, 90, 112
movement between organisations/sectors 65–6
mulitagency welfare partnership 112
multifaceted leadership 114

N

negotiation 39, 45, 89, 104, 114
nesting 113
Netherlands 13
network brokers 41–2
network governance 13, 95, 96–7
network management 41–2, 96–8, 100
network managers 85, 97–8, 100
network tensions 98, 143
networking 40, 41, 42, 71, 72–3, 75, 132
networking judgements 38
networks 19, 20, 38, 40–1, 132
    see also communities of practice
New Labour governments 10, 12
new leadership theories 101, 104–5
new public management 12, 13
Newell, S. 49
Newman, J. 46–7, 98
Noble, G. 2, 89–90
Nocon, A. 44

Nonaka, I. 122
Nooteboom, B. 122
norm-based trust 47–8

O

Oborn, E. 57
O'Leary, R. 99
Oliver, C. 16, 18
openness 66, 121
operational learning 121
opportunism 59, 67, 74
organisational identity 17
organisational self-interest 149
Osborne, S.P. 133, 150
Ospina, S. 111
O'Toole, L.J. 40, 98, 147

P

Page, S. 49, 111
paradoxes 70, 115, 146–9
Parry, K.W. 101
partnership game 52
partnership structure, Cardiff 10, 11
partnership working 86
  costs of 17
  management training in 124
partnerships 9, 10–12, 98
  see also public-private partnerships (PPPs)
  life cycle of 103
  types of 19
  welfare partnerships 112
Pasquero, J. 42
Payne, M. 16
Perren, L. 133
Perrone, V. 86–7
personal attributes *see* personal qualities
personal characteristics *see* personal qualities
personal networks 87
personal qualities 37, 67–8, 128, 142–3, 145
  alliance managers 87, 88, 143
  leaders 102, 112, 115, 143
  managers 143
personal relationships 38–9, 43–5, 50, 90
  potential problems with 79, 147
  private sector 86–7, 88
  and professional relationships, blurring 71–3
personality 55, 66–70
  see also personal qualities
Pettigrew, A. 70
Pittinsky, T.L. 111
police leadership structures 107

policy brokers 29
policy entrepreneurs 54–5, 56–7, 67
policy networks 13
policy windows 56–7
political economy approach 18
Porter, M.E. 85
Posner, P.L. 28, 63, 134
Powell, M. 119
power 29, 40–1
  managing without 87, 91, 147–8
  and status 45–6
power relationships 17, 18, 45–6
power sharing 113
power-based trust 49
power/resource dependency perspectives 18
Poxton, R. 23
PPPs *see* public-private partnerships
private finance initiatives (PFIs) 12, 89
private sector 9–10, 12, 16, 83–4, 149–50
  see also public-private partnerships (PPPs)
  alliance management 85–8
  cooperative strategies 84–5
  personal relationships 86–7, 88
  and public sector comparison 90–2
  tensions 87, 88
process-based leadership 113
process-based trust 48
professional and personal relationships, blurring of 71–3
professional boundary spanners 126–32
professional qualifications 66
  see also academic programmes
professional-based trust 52
professionalism 126, 127
project champions 89
Provan, K.G. 96–7
public entrepreneurs 55, 59, 67
public governance 150
public integrative leadership 109–10
public management 13–14, 95, 108, 145
public managers 33, 95, 96–100, 134, 135, 147
  see also alliance managers; managers
public sector and private sector comparison 90–2
public sector leaders 104
  see also leaders
Public Service Management Wales programme 131
public-private partnerships (PPPs) 12, 88–90
  see also partnerships

Q

qualifications 66
  see also academic programmes

R

Radin, B.A. 31, 124
Rainey, H.G. 101
Rangan, U.S. 86, 87
reciprocity 50, 72
reframing 113
Rein, M. 28, 29
relational capital 86, 90
relational pragmatics 30
relationship building 72–3, 76
relationships 19
  exchange 18, 46
  interorganisational 14, 18, 24, 86–7
  personal 38–9, 43–5, 50, 90
    potential problems with 79, 147
    private sector 86–7, 88
  personal and professional, blurring of 71–3
  power relationships 17, 18
  romantic 47, 48
  trust-based, fragility of 51–2
research, future agenda 150–3
respect 50, 66, 67, 72, 86
Rethemeyer, R.K. 98
reticulist role 38–42, 58, 72, 79, 90, 142
  network management 41–2
  power of 40–1
Rieple, A. 44, 140–1
Ring, P.S. 72
risk taking 50, 55, 59
Roberts, N.C. 55
romantic relationships, trust in 47, 48
Rubin, H. 150
Rugkasa, J. 4

S

Sabatier, P.A. 29
Saint-Onge, H. 108
Sarason, S.B. 66, 145, 149
Scanlan, T.J. 83
Schon, D.A. 28, 29
Scully, M.A. 75
selfishness 67
sensemaking 28, 29–30
Sewell, W.H. 24
shadowing 130
shared leadership theory 105–7
Shortell, S.M. 20
Silvia, C. 115

simulated trust 48–9
situated learning 125–6
  see also learning
Skelcher, C. 58, 66, 103
Slater, L. 109
Snow, C.C. 42
Snow, D.A. 29, 77
social bonding 72
social capital 41, 121, 125
social learning 29–30
social network approach 18–19
social networks 86, 126
Speckman, R. 87
Spillane, J.P. 105, 106, 107
status 45–6
Stogdill, R.M. 101
Stohl, C. 71
Stoker, G. 95
Stone, D.A. 32
strategic alliances 16, 86
strategic uncertainties 98
structuration theory 24
structure 24, 27, 28, 30, 88
  ideational influences 25–8, 30
  structure-agency debate 24–30, 87
style leadership theory 101, 102–3
substantive uncertainty 98
Sullivan, H. 14, 24, 58
Sure Start programme 54–5
suspending 113
sustainable development 27
Swan, J. 49
Sydow, J. 48, 49
systems thinking 55, 113, 134

T

tacit knowledge 121, 122, 132, 135
tacit learning 86
tact 66
Taylor, M. 70
technical-based trust 52
tempered radicals 74–5
tensions 91, 142–3
  accountabilities 73–6
  framing processes 77–9
  governance, multiple modes 70–1
  of leaders 115, 143
  of managers 98, 100
  private sector 87, 88
  relationships, blurring of 71–3
Thomas, J.B. 42
Thompson, J.D. 83, 98
Thomson, A.M. 15

time management 41
training and development 123–4, 133–5
  academic 129, 134–5
  capacity building 130–2
  communities of practice 133
  of competencies 124, 127–8, 131, 134
  experiential 129–30
  networking 132
  professional 126–32
  programme design 124–6
trait leadership theory 101, 102
trait theories 69
traits 67, 69, 102
transactions costs 18
transformational leadership 104
transparency 121
  lack of 17, 73
Trevillion, S. 40, 44, 67
Trist, E. 40
trust 41, 46–52, 72, 86, 87, 90, 147
trust building 51, 52
trust-based relationships, fragility of 51–2
trustworthiness 46, 66, 67
Tsasis, P. 49
turf 45
Tushman, M.L. 83

U

Uhl-Bien, M. 109
uncertainty 98, 145
United States 13–14
urban partnerships 103
urban regeneration projects 90–1

V

value-based trust 47–8, 52
van de Ven, A.H. 72, 119
van Wart, M. 102, 114, 115
Vangen, S. 20, 49, 113
Vincent, S. 24
vision-based leadership 104–5, 113
voluntary sector 107, 112
voluntary services' director 112

W

Waldman, D.A. 105
weaving 113
Webb, A. 39, 46
Weick, K.A. 64
Weiss, C.H. 119
welfare partnerships 112
  see also partnerships

Wenger, E. 31, 54, 139, 145–6
whole systems thinking 55, 113, 134
wicked issues 10, 110, 111, 139
Wildavsky, A.B. 64
Wilson, A. 40, 45
Wood, D.J. 20
Wright, C. 74, 87, 88, 148

Y

Yip, J. 113
Yoshino, M.Y. 86, 87
youth offending manager 76

Z

Zaheer, A. 87